What people are saying about

Irreducible

Federico Faggin is probably the most well-rounded Idealist alive. He embodies the near-perfect combination of hard-nosed, scientifically informed thought with direct introspective insights into the primacy of consciousness. This book is a true philosophical treasure and, in some ways, a culmination of Western thought; an absolute must-read.

Bernardo Kastrup

T0245773

Irreducible

Consciousness, Life, Computers,
and Human Nature

Irreducible

Consciousness, Life, Computers,
and Human Nature

Federico Faggin

Winchester, UK
Washington, USA

JOHN HUNT PUBLISHING

First published by Essentia Books, 2024
Essentia Books is an imprint of John Hunt Publishing Ltd., No. 3 East St., Alresford,
Hampshire SO24 9EE, UK
office@jhpbooks.com
www.johnhuntpublishing.com/essentia-books/

For distributor details and how to order please visit the 'Ordering' section on our website.

ISBN: 978 1 80341 509 3
978 1 80341 510 9 (ebook)
Library of Congress Control Number: 2023931858

A CIP catalogue record for this book is available from the British Library.

Design: Matthew Greenfield

UK: Printed and bound by CPI Group (UK) Ltd, Croydon, CR0 4YY
Printed in North America by CPI GPS partners

We operate a distinctive and ethical publishing philosophy in
all areas of our business, from our global network of authors to
production and worldwide distribution.

Contents

To Elvia, to our children, Marzia, Marc, and Eric, and to Viviana, Irene, Cecilia, and Daniela Sardei for their example of love and cooperation

Preface

This book follows my autobiography, titled *Silicon: From the invention of the microprocessor to the new science of consciousness* (Waterside, 2021), and describes the latest developments of my continuing research on the nature of consciousness and reality.

Since 2010 I have deepened the study of consciousness as an irreducible phenomenon and developed the CIP framework (acronym formed by the initials of Consciousness, Information, and Physical). In this conception, the nature of reality consists of two complementary and irreducible aspects: the semantic space of conscious experiences, called C-space, and the informational space of symbolic forms, called I-space. Symbols are created by conscious entities to communicate and explore their inner meaning for the purpose of knowing themselves ever more. Physical space, called P-space, is a virtual space experienced by those conscious entities that control living organisms. The organisms are symbolic structures that interact with the other I-space symbols and generate within themselves symbolic representations of I-space that are perceived as "reality" by the conscious entities. In this framework, consciousness exists only in C-space.

In March 2017, I received the following email from Professor Giacomo Mauro D'Ariano:

> We met briefly on Vieques Island in January 2014 at the fourth FQXi conference on "Physics of Information". On that occasion I gave a very short talk of only five minutes on the derivation of Dirac's equation from information-theoretic principles. You gave me a very nice compliment. Unfortunately, not knowing you, I had no way of answering.

An invitation to meet followed.

In April 2017 I replied via email:

Dear Giacomo, sorry for the delay with which I reply to your welcomed e-mail. My dream is to derive physics from cognitive rather than materialistic principles. Of course, you are doing the first step, to prove that quantum mechanics is about information, hence syntax. For me, syntax is evidence that semantics must exist somewhere.

What is the meaning of the existence of a hierarchy of languages (the physical world), if no one is using them? In my opinion there is a semantic reality that consists of a parallel hierarchy of conscious entities that use particles, atoms, molecules, cells, animals, etc. as symbols for their communications. The materialist only sees the symbolic aspect, and does not realize that behind the stage there are "puppet masters".

This is why information theory is essentially isomorphic with quantum mechanics! This is why quantum mechanics must use a probabilistic language! The meaning of a book is free even if the symbols obey deterministic laws (in terms of probability). This is why physics can only guarantee that the next book to be written will obey the laws of symbols, but cannot predict the semantic content of a book that has not yet been written. I think semantics is the real ontology. Therefore semantics is free, even if the syntax is deterministic.

These are the issues that fascinate me. And I think this is the right way to restore meaning to a universe that has been declared "pointless" by those who have forgotten that the meaning of existence resides "inside" matter. Today I would say: "It exists in a deeper reality than what manifests itself in space-time"; an interiority that is denied by a zealous materialistic *fiat*.

I'd love to discuss these issues with you if you're interested. I will be in Milan around July 21, where I will be one of the presenters at an event called Campus Party. It would be a good opportunity to meet.

Thank you for expressing your gratitude for my heartfelt compliment, and congratulations on your progress in completing Wheeler's dream. Best regards and best wishes, Federico.

A few days later, D'Ariano replied by telling me that he would be very pleased to meet for us to discuss "the ontology of information," characterized by the phrase "software without hardware," "which perhaps is very close to what you call ontology of semantics, which I believe you mean that it also involves the 'observer,' i.e., the 'puppeteer.'"

This was the beginning of a fruitful collaboration, which a couple of years ago allowed us to understand that the pure state of a quantum system can represent the state of consciousness of the system, since it has all the crucial characteristics of a conscious experience made of qualia. This important step brought into focus the "core" of the enigma of consciousness, which made it possible to connect the philosophical notions of the CIP framework with the OPT (Operational Probabilistic Theory), the theory that D'Ariano and his collaborators had developed to demonstrate that quantum physics can be entirely derived from quantum information postulates.

This new axiom allows us to claim that consciousness is a quantum phenomenon because it has all the peculiar characteristics of a pure quantum state, i.e., it is a *definite* and a *private* state, and so is a pure state which is not clonable, i.e., cannot be copied and therefore cannot be known by any observer. Therefore, such a state, if knowable at all, is knowable only by the system that is in that state. This crucial insight reflects remarkably the phenomenology of our inner experience.

If the current idea that consciousness emerges from the functioning of the brain were correct—where the brain is thought to be like a classical computer—then a computer could be conscious. But then consciousness could be copied like we routinely copy computer programs, which is classical information. Yet we know perfectly well that our experience is in constant evolution and is private, knowable only within ourselves. Moreover, the meaning we feel always exceeds any symbolic description we may produce to describe it. Therefore, even the owner of the experience (described by quantum information) can only translate a portion of its experience into symbols (described by classical information).

Consciousness is the ability to experience through qualia and know the meaning of the experience. Qualia are the private sensations and feelings that reveal the meaning of the experience to the entity. The ability to know must therefore exist before the knowing, and knowing brings into existence what is known for the first time. Knowing therefore becomes synonymous with existing, and this "miracle" cannot be explained in simpler terms than these. If we accept this principle, the fundamental entities from which everything that exists emerges must be conscious entities similar to the *monads* of Leibniz.

This is the view that will be articulated in *Irreducible*, a title that refers to the crucial property of the conscious entities endowed with free will that emerge from One, the totality of what exists, and cause the continuing creation and evolution of the universe.

One is a Whole, both in potentiality and in actuality, irreducibly dynamic and holistic, that desires to know itself to self-realize. From One emerge monads, or consciousness units, i.e., parts-whole that are inseparable from One and in continuous evolution. These units communicate with each other to know themselves, thus realizing the intention and purpose of

One they all share. Therefore, there is *becoming* in the universe, and the future is not predictable, not even by One.

This view is in full agreement with what quantum physics has already revealed to us. Therefore the idea of producing a Theory of Everything (ToE) that can predict the future of the universe is contrary to the deepest message of quantum physics. This does not mean that the search for a theory that reconciles quantum physics with general relativity is not desirable; quite the contrary. The new vision, however, shows us that the most reasonable ToE is a theory in which consciousness and free will have always existed and in which the universe—that is, One—is open because its evolution is the evolution of its knowing. The ToE can only tell us the characteristics of the outer world as symbolic correlations of the inner world of meaning.

It is becoming ever more evident that unconscious matter cannot produce consciousness, while conscious entities can produce phenomena that behave like unconscious matter. "More" cannot come out of "less," though the opposite is clearly possible. Crucially, when consciousness and free will are irreducible properties of nature, the evolution of the physical universe can no longer be the work of a "blind watchmaker," but the result of cooperating and intelligent conscious entities that have always existed and are the ultimate cause of the universe's eternal becoming.

In this book there is a crucial distinction between conscious and unconscious knowledge that is generally neglected in the scientific literature since consciousness is considered epiphenomenal. This confusion is further facilitated by the lack of appropriate words in the English language to discriminate the two. In the Italian language there are two verbs, *conoscere* and *sapere*, instead of only "to know." *Conoscere* is a deeper form of knowing than *sapere* because it refers to the knowing that is based on experience and comprehension, whereas *sapere* can describe the knowing by heart of someone who repeats what he does not understand. In the Italian version of this book I have consistently used *conoscere* with the meaning, "conscious knowledge," and *sapere* to mean "unconscious knowledge," even though in their common usage the two verbs are often used interchangeably. In the English version, I have consistently translated *conoscere* as "knowing" and *sapere* as "knowledge." This distinction is essential to discriminate between the symbolic-only knowledge of computers or brains and the semantic knowing of a conscious entity.

Introduction

The search for truth must be the ultimate goal of any science.

— Augustin-Louis Cauchy, *Seven General Physics Lessons*

I am a physicist, inventor, and entrepreneur. I was born in Vicenza, Italy during the Second World War in a Catholic family and I received a *Laurea* degree in physics from the University of Padua in 1965, *summa cum laude*.

In 1968, I moved to Silicon Valley, California to work at Fairchild Semiconductor, where I developed the original silicon gate MOS technology, the process technology that made possible microprocessors, dynamic random access memories (DRAM), non-volatile memories, and CCD image sensors, the key components of the information revolution. In 1970 I moved to Intel where I designed the world's first microprocessor, the Intel 4004, and for five years I led the team that created the 8008, 4040, 8080, and other components that have revolutionized information technology.

In late 1974 I founded Zilog, the world's first company entirely dedicated to the microprocessor market, thus starting an entrepreneurial career that occupied the rest of my professional life. Zilog's first microprocessor, the Z80-CPU, became a bestseller and is still in production today (2022).

During the second half of the 1980s, I became interested in artificial neural networks and founded Synaptics to develop analog chips capable of *emulating* neural networks using floating-gate transistors. At that time, neural networks were considered a bad idea by the artificial intelligence (AI) experts. Twenty-five years later, however, they became the only practical solution to the recognition of complex patterns, a very difficult problem.

Up to the age of 40, I lived doing what most of us do: I sought happiness outside myself, convinced that to be happy I would have to fulfill everything the world prescribes to that end. I buried myself in work and deeply repressed any interference that might distract me from my objectives, thinking that the harder the goals, the more happiness they should bring me if I succeeded.

I rushed to check all the boxes on my imaginary "happiness list," pushing down any inner turmoil. I didn't want to be distracted from my goals for any reason. I told myself that to be happy, I had to first get to the end of that list.

I was hostage to a kind of hypnotic trance and I had embraced the competitive and consumerist vision that dominates our society. I had lost the connection with my emotions and my inner reality. I had fallen into the trap most of us fall into.

Looking back, I'm sure that, if I hadn't reached the bottom of the list, I would have continued to struggle until my death, without ever realizing that I was confusing an imaginary happiness with a real one.

It was only because I crossed the finish line and took a break from the race that I was able to look inside myself. What I found was a deep suffering that I pretended not to feel. My first reaction was: What's wrong with me? How is it possible not to be happy when I have achieved everything that should make me so?

As Simone Weil says: "Suffering is a door that we can choose to go through and then we learn something, or we refuse to open, and then nothing is added, rather, it takes everything away from us."

The Search for Truth

While studying neuroscience I wondered if it was possible to build a conscious computer. If materialism were right—as I then thought—the answer had to be yes. Therefore I explored all possible ways I could think of to achieve such a goal, reflecting deeply on the attributes of awareness. It didn't take long to recognize the big obstacle: the complete lack of understanding of the nature of sensations, feelings, and emotions, what philosophers call *qualia*. No matter how hard I tried, I could not find any way to convert the electrical signals of the computer into qualia, because qualia belong to a different kind of reality with no apparent connection to symbols. It was like trying to transform the feeling of love one feels for a child into a computer program.

I also sensed that the cause of my despair was deeply connected with the mystery of consciousness and that further motivated me to try to understand. My situation placed this enigma at the center of my midlife crisis and led me to an experience of unexpected, unsolicited, and spontaneous awakening, which made me realize that consciousness is fundamental and beyond matter.

From that point on, I embarked on a new path of searching for truth, which led me to investigate all aspects of reality, even those that I previously had taken for granted and would have never thought of taking into consideration. I realized that just as I had uncritically accepted religious dogmas as a child, I also had accepted those of science, replacing the old dogmas with the new ones.

My awakening experience has already been described in my autobiography, entitled *Silicon: From the invention of the microprocessor to the new science of consciousness*, first published in Italy in 2019 and in 2021 in USA [1]. For the convenience of the reader, I report the experience below with minimal changes.

The Awakening

In December 1990, while I was at Lake Tahoe, California with my family during the Christmas holidays, I woke up around midnight thirsty. I poured myself a glass of water from the refrigerator in the kitchen and, sipping it, I moved into the adjacent living room to contemplate the lake, now dark and mysterious.

I went back to bed and while I was waiting for sleep to return, I suddenly felt a powerful rush of energy emerge from my chest like nothing I had ever experienced before and could not even imagine possible. This *alive* energy was love, yet a love so intense and so incredibly fulfilling that it surpassed any other notion I previously had about love. Even more surprising was the fact that the source of this love was me.

I experienced it as a broad beam of shimmering white light, alive and beatific, gushing from my heart with incredible strength. Then suddenly that light exploded. It filled the room and expanded to embrace the entire universe with the same white brilliance. I *knew* then, without a shadow of a doubt, that this was the substance out of which everything that exists is made. This was what created the universe out of itself. Then, with immense surprise, *I recognized that I was that light!*

The whole experience lasted perhaps a minute, and it changed me forever. My relationship with the world had always been as a separate observer perceiving the universe as outside myself and disconnected from me. What made this event astonishing was its impossible perspective because I was *both* the experiencer *and* the experience. I was simultaneously the observer of the world and the world. I was the world observing itself! And I was concurrently *knowing* that the world is made of a "substance" that feels like love and that *I am* that!

In other words, the essence of reality was revealed to be a "substance" or *nous* that knows itself by self-reflection, and its self-knowing is experienced as an irrepressible and dynamic love full of joy and peace.

This experience contained an unprecedented force of truth, because it felt true at all levels of my being. At the physical level, my body was alive and vibrant like I had never felt before. At the emotional level I perceived myself as an impossibly powerful source of love, and at the mental level I knew with certainty that everything is "made of" love. For the first time in my life I had experienced the existence of another dimension of reality, a dimension that previously could only be known intellectually by reading about it, but not by living it: the spiritual level in which a person is one with the world.

It was a form of *direct knowing*, stronger than the "certainty" offered by logic; a knowledge from the inside rather than the outside, which simultaneously involved all aspects of my consciousness: the physical, emotional, mental, and spiritual levels.

I like to think that I have experienced my nature both as a particle and as a wave, to use an analogy with quantum physics that is impossible to comprehend with ordinary logic. The particle aspect was the ability to maintain my identity despite experiencing myself as the world (the wave aspect). But my identity was also part of the world, because I felt myself to be the world with "my" point of view. So now I think that my identity is like one of the infinite points of view with which One—the totality of what exists—observes and knows itself. In other words, each one of us is a point of view of One, a part of One indivisible from It that contains Its essence and, as such, is eternal.

That experience made me understand that, as the famous Lebanese aphorist Kahlil Gibran said: "Spiritual awakening is the most essential thing in human life, it is the only purpose of existence." That experience has completely changed my life and has retained its original intensity and clarity over the years. Even today it continues to have a powerful impact on my life.

Key Questions

Live the questions now. Maybe in the future, gradually, without noticing, one day away, you will live the answers.
—Rainer Maria Rilke, 'Be Patient'

The encounter with my spiritual nature began a path of personal investigation into the nature of *my* consciousnes, the only one I can experience and know. Driven by the desire to understand and reconcile the ineffable unitive experience of awakening with everyday reality, I worked intensely on myself for the following 20 years, during which I continued to carry out my professional activity, first as CEO and then as Chairman of Synaptics.

During that time I thoroughly explored my hitherto neglected inner reality, and tried to integrate it with the outer reality, living in and out of the world at the same time, so to speak: "in the world but not of the world." I also understood that the experience of the outer world is based on the reproducibility of shared events, while that of the inner world is strictly private and can be known by others only to the extent that we communicate it.

This inner work was the source of many intuitions and spontaneous transformations of thoughts and attitudes which gradually led me to an integration and harmonization of the two worlds, changing me profoundly. The most evident aspect has been the almost complete disappearance of a type of restlessness and mental anxiety that had always been part of my inner landscape.

I then began to question the theory that describes us as biological machines similar to computers because, based on the known laws of physics, we should be completely unconscious, just like our computers are. In fact, the taste of wine, the scent of a rose, the color orange, and the love for a son should not exist, because no scientist can explain how electrical or biochemical signals can produce these qualia. The fact that each of us feels them, and "knows" because of them, is indisputable, and this falsifies the idea that current physical theories are complete, i.e., they describe all of reality.

We are repeatedly told that we are biological robots, while the intense personal investigation that occurred after my awakening revealed otherwise, through many other extraordinary and spontaneous experiences of consciousness.

I felt that, rather than a body, we are spiritual beings temporarily imprisoned in a physical structure similar to a highly sophisticated drone. But if we allow ourselves to be convinced by those who insist we are only our mortal body, we will end up thinking that everything that exists originates only in the physical world. In that case we will not even ask ourselves questions about the nature and purpose of our creative impulses and emotions. In so doing we will also avoid investigating the meaning of our life which, as I now understand, is the most important part of our human existence and experience.

In summary, if we believe that the inanimate matter can explain all of reality, we will support an assumption already falsified by the fact that we are conscious.

As I progressed in my study, I gradually realized that, if we hypothesized that consciousness and free will are irreducible properties of nature, the scientific vision and narrative of reality would radically change and legitimize a profound spirituality, with unexpected consequences for both science and spirituality. But how could such a drastic change occur?

In my opinion, science should try to answer all our fundamental questions, not eliminate from reality what it cannot explain. I therefore decided to devote myself full-time to the scientific study of consciousness, and, in 2011, I created with my wife the Federico and Elvia Faggin Foundation to support basic research on consciousness starting from the premise that it is a fundamental and irreducible aspect of reality. The stakes are too high not to seriously consider the hypothesis that consciousness may exist before matter, or perhaps simultaneously with it.

The New Science of Consciousness

If we start from consciousness, free will, and creativity as irreducible properties of nature, the whole scientific conception of reality is overturned. In this new vision, the emotional and intuitive parts of life—ignored by materialism—return to play a central role. Aristotle said: "To educate the mind without educating the heart means not educating at all." We cannot let physicalism and reductionism define human nature and leave consciousness out from the description of the universe.

The physicalist and reductionist premises are perfect for describing the mechanical and symbolic-informational aspects of reality, but they are inadequate to explain its semantic aspects. If we insist that these assumptions describe all of reality, we eliminate *a priori* what distinguishes us from our machines and we erase our consciousness, our freedom and, above all, our humanity from the face of the universe.

If, on the other hand, we take our inner world seriously and begin to investigate it with love and determination, we will discover a new *Weltanschauung* that promises a creative and cooperative future for humankind, full of profound satisfactions. Life cannot be defined only by mere biological aspects, but, above all, by the triumph of the spiritual nature of the universe which silently guides us.

Quantum physics is already telling us that the universe is holistic and creative, and the new developments in quantum information theory justify, as we will see later, a new and revolutionary theory of consciousness and free will.

From my perspective, the only possible way to explain how the universe can create life and consciousness is that the universe is itself alive and conscious from the outset. If you take this hypothesis seriously, the entire conception of reality is transformed, with enormous consequences that point to a brilliant and fulfilling future. Creativity, ethics, free will, and joyful love can only come from consciouness. The immense mechanical intelligence, beyond the reach of the human brain, that comes from the machines we have invented will then add tremendous strength to our wisdom. Otherwise our technology will be used against humankind by those who promote the materialistic vision of the survival of the self-proclaimed fittest.

PART ONE

If this science, which will bring great benefits to man, does not help man to understand himself, it will end up turning against man.

—Giordano Bruno, *Of the Infinite, Universe, and Worlds*

1

The Nature of Physical Reality

In science everything is always different from what it would
seem according to common sense.
—Bertolt Brecht, *Life of Galileo*

What Is the World Like?

Today we are still grappling with this question, which human
beings have always asked themselves. For centuries it was
believed that the world consisted of earth, water, air, and fire in
various proportions.

Only in the last hundred years, with the advent of quantum
physics, have we made great strides in understanding the nature
of reality. We have in fact discovered that matter, which seems
solid and compact, is instead made of vibratory energy!

During the last 20 years we have then understood that
everything is made up of quantum information. However, there
is still no theory capable of giving us a vision of the world that
is consistent with both general relativity and quantum physics.
In this book I put forward the hypothesis that the universe has
been conscious and had free will forever. Therefore, nothing
is as it appears: Not only is the world much different than we
imagined, but reality is even more unbelievable and fantastic
than we ever thought possible because the evolution of the
universe reflects its ever-increasing self-knowing.

At the Dawn of Science

Homo sapiens lived a nomadic existence for millennia. Then,
about 10,000 years ago, with a flash of intuition, they learned
to "domesticate" vegetation. This led to the birth of agriculture

and caused human beings to settle in ever larger communities, giving rise to different professions and specializations.

At a certain point, the need to permanently document fleeting verbal agreements promoted a very important invention: writing.

The first Sumerian cuneiform script dates back to about 5000 years ago and the first religious-spiritual-philosophical text, the *Rigveda*, is about 3500 years old.

Writing also allowed us to record thoughts and ideas to be able to later reflect on and further develop them, an otherwise nearly impossible task given the dynamism and limited memory capacity of our mind. Furthermore, the written thoughts could be faithfully copied and shared with many other thinkers, and thus spread beyond the fading boundaries of words which persist only for a few seconds around the space in which they are pronounced. Writing was a necessary step in the development and perfecting of cooperative thinking, logic, and rationality.

About 2500 years ago, Greek philosophers developed rational thinking to a level never reached before. The philosophical-mathematical ideas of Pythagoras provided the foundations of physics and mathematics, which two centuries later brought us Euclid's *Elements*, the text that founded axiomatic mathematics. However, it took almost 2000 years to see the birth of experimental science, thanks to the awakening of humankind during the Renaissance, which brought us a new consciousness. Science and mathematics allowed us to regain freedom of thought, after a long period in which it was not legitimate to question the religious dogmas that dominated every act of daily life.

The scientific method was born with the innovative and courageous ideas of Copernicus, Galileo, Newton, and many others. By using observations, mathematical reasoning, and carefully crafted experiments to validate rational hypotheses, the scientific method allowed unprecedented progress in our understanding of the world.

Just like matter transformed by writing could faithfully reflect our ideas back to us, the same matter could also reveal its functioning to curious and sharp-witted minds who knew what questions to ask and what experiments to invent. Mathematics, then, made it possible to precisely formulate the abstract models followed by matter.

During its four centuries of existence, physics has immensely clarified our ideas about how the physical world functions, and it also provided the theoretical foundations for the development of many other scientific disciplines and technologies that have profoundly affected our life and the planet.

Physics is rooted in the experimental proof of the predictions made by its mathematical theories, which must be verified (or falsified) by experiments before they are accepted. Over the years, the physical world has revealed an ever-increasing complexity and has required the use of highly sophisticated and abstract mathematical theories, to the point where physics today resembles applied mathematics rather than the experimental physics of the nineteenth century. Nonetheless, the experiment has the last word, no matter how elegant or rational is the mathematical model. If the experiment fails, the beautiful theory must be changed or abandoned. In fact, Einstein said: "No amount of experiments will prove that I am right; a single experiment can prove that I was wrong."

This pragmatism led to constant progress, especially when new experiments showed inexplicable anomalies with existing theories. In a sense, the process is similar to the variation and selection principle used by life, because the theory surviving the selection made by many experiments becomes the winning one.

Until the late nineteenth century, classical physics provided the basic concepts and laws that fueled the industrial revolution. During the 1930s and 1940s, it also gave birth to the information age, based on the extraordinarily fertile idea of the computer. Computer technology then blossomed thanks to the solid-state microelectronics that emerged from quantum physics, the physics of the twentieth century, applied to crystals. Each era "rests on the shoulders" of the previous ones, and the new one is transforming our way of living even more rapidly than the industrial revolution that preceded it.

The Worldview of Classical Physics

In the early sixteenth century, Copernicus's heliocentric system found direct experimental confirmation in the work of Galileo Galilei, who turned the newly invented telescope to the sky and discovered four satellites orbiting Jupiter, and the phases of the planet Venus. His experiments provided incontrovertible evidence that not all celestial bodies revolve around the Earth, as was believed according to the Ptolemaic system.

Galileo gave us the first clear demonstration of the scientific method, stating that the physical world follows natural laws that can be expressed with the language of mathematics, an idea that dates back to Pythagoras. He also stated that mathematical theory must be tested experimentally, and that the final verdict must be based on the supreme authority of repeatable experiments. He was also the first scientist to postulate the invariance of physical laws in any reference frame that moves with uniform motion (called inertial frame). Galileo also experimentally derived $F = m \cdot a$, the empirical mathematical law that describes the accelerated motion of terrestrial objects.[1]

Isaac Newton, born the same year in which Galileo died, conceived the idea that the physical laws valid on Earth should also apply throughout the universe. His bold conception allowed him to formulate the law of universal gravitation and

---

1 Galileo made a series of experiments with an inclined plane on which a ball was made to roll at different angles, thus varying the propulsive force acting on the ball. In this way, Galileo proved that the motion was accelerated, with the acceleration proportional to the force.

to extend the principles of Galileo's mechanics with precise definitions of space, time, mass, force, and energy. Starting from a purely mathematical theory, Newton then proved Kepler's empirical laws describing the motion of the planets around the Sun. To this end, Newton also invented a new field of mathematics called differential calculus. This work provided the first example of how to do theoretical physics, that is, how to do science starting from a general mathematical theory. From such theory any particular case could be derived by specifying some parameters and the initial conditions of the system: an exceptionally fruitful paradigm.

The success of Newton's mechanics provided the theoretical basis for a technology that was no longer purely empirical but also based on solid mathematical foundations, thus leading to and fueling the industrial revolution.

The scientific method became the new methodology for investigating nature, and changed the traditional way of thinking. With it, rationality and experimental evidence superseded speculative and intuitive thinking, not to mention the respect (or fear) of authority that characterized previous practice. Scientific positivism became the new creed, founded on reductionism, materialism, and the absolute faith in mathematical logic, considered free of internal contradictions. This vision allowed us to mathematically study with great success many complex systems by reducing them to the sum of their parts.

A New Way of Thinking

The intellectual euphoria that characterized the early nineteenth century can be succinctly described by Pierre-Simon Laplace's famous statement in the Introduction to his *Essai philosophique sur les probabilités* of 1814:

We can consider the present state of the universe as the effect of its past and the cause of its future. An intellect that at a certain moment knew all the forces that set nature in motion and the positions of all the elements of which nature is composed, if this intellect were also vast enough to subject these data to analysis, it could embrace in a single formula the movements of the largest bodies in the universe and those of the smallest atom; for such an intellect nothing would be uncertain and the future like the past would be present before his eyes.

This position of extreme determinism and reductionism was called "Laplace's demon" and was also used to claim that free will is an illusion. This point of view is still prevalent today among most scientists and philosophers, despite the indeterministic, probabilistic, and holistic character of quantum physics. I will return to these crucial points in later chapters.

The nineteenth century marked the maturation of classical physics with the development of thermodynamics, statistical mechanics, and electromagnetism. The latter was a completely new field of physics about which, just a century earlier, almost nothing was known. The discovery of electromagnetic waves as oscillations of an "energy field" marked the triumph of classical theoretical physics. The unsuspected existence of these waves was first predicted by James Clerk Maxwell's equations in 1865, and experimentally verified by Heinrich Rudolf Hertz in 1887.

Electromagnetism changed our fundamental ideas about the nature of the physical world, previously considered essentially mechanical, and heralded a new world full of unsuspected technological and application possibilities.

At the end of the nineteenth century, classical physics dominated the scientific view of the world that can be summarized as follows:

1. The physical world is all that exists (naturalism) and its existence is independent of the observer (realism).

2. Physical reality is created by the interactions of "particles" of matter in space and time (atomism). These particles are imagined as Democritus's atoms: irreducible, indestructible, hard, microscopic, separate, and ontological objects.
3. Space and time are independent and absolute. They are the stage on which particles of mass and electricity interact. Mass particles move in space and time following gravitational and other mechanical forces, while the movements of electrical particles follow Maxwell's equations and produce an electromagnetic field that influences and is influenced by all other electrical particles.
4. The behavior of a complex system can be completely described as the sum of the behaviors of all its parts (reductionism).
5. If we know the initial conditions of all the particles of a system, we can, at least in principle, predict all the past and all the future evolution of the system (determinism).
6. We live in a static and closed universe in which entropy (disorder) is constantly increasing.
7. One can observe the world without disturbing it.
8. Mathematics can give us a true and comprehensive description of reality.
9. The evolution of all living species follows the Darwinian principle of random variation and natural selection.
10. The nature of mind and matter was debated primarily by philosophers. Cartesian dualism claimed that mind and matter are completely different "substances," while materialism claimed that only matter exists (monism). For the materialist, the mind is simply one of the functions performed by the brain.

The materialist was convinced that classical physics would be able to fully explain the nature of life and consciousness, using the same method and the same assumptions that had produced the enormous amount of knowledge and progress witnessed in the previous two centuries.

The End of Classical Physics

In one of his splendid books, Thornton Wilder said that the bridge of San Luis Rey—an ancient, aerial, beautiful bridge, the most beautiful in all of Peru—was apparently part of the things that last forever: it was unthinkable that it could break. However, one Friday at noon, all of a sudden, that bridge fell apart.

At the end of the nineteenth century, the fundamental assumptions of classical physics seemed universal truths, solid, and unassailable. The remarkable successes of science and technology had brought with them the false impression of knowing much more than was really known, backing up the strong belief that those basic ideas and principles were a reliable guide for the future. On the threshold of the twentieth century, the famous physicist Lord William Thompson Kelvin had stated: "By now there is nothing new to discover in physics; all that's left to do is more and more precise measurements." And this certainty (some would say arrogance) was expressed despite the presence of some anomalies that classical physics could not explain, and which would soon cause the collapse of the entire intellectual structure of classical physics.

It took a quarter of a century to explain the phenomenology of these persistent anomalies, and to do so it became necessary to replace almost all the fundamental assumptions of classical physics. This profound revision led us to special and general relativity and to quantum mechanics: a new physics that replaced determinism and reductionism with indeterminism and holism.

However, the needed change in perspective was so difficult to accept that, a century later, we are still trying to come to terms with the conceptual revolution brought about by these new theories. In particular, we still have difficulty understanding the indeterminism of quantum physics, which has eliminated the possibility of knowing the whole truth about the physical world: not only in practice, but also in principle. The *interpretation* of reality provided by classical physics could not have been more wrong!

In 1899 three main phenomena were unexplainable by classical physics: black body radiation, the photoelectric effect, and the Lorentz transformations.

Black body radiation refers to the frequency spectrum of the light emitted by a hot object as a function of its temperature. The anomalous behavior of this radiation[2] was explained by Max Planck in the year 1900 using a mathematical device that at first seemed unjustified. Planck found that, if the exchange of energy between matter and radiation had occurred only in integer multiples of a discrete value of energy—called the quantum of energy—then the mystery would be solved, at least mathematically. In other words, Planck hypothesized that there must be a minimum energy exchange, greater than zero, and proportional to the frequency of the radiation, and that all exchanges should occur in *integer* multiples of this minimum. Fractional quanta were not allowed.

---

2   According to classical physics, the amount of electromagnetic radiation emitted by a body in thermal equilibrium with the environment (called "black body") had to increase without limit as the frequency increased, whereas the measured behavior tended to zero. This was such a glaring discrepancy that it was called the "ultraviolet catastrophe." At the beginning of the twentieth century, this anomaly was a big thorn in the side of physics.

In 1905, a young Albert Einstein was able to explain the photoelectric effect[3] by assuming that the interaction between light and matter that produces electrons is caused by "particles of light" having energy quanta provided by the Planck relation. Einstein hypothesized that light, when interacting with the atoms of matter, behaves like many particles, and not like a wave, as Thomas Young had shown almost 100 years earlier.

Einstein's explanation contradicted the established principles of classical physics and earned him the Nobel Prize. The quantum of light was later called a *photon* and its implications were astounding. Hence photons were found to have a double personality because they acted both as particles and as waves: an almost contradictory and quite disturbing behavior. According to Einstein, the energy E, needed to extract an electron from an atom, had to come from a *single collision* with a "particle of light," whose quantum of energy had to be equal to, or greater than, E. Furthermore, that energy could not originate from a sum of quanta in which each quantum had energy less than E; it had to be a single-event process. This intuition explained why the photoelectric effect had a threshold that depended only on the frequency of the incident light and not on its intensity.

The profound impact of Einstein's explanation was to show that light could be understood as composed of many individual photons which did not lose their individuality once they were added.

In 1905 Albert Einstein also explained the mysterious Lorentz transformation, i.e., the fact that the objects described

---

3   The photoelectric effect is produced when a beam of intense light illuminates matter and produces electrons. The puzzling and unexplained behavior was the following: when the light frequency was below a certain value, there was no emission, even when the light intensity was very high. Maxwell's equations instead predicted that the number of electrons should be proportional to the intensity of light without regard to its frequency.

by Maxwell's equations violate the simple Galilean inertial transformation when their relative speed is close to that of light. This anomaly was elegantly solved by assuming that the speed of light, c, is the same in all inertial frames of reference, i.e., those frames that move at a constant speed. The consequences of this simple assumption were devastating, because it was discovered that time and space, considered independent and absolute since Newton's time, depended instead on the relative velocity between observer and observed. As their relative speed approached c, the time marked by a clock that was part of the observed system slowed down and the length of a stick aligned with the direction of motion was shortened, as compared to the time and length of identical clocks and sticks within the observer's frame of reference!

This theory was called special relativity. According to it, no material object with mass m greater than zero could accelerate and reach a speed equal to c, because its mass would increase without limit as its relative speed approached c.

Einstein also discovered that the notion of simultaneity of events was not as absolute as it was thought, but was relative to the motion of the observer. For example, when an observer A sees event 1 happen *before* event 2, a second observer B, who moves with respect to A, could see event 1 happen *after* event 2! The concept of causality also lost its absolute status.

Finally, Einstein discovered that the rest mass of an object m and its energy E are proportional, according to the famous relation $E = mc^2$. The mass of a resting particle is therefore energy confined into a microscopic portion of space. Incredible!

After 1905, physics could never be the same.

The Revelation of a New World

In 1911 Lord Ernest Rutherford discovered that the atom, considered a particle of solid and indivisible matter since the time of Democritus, turned out to be almost empty and divisible, composed of a tiny nucleus surrounded by electrons, similar to a miniature solar system. Two years later, Niels Bohr was able to explain the discrete spectrum of light emitted or absorbed by a hydrogen atom by combining Maxwell's equations, Rutherford's discoveries, and Einstein's photon in a semiclassical theory. Once again the incredible fecundity of Planck's quantum of action was confirmed by revealing a further quantum aspect of the real world, in contrast to the continuum described by classical physics.

In 1915 Einstein completed his theory of general relativity (GR), showing that the gravitational force could be explained as a geometric effect on spacetime due to the mass of objects. Consequently, when a planet orbits a star, it actually moves in a "straight line," but since the surrounding space is "curved" by the enormous mass of the star, the planet ends up moving in an elliptical orbit around it. The physics community was stunned!

GR can be concisely described in the words of physicist John Archibald Wheeler: "Space-time tells matter how to move; matter tells space-time how to bend." In other words, the global distribution of matter affects the local properties of spacetime, and the local properties of spacetime determine how matter moves. When matter moves locally, its global distribution changes, and this in turn changes the local properties of spacetime.

It almost looks like a "snake biting its tail," yet the same analogy can also illustrate how electromagnetic waves propagate, because a change in the electric field causes a change in the magnetic field, and a change in the magnetic field causes a change in the electric field. These reciprocal changes occurring within the electromagnetic field, a real but *immaterial* "field," cause the propagation of a wave in spacetime without the need for any physical means. At the end of the nineteenth century it was thought that waves required a medium such as air or water to propagate. Sound waves, for example, cannot propagate in a vacuum. Therefore, empty space was thought to be filled with a "luminiferous ether," a physical medium capable of vibrating to carry light waves. A famous experiment in 1887 by Albert Michelson and Edward Morley showed instead that the ether did not exist. Einstein's special relativity theory was in fact motivated by the desire to understand the consequences of the experimental absence of the ether.

GR expresses the existence of *feedback* from the whole to the parts as well as the existence of *feedforward* from the parts to the whole. Feedback is a top-down influence in which the global distribution of matter (the whole) determines the local properties of spacetime that inform the local behavior of matter (the parts). Feedforward is a bottom-up influence in which the local behavior of the matter determines the future global distribution of the matter that constitutes the whole.

GR contradicts the principles of *classical* physics, in which space and time are absolute and the behavior of the whole is determined solely by the behavior of the parts, meaning that only feedforward exists. The story does not end here, however, because the first decades of the twentieth century had many other big surprises in store.

Quantum Mechanics

In 1926 Erwin Schrödinger extended the principle of minimum action[4] to the quantum reality that was gradually emerging, and his wave equation gave birth to quantum mechanics. The discrete

---

4   The principle of least action is central to physics and has been applied to mechanics, thermodynamics, quantum mechanics, and string theory. It is quite technical and difficult to explain correctly without high-level math. To give an intuitive but imprecise understanding, imagine a mechanical system undergoing a change from an initial to a final configuration. The principle of least action states that, of all the possible paths that a system could follow, the path taken is the one that minimizes the action, where action is defined as the path integral of the system's energy over time.

solutions of the Schrödinger equation are called wave functions, and represent the temporal evolution of the state of a system, for example a particle. Furthermore, the square of the absolute value of a wave function defines the probability of finding such a particle in a certain region of space.

We owe this probabilistic interpretation of the wave function to Max Born, who formulated it in the same year (1926). Interestingly, Max Born and Werner Heisenberg had developed matrix mechanics in 1925, a different formulation of quantum physics, which later proved to be equivalent to Schrödinger's wave mechanics.

Two years later, Heisenberg postulated the "uncertainty principle." It is a mathematical relationship that shows the impossibility of measuring two "conjugate" variables with arbitrary precision, such as the position and momentum of a particle, or the energy and time of the same.[5]

The precious determinism of classical physics was falsified where it hurt most, because the nature of the elementary particles that should have determined everything else proved itself to be indeterministic and probabilistic. The theory no longer tells us the specific state that will manifest but only its probability. This is a different type of "indeterminism" than the one expressed by the Heisenberg principle, revealing an irreducible knowledge gap between the quantum evolution of the system and its measurement. This gap is called "the measurement problem" of quantum physics because it requires something to occur between the quantum system and the measuring apparatus—called the "collapse of the wave function"—which is not described by the theory. Much has been written about this problem, and yet there is still no solution that a majority of physicists agree upon.

---

5 A detailed explanation of the key concepts and terms used by quantum physics can be found in the Glossary at the end of the book.

Wolfgang Pauli, Nobel Prize in Physics, said in his speech on 13 December 1946: "I was not spared the shock that every physicist accustomed to the classical way of thinking suffered when he first heard of the fundamental postulate of Bohr's quantum theory." And, in 1950, in a letter to A. Pais, Pauli wrote: "It is my personal opinion that for the science of the future, reality will be neither psychic nor physical: in some way, it will be both and neither one of them."

In 1928 Paul Dirac combined Schrödinger's non-relativistic equation with Heisenberg-Born's matrix mechanics, and extended it to the relativistic case, thus creating the first quantum field theory of electrons. His equation predicted the existence of antielectrons (positrons), which were later discovered experimentally.

Physical reality was gradually revealing a completely unsuspected nature.

The End of Certainty

In conjunction with the many shocking discoveries in physics, extraordinary developments were also occurring in the field of mathematics. It was the mathematician Kurt Gödel in 1931 who delivered the *coup de grâce* to the logical positivism that dominated the philosophical-scientific thought at the end of the nineteenth century. Gödel demonstrated the *incompleteness* of mathematics, proving that classical logic was insufficient to establish the truth of all possible statements that obeyed the rules of an axiomatic system sufficiently complex to contain arithmetic.

Having proved that there are *undecidable* sentences, that is, sentences that cannot be formally proved to be either true or false without introducing new axioms, Gödel's theorem eliminated the completeness and absolute certainty that mathematics was thought to have.

Another important aspect of mathematics, which is often underestimated, is that the truth of its statements is entirely based on the unproven truth of the set of axioms on which there is agreement. These axioms are in fact considered *self-evident truths*, accepted as such by convention because their truth cannot be proven. The presumed objectivity of mathematics is therefore based on the subjective acceptance of what is considered self-evident. It is therefore legitimate to have some doubts about the absolute certainty that we can attribute to mathematical statements, especially when they are applied to the real world.

In fact, with quantum physics the world ceased to behave in a self-evident way! How, then, can we choose the postulates of quantum physics when we have yet to solve the measurement problem? Self-evidence lost its supposed universal validity. The physicist Leon Max Lederman put it this way: "It is not the uncertainty of measurement that hides reality; on the contrary, it is reality itself that never provides certainties in the classical-Galilean sense of the term, when examining phenomena at the atomic scale."

In the 1960s, mathematicians rediscovered and formalized another great surprise: *chaotic* systems. A chaotic system is a system whose behavior depends so sensitively on its initial conditions that it diverges exponentially when tiny variations of those conditions occur. Said differently, to predict the future behavior of a chaotic system, it is necessary to know the initial conditions with more precision than is possible to know, even in principle, given Heisenberg's uncertainty principle.

This means that even simple classical systems, such as three objects in mechanics,[6] can behave in a chaotic way.

---

6   The "three bodies problem" in classical physics is the following: when three objects interact gravitationally, there are regimes of initial conditions (the position and the linear and angular momentum of each object) in which the behavior can be stable, unstable, or chaotic. *The behavior is actually chaotic for most of the initial conditions.*

Before the discovery of chaotic systems, determinism was considered synonymous with predictability. Classical physics is deterministic, but now we know that determinism is necessary, but not sufficient, to guarantee predictability because chaotic systems stop being predictable after a while. Laplace's characterization of reality was erroneously based on the idea that predictability and determinism were synonymous. Laplace's demon, the powerful intellect that in principle could have known everything, turned out to be an illusion.

The conclusion is that any mathematical theory of physical reality is a valid model only within certain limits, and therefore it is not totally dependable. The real world outclasses any attempt to completely describe it.

2

The Nature of Quantum Reality

The universe is not made up of things, but of vibratory energy networks that emerge from something even deeper and more subtle.
—Werner Karl Heisenberg

Between 1928 and the late 1960s, Dirac's quantum field theory was extended to the interactions between electrons and photons (quantum electrodynamics, or QED theory) and later to nuclear interactions involving the *strong* and the *electroweak* forces (quantum chromodynamics, or QCD theory). Finally, in 1975, the Standard Model of quantum physics emerged, according to which there are six quarks for the strong interaction and six leptons for the weak one. Each quark and each lepton have an antiparticle, and the interactions between particles are mediated by the gauge bosons—the carriers of the strong, the electroweak (two bosons), and the electromagnetic force—and by the Higgs boson, the carrier of mass.

Therefore, all that exists are spacetime, described by general relativity, and 17 quantum fields, described by quantum field theory (QFT). Each elementary particle is an excited state of the homonymous field. Within QFT the particles are no longer objects and the ontology resides in the fields, away from the particles of classical physics.

Quantum Field Theory and General Relativity
According to QFT, elementary particles, atoms, molecules, proteins, cells, organs, and living organisms constitute hierarchical organizations of states belonging to the quantum fields, with ever-growing complexity. These fields have space

and time in common and are the fundamental entities that, interacting with each other, create everything that exists physically. For example, all the electrons in our body and in the rest of the universe are waves or "quantum states" of the same quantum field of electrons. Each quantum wave describes the superposition of the possible states of an electron with probabilities specified by the square of the amplitude of the component waves representing each state.

I know that this explanation seems far-fetched; however, for the moment there is no simpler way to express it.

The view of the universe that emerges from the description of quantum states (particles) is very strange, because the variables assume a defined value only when two particles interact, but none of the variables are defined prior to their interaction. Furthermore, the basis of reality is indetermination and granularity instead of continuity. A particle behaves like a probability wave that can take all possible paths, and thus it may be found in a volume of space, rather than moving with a precise trajectory.

However, the probability wave has little in common with the waves of classical physics, which are collective phenomena produced by a vast number of classical particles. In other words, particles do not exist as we imagined them, for they can only be described as probability waves that allow us to predict the probabilities of all possible states in which they could be detected. And yet the specific state that will manifest is not predicted by the theory when the "collapse of the wave function" occurs.

Today, quantum field theory (QFT) and general relativity (GR) constitute the two pillars of theoretical physics. However, GR describes a classical and continuous field rather than a discrete quantum field, in contrast to the fundamental quantization of the other three forces of nature. For more than 70 years the community of theoretical physicists has labored to unify QFT with GR, but so far without success despite enormous efforts. If that unification were to happen, it would describe spacetime, the gravitational force and all the quantum fields as a single unified field.

Particles Are Waves of Probability

When physicists say that "a particle interferes with itself," they mean that the probability waves that describe the possible states of a particle interfere with each other when they are allowed to take more than one path. This is the case with the famous and puzzling double-slit experiment. The interference produces a probability of finding an electron in a large region of space, telling us that the electron cannot be a classical particle that moves along a well-defined trajectory, but behaves instead like a "probability cloud" described by the wave function.

In this experiment, particles are sent one at a time through a barrier with two slits and are detected on a screen placed on the other side of the barrier. If particles were classical, each of them would always pass through one of the two slits and would be detected in a small portion of the screen corresponding to each of the slits. However, a quantum particle behaves like a probability wave. When the wave hits the barrier, it splits into two branches that combine and produce an interference pattern, much like when we throw two stones into a pond. The square of the amplitude of the combined wave hitting the screen represents the probability of detecting the particle at the various points of the screen.

Amazingly, even an atom or a macromolecule can interfere with itself! This experiment clearly shows that the particle is not a tiny ball, even though it is always detected in a point of the screen. In other words, when the particle is not observed, it can be *represented* as a cloud of probability, but this does not mean it is a cloud. When it is finally observed, the particle always behaves like a little ball, but this does not mean it is a ball.

What is it then? No one knows. When a quantum particle is not observed, it cannot be located in space like a classical particle, otherwise it could not pass through both slits at the same time. What "crosses" both slits is a "probability wave," which is a *representation* of the particle, not the particle as a wave.

In other words, we know next to nothing about what a particle is when it is not measured. *The probability wave does not describe the particle, but what we can know about the particle when we measure it.* The wave only gives us the probability of detecting the particle at every point on the screen. But knowing the probability does not tell us where the particle will actually hit the screen. To show that a particle "behaves like a wave," we have to repeat the experiment with many particles all prepared the same way. Then, each particle will hit the screen at different points, and *collectively* they will show the interference pattern calculated by the mathematical theory.

Quantum theory therefore allows us to calculate very well the interference pattern produced by a large number of particles, but it cannot tell us where each particle will manifest itself. A quantum particle behaves like an extremely complex system, not like a classical particle, and quantum physics cannot describe the trajectory of a single particle, not because the theory is incomplete, but for the simple reason that quantum particles are not objects. They are "something" we have yet to fully understand.

We Don't Know What a Particle Is

Classical physics described physical reality as if its description were the truth. It described instead the illusory model of reality created by our senses. Quantum physics does not describe reality either. It can only tell us what we can know about a deeper reality that always presents itself as "particles," quanta, in our measurements. This also includes electromagnetic waves that manifest only as photons, i.e., as particles. In other words, the probability waves of quantum physics do not describe reality but only what we can possibly measure of a deeper reality that manifests itself in the spacetime screen of our senses.

It is astounding to find that a classical object that we thought was real is instead the collective behavior of gazillions of invisible and interacting probability waves that do not exist as such in our world until they manifest as particles in spacetime. Where and how, then, do "particles" exist when we do not observe them? And what makes them show up as particles?

Quantum particles reserved another great surprise because they can do something that no classical particle can do: they can be "entangled." This phenomenon consists in the existence of particles that have joint properties. For example, two electrons can have their magnetic spin entangled in such a way that the sum of the two spins must be 0. Therefore, if we measure the spin of electron A and find that it is $+1/2$, the spin of electron B will simultaneously be $-1/2$, and vice versa. These are called entangled states.

The strange thing is that, when the spin of A is measured, this measurement disturbs A in an unpredictable way, so much so that the probability of obtaining $+1/2$ or $-1/2$ is the same, just like when we toss a fair coin. But then, how does B *instantly know*, regardless of its distance from A, that the measure of A gave $+1/2$ when it could just as likely have been $-1/2$? The principle of locality is no longer respected since no influence should move faster than the speed of light. No one can explain why the spins of the distant particles are *always* correlated, regardless of their distance, and without particle A being able to communicate with B.

Yet this phenomenon cannot be exploited to communicate faster than the speed of light for, to communicate, Alice must have control over the message it sends to Bob and this is impossible given the 50-50 probabilistic behavior of the particles. If classical correlated states existed before the measurement, by repeating the measurement on many similarly prepared systems, the percentage of correlations should not exceed a certain maximum value determined by Bell's theorem. Entangled quantum systems, however, may exceed this limit. The only way to explain this phenomenon is that the state of the two systems cannot exist prior to the measurement; it must be created during the measurement process. How correlations can violate Bell's theorem is still a mystery (see also the entry *Quantum entanglement* in the Glossary).

This quantum property is called *nonlocality*, because it behaves as if the two particles were a single system manifesting in two different positions as if space did not exist. In other words, while the physical result of the measurement can propagate only at the speed of light, the "knowledge" by the two-particle is instantaneous. Entanglement is telling us that spacetime may not be what we generally imagine it to be, since these nonlocal properties are inexplicable.

The Worldview of Quantum Physics

The world as we created it is the result of our thinking. We cannot change it without changing our way of thinking.
—Albert Einstein

The changes to our worldview brought about by a century of scientific breakthroughs have been so numerous and astonishing that their implications have yet to be fully metabolized. In summary, the physical world described by contemporary physics has the following extraordinary properties:

1. Nature is not continuous, but discrete. There is a limit to the divisibility of space, time, and matter. All properties, both of fields and states (particles), are discrete. The fundamental nature of physical reality is quantum.

2. Elementary particles appear in spacetime only when fields are excited or interact with other fields. Particles do not exist as objects, but only as excited states of the homonymous fields.

3. When an interaction occurs between two quantum systems, the states of both will change, with the creation of an "entangled state," having new properties that are not the sum of the properties of the component states. For example, when the electron field interacts with the proton field, the result could be a hydrogen atom, a structure with entirely new properties.

4. Indeterminism is an irreducible property of nature. We cannot measure two non-commutable variables at the same time, and we cannot even predict where a particle will be, not even in principle. We can only predict the probabilities of finding a particle in a certain region of space.

5. A measuring apparatus that interacts with a quantum system is a quantum-classical system that amplifies the result of a quantum interaction to produce a classical signal that can be shared. The many states that are possible in the quantum world will "collapse" into a single reality in our physical world. However, the specific state that will occur cannot be predicted before the measurement, unless the probability of occurrence is 1.

6. Particles are not subject to "forces" as classical physics describes. Quantum particles interact by exchanging other particles. In this way they behave as if there were a force acting between them.

7. Physical reality is described by a set of fields subject to the laws of quantum field theory (QFT) and general relativity (GR). Everything we observe derives from the action of these laws upon the fields.

8. The union of QFT and GR in a single coherent theory promises to reduce physical reality to a single unified quantum field. However, this theory does not yet exist.
9. Nonlocality reveals the existence of a totality that cannot be divided into separable parts. This totality escapes any human description or representation because it cannot be described by the properties of its separate parts. A compound quantum system has *properties that are incompatible with any property of its parts*. This type of holism does not exist in classical systems because the properties of a classical system are compatible with the properties of its parts [2].

The impact of nonlocality, quantum uncertainty, and the incompleteness of mathematics is enormous:

1. There is no longer a one-to-one correspondence between an element of theory and an element of reality. Determinism and reductionism do not exist, not even in principle.
2. Reality is one. Its existence is manifested in the interactions with observers that are indivisible parts of the same reality. Moreover, the idea that reality exists whether we observe it or not (realism) is false. The local realism that Albert Einstein strongly supported has been proved false.[1] In the

---

1 In 1935, Albert Einstein, Boris Podolsky, and Nathan Rosen published an article arguing that quantum physics was incomplete because it violated the locality principle. The argument was based on a thought experiment which produced a contradiction (later called the EPR Paradox, from the authors' initials). It took almost 50 years to be able to carry out the first experiment that could confirm or falsify Einstein's statement. That experiment and all subsequent ones have shown that quantum physics is correct and that Einstein's objections were not valid. The implications of nonlocality are staggering and have not yet been fully understood.

words of John Archibald Wheeler: "No phenomenon is a phenomenon until it is an observed phenomenon."

3. Reality is continually created by the interactions that take place between its "parts" (parts that are not separable, however). And each observation changes both the observer and the observed. There is no privileged position: in an interaction of two "parts," the positions of observer and observed are symmetrical.

As Werner Heisenberg said: "The idea of an objective real world whose smaller parts exist objectively in the same sense as stones or trees exist, regardless of whether we observe them or not... is impossible."

According to Wheeler, "The term 'observer' should be replaced by the term 'participant.' This replacement could indicate the radically new role of consciousness in physics... subjective and objective reality in a sense create each other." It is legitimate, on the basis of his reflections, to ask ourselves whether "It is possible that the universe in a strange sense is 'brought to light' by the participation of those who participate."

Nonlocality implies that the Whole cannot be the subject of scientific investigation, not even in principle. There is an "epistemic horizon of events," which precludes the Whole being entirely derivable from the properties of its parts. The Whole is more than the sum of its parts. By breaking down the Whole into parts (reductionism), we create a model that differs from the Whole according to how we have divided it.

A Monistic Conception of the Universe

The Cartesian dualism proposed a vision of reality in which mind and matter are fundamentally separate substances. Materialism is a monism based on classical physics, which identifies reality with the matter from which the mind also derives. The mind, however, is considered *epiphenomenal* because only matter can influence reality. Idealism, on the other hand, is a philosophical monism that supports the idea that the mind is fundamental and that matter derives from mind. Hence, the mind "commands" matter.

There is another position in which mind-and-matter are two irreducible aspects of the same reality, that is, they are like two sides of the same coin that cannot be separated. It is a form of panpsychism that I will talk about a lot in the second part of the book. This is a monism that is like the wave-particle nature of quantum physics, i.e., the two complementary and irreducible aspects of the same entity. I think that the universe, in its essence, must contain the seeds of both mind and matter. Mind and matter are like the inner and the outer surfaces of a sphere, and ontology belongs to the whole sphere and not just to what can be observed from the outside or from the inside.

The whole of current physics corresponds to the unified field that combines QFT with GR to describe the outer physical reality, what we call matter, but also includes energy, space, and time. My position is that physics needs to also deal with the interiority of reality, what we call mind, which includes consciousness, free will, and life in its most general manifestation.

How Do We Know?

The only task of science is to light the way.
—Mikhail Bakunin

What proof do we have that we perceive reality as it is? How do we decide that something exists and has certain properties worth exploring? How do we determine that a particular search makes sense?

It always starts from our conscious experience of the world and from our inborn desire to understand and to imagine, together with our ability to reason. This allows us to make assumptions about what the "objects of reality" are and how they interact. We do this by replacing physical objects with mental abstractions, and then constructing theories that attempt to explain our experience by making predictions that may or may not be verified. In the event that the predictions do not correspond to the experience, we must go back to where we went wrong and change something. Discovering and fixing anomalies is what often allows us to make progress.

In the last few millennia, our reasoning has been formalized with the concept of an axiomatic system exemplified by Euclidean geometry. This method makes it possible to logically prove the truth of a sentence on the basis of the presumed truth of a small number of axioms or postulates. In mathematics, the objects of study and the choice of axioms come from our intuition, whose origin is a mystery. The axioms are statements assumed to be true without proof, because they are held to be self-evident. But would an axiom be self-evident to a monkey or to a computer? When we believe that "A" is self-evident, we assume that the way we imagine or perceive A corresponds to reality. This is an understandable position, but it could also be wrong.

We create the mathematical axioms, but the physical world is not our work, so the world could be very different from what we think is self-evident. Quantum theory has amply shown to us that the reality of classical physics, considered almost universally self-evident a century ago, turned out to be a great self-deception. In fact, the deception is so convincing that many scientists still refuse to fully accept the disturbing philosophical and interpretative implications of phenomena such as quantum superposition, entanglement, and indeterminism.

One hundred years ago, most scholars were sure that classical physics faithfully represented the ontology of the universe, but then, the experimental evidence that falsified the postulates of classical physics required new axioms which barely make sense to the insiders, never mind to the rest of us. How do we know then that the new axioms are correct? The only way to know is to falsify the predictions of the theory that is based on those axioms. But how do we choose the new axioms to replace those that have been falsified? What is it that makes us know? Does a robot know?

Semantic and Symbolic Knowledge

I know I exist because I am *aware* of knowing what I affirm to know, i.e., that I exist. This is Descartes' *cogito ergo sum*: I know I exist because I experience "existing." I call this type of knowledge *direct semantic knowledge*, because it refers to my own private experience: it is a reflection of my consciousness upon itself and produces qualia whose meaning is, "I exist."

I call *indirect* semantic knowledge that which refers to knowledge obtained by observing the external world through my senses. For example, I can say that I saw a dog because I experienced it in my consciousness by looking at it. Indirect semantic knowledge, however, does not assure us that what we know is completely true. It is only a necessary, but not sufficient, condition for knowing the truth.

A machine, on the other hand, "knows" without knowing that it knows and without even knowing what it means to know. Its knowing is unconscious and mechanical and cannot be called knowledge: it is simply *information* made up of meaningless symbols, which can be mechanically linked to some other deterministic information or action. The robot's actions do not involve free and conscious choices made by the "robot" as an independent entity from the sum of its parts.

I should point out that we too have the same type of automatic behavior as robots in many situations, for example when we drive a car. In this case, together with the pure symbolic information that a robot has, we also have the conscious experience of the landscape, the road, and the situation in which we find ourselves. Consciousness performs the function of supervisor of the mechanical processes of our body. It does not contribute to driving, however, unless it is necessary to intervene, in which case it takes over the conditional autonomy it granted to the body.

It is consciousness that understands the situation and therefore "knows" when to intervene. And this makes all the difference between a robot and a human being.

In a robot, there is no conscious self-reflection that is independent of the algorithmic program and can thus change the decisions hardwired in the program. In a robot, there is no "self" and no self-witness. In a machine there is no "pause for reflection" between symbols and action, because only within our consciousness can we find the meaning of symbols, a possible doubt, and the free will to choose differently than the dictates of the mechanism.

There is a clear distinction within us between the symbolic "knowledge" of the machine and our semantic knowledge. The first is not knowledge but objective information that can be copied and shared; the second is a subjective and private experience that occurs in the intimacy of a conscious entity. As such, semantic knowledge is a dynamic state of consciousness that contains within itself also the sense of its own dependability, i.e., the sense of how much one can trust one's own knowledge.

I know that I know; I know that I don't know; I also know when I am not sure I know and when I pretend to know. Semantic knowledge is a property of a conscious entity; it is not a property of a machine.

What Is Consciousness Good For?

It is our consciousness that makes us human. Without it we would be acting as a robot, and life would have no meaning.
—David Chalmers

Someone might ask: "What good is consciousness if a robot can drive a car better than us?" This is a typical question based on the assumption that we are biological machines existing in a world governed by the laws of classical physics and by the survival of the fittest. If we believe in this interpretation of reality, any subjective value will appear illusory to us. Within this perspective, our inner experience, emotions, dreams, aspirations, joys, sorrows, curiosity, music, art, love for life, and our rare but exhilarating sense of oneness with the universe and with all of life are only illusions.

But how can we compare ourselves to a mechanism when a living cell is not even close to a mechanism like a computer? Have you ever seen a computer give birth to another computer, hardware and software included? Have those who promote the idea that computers might become conscious someday ever given you a convincing explanation of how this might happen?

Are you willing to throw away everything that gives meaning and purpose to your life for an idea based on the desire of materialists to uphold their belief? How can consciousness arise "somehow" when the complexity of a classical system becomes big enough? How can complexity generate consciousness and free will from a deterministic system? What is the mechanism by which a new quality emerges from something that does not possess such a quality? At most, complexity is a necessary condition to *harbor* consciousness, but not to create it!

Do you believe that large and complex computers that contain millions of microprocessors and consume megawatts of energy are conscious?

Each one of us can say, "I am conscious," not because we repeat a meaningless collection of bits from memory, like a computer would, but because the meaning of that sentence exists *prior* to the words we pronounce. Meaning is also the reason why words exist. And consciousness is what allows us to know the meaning of the symbols that our senses capture. Consciousness also gives us the freedom of choice that many scientists and philosophers consider illusory because it is falsified by the axioms of classical physics that they have chosen to accept.

If the only reality we admit is the one we can measure with rulers and clocks, we have already eliminated the inner reality that makes us love life and enjoy the great gift of human existence. By doing so, we accept the prejudice of those who consider real only what is repeatable and measurable in a laboratory, i.e., the idea that only objective reality exists, whereupon consciousness and free will are declared illusions despite the evidence of their existence within each of us. I am referring to our thoughts, emotions, sensations, feelings, common sense, and creativity, the phenomena that no machine possesses.

Mahatma Gandhi liked to say: "I don't need to go far to look for the sacred cave, I carry it inside me." Why do we want to give credit to those who want to convince us otherwise? We need to wake up from this sort of trance and trust instead our inner voice, which whispers the words of Richard Bach in *A Bridge to Eternity*: "Intuition does not lie when it whispers to us: 'You are not dust, you are magic!'" You are not a machine! You are consciousness! And, as Gautama Buddha said: "When you find out who you are, you will laugh at what you thought you were..." I am convinced that when our rationality is uniquely informed by the principles of materialism, reductionism, and the survival of the fittest, it can only lead us to unbridled competition, racism, and war. Indeed what has characterized much of human history. However, the unconsciousness of robots and the discoveries of quantum physics are telling us that materialism and reductionism are only approximations of a deeper and more mysterious reality, something we have yet to recognize and understand.

3

The Nature of Machines

One day the machines will be able to solve all the problems,
but none of them will ever be able to pose one.
—Albert Einstein

I remember that when I was a kid I was fascinated by machines,
so much so that I used to run to the balcony of the house to
see the steam locomotives pass by, as they announced with a
prolonged whistle their approach to the railroad bridge not far
from my home. Machines, and especially airplanes, have always
held a special fascination for me.

As I grew up, my interest gradually shifted to computers,
which at that time filled large rooms and displayed panels of
mysterious lights turning on and off at great speed. Towards
the end of the 1950s, as a teenager, I wanted to understand
how computers worked. I could never have imagined that ten
years later I would create the technology that would allow
us a few years hence to integrate an entire computer on a
small silicon crystal. In fact, I used that technology to design
two years later the world's first microprocessor (Intel 4004).
Those accomplishments made it possible to reduce the size
of computers and increase their performance to the point of
creating the smartphones we now take everywhere.

Computers and robots are among the most complex systems
we can imagine and build today, and they encompass the basic
principles used in all other machines.

These are by design classical, deterministic machines, in
contrast to living organisms, which are both quantum and
classical systems. We will see later that these organisms are

much more sophisticated than microchips, because they can "host" the consciousness and free will that make us human. In other words, the widespread opinion today that living organisms are classical machines based on biology instead of silicon—and therefore, in principle equivalent to computers—could not be more wrong.

The Evolution of Machines

Today's technology was unthinkable fifty-sixty years ago. But technique alone is not enough, we need a broader vision.
—Rita Levi-Montalcini

Before the discovery of electricity, all machines were mechanical and were based on levers, wheels, pulleys, gears, springs, and so on. For millennia, the energy source of machines came from wind, water, or animal muscles. At the end of the seventeenth century, the invention of the coal-fired steam engine was the spark that ignited the industrial revolution. About 150 years later a more efficient and compact thermal engine was devised: the gasoline engine, still widespread today.

The discovery of electromagnetism in the early nineteenth century brought a new form of energy to the attention of the world, energy acting without any apparent physical movement. Just think of an electrical signal that propagates almost at the speed of light within a telegraph or a telephone cable. Physicists assure us that there are electrons moving inside that wire, but who has ever seen these electrons?

With electromagnetism, even matter began to reveal "inner movements" never observed before, which could be exploited in various ways. For example, an electric generator could convert mechanical motion into electricity, and vice versa—a more cost-effective, reversible transformation than heat engines.

And electric cables could carry electricity from a distant generator into our homes to produce any kind of work without physically transporting anything.

In 1844 the telegraph was invented to carry information, rather than energy, by using only one cable and by assigning to each number and letter of the alphabet a unique binary code represented by a sequence of electrical impulses of two different durations (Morse code). Thirty-two years later the telephone was invented by using a continuously variable electrical signal—called analog signal—to connect people located at great distances from each other. Soon a dense network of cables covered the cities, to distribute energy and information without moving anything but electrical signals. In more recent years, electromagnetic waves—a form of energy simply unknown 160 years ago—have allowed us to achieve "wirelessly" most of the tasks that were previously entrusted to electrical cables.

Today we take for granted the smartphones that we carry everywhere. They allow us not only to video call anyone in every corner of the planet, but also to take photographs, videos, and audio recordings, and finally to compose messages similar to the telegrams of the past, but now relying on microwaves. We can also store and recall books, photos, music, and videos, where only 40 years ago we would have used a different and bulky device for each function. Smartphones also give us access, inside and outside our homes, to services such as GPS, maps, and thousands of other applications that were simply unthinkable 40 years ago.

We are discovering that a large portion of what matters in our life has to do with information: creating, transforming, moving, and "consuming" information represent a growing portion of what interests us. If we think about it, much of the physical movement in the past was also connected with information. For example, 200 years ago, what we accomplish with a phone call or by downloading some data to our computer would have required a trip of several days on horseback. Forty years ago we physically went to the library, to a record store, or to a movie theater to do what we now do at home or on the go.

And let's not forget that to transmit information in the past, one could even lose one's life, as happened in 490 BC to Philippides, who, to bring to the Athenians the news of the victory of the Greeks over the Persians, had to run at breakneck speed for over 40 kilometers, from the plains of Marathon to Athens. And when he reached his destination, he managed to pronounce a single word, "Victory," before collapsing due to the effort he had made. In this case, the cost of that information was really very high.

Today, computer technology allows us to create and manipulate information at such a low cost that, compared to just 50 years ago, our capacity for obtaining knowledge has increased exponentially.

Before the Information Revolution

The second industrial revolution does not appear as the first with overwhelming images such as sheet metal presses or steel castings, but as the bits of a flow of information that runs on the circuits in the form of electronic pulses. Iron machines are still there, but they obey weightless bits.

—Italo Calvino, *American Lessons*

Even before the information revolution there were simple tools for writing, measuring and calculating: the abacus, for example, has been around for millennia and is still in use in some developing countries. All the first computing machines processed information through physical movement and used rudimentary analog and digital mechanical contraptions. Even the abacus, which mainly performs a memory function, requires movements controlled by our fingers.

The first mechanical four-function calculator—the arithmomètre—was invented by the Frenchman Thomas de Colmar in 1820 and was first commercialized in 1851. This machine could finally speed up calculations considerably compared to the abacus—an important difference for a banker or for an engineer.

Seventy years ago, electromechanical calculators had about 1000 moving parts, were manually controlled, and could operate 100 times faster than a person armed with pen and paper. They were computing machines in which levers and gears, driven by an electric motor, did all the work.

Created by Joseph Henry in 1835, the relay was an electrically activated switch: a hybrid device—electrical and mechanical—in which an electrical signal could operate a mechanical switch that could connect or disconnect two electrical wires. A relay allowed a relatively weak signal to activate a switch that could transfer a much stronger signal to power many other relays. This allowed an elementary form of signal processing and amplification, which in turn made possible the creation of the first automatic telephone switchboards and exchanges, and even the creation of the first programmable digital computer—the Z3—conceived and built in 1941 in Germany by Konrad Zuse.[1]

Henry's relay was the bridge that allowed the transition from mechanical to electromechanical processing and from special purpose to general purpose. However, a relay computer was so slow that it was almost useless. The task of speeding up the calculations fell to electronics.

---

1   The Z3 computer operated at a frequency of 5 Hz (cycles per second), very slow compared to the first electronic computer completed in 1945—the ENIAC—which operated at a frequency of 5000 Hz. A factor of 1000 made a crucial difference. Today the most advanced microprocessors operate at a frequency of 5,000,000,000 Hz.

Electronics was born with the invention of the triode, a vacuum tube conceived by Lee De Forest in 1906. It was a device that modulated the current flowing between two electrodes—called cathode and anode—by applying a small voltage to a third electrode called a grid, placed between the two. The electrodes were located inside a glass tube in which a vacuum had been created. The triode was the bulky forerunner of the MOS transistor, in which the current between two electrodes—called the source and the drain—is modulated by the voltage applied to a third electrode called a gate.

Invented in 1959, MOS transistors are solid-state devices used in almost every chip manufactured today. Thanks to the amazing advances in semiconductors, the space occupied by a single triode of 1906 could today contain an entire computer system made of more than ten trillion MOS transistors (10^{13}), including all their interconnections! It is interesting to note that the volume occupied by the interconnections far exceeds the volume occupied by the transistors, just like we find in our brains with neurons and their interconnections.

Today, a single microchip may contain up to one trillion transistors (a flash memory chip), and can speed up human calculations nearly a quadrillion times, with nothing moving. Moreover, a chip is "monolithic" in the sense that all its parts are made and assembled simultaneously. What moves in a chip are "electrical signals," but that motion is more like the propagation of light than the motion of objects. In a chip, the electromagnetic energy that carries the information flows through a labyrinth of "streets" and "doors" at close to the speed of light, following paths established by a program, thus transforming the information according to human desires.

Computers Are Universal Machines

Almost all information-processing systems prior to computers were special purpose, i.e., they could perform only a small set of specific functions defined by the designer *before* the machine was built. Computers, on the other hand, are general purpose, because the same machine can perform an almost infinite number of different functions, which often exceed the wildest imagination of the computer hardware designer!

This prodigious result is due to the separation of the physical machine from the program, the hardware from the software. The software is the nonphysical part of the computer, which specifies its function. What is surprising is that the same relatively simple organization of matter, the hardware, can perform an infinity of algorithms, as long as it has sufficient memory and speed.

It was Alan Turing, in 1936, who conceived such a "universal machine" with a thought experiment aimed at demonstrating that the so-called *decision problem* posed by the mathematician David Hilbert in 1928[2] was unsolvable. The Turing machine gave us an abstract model of a class of universal machines capable of executing any general algorithm. And this invention created theoretical information science and showed the deep and stimulating links between mathematics, information, and intelligence.

It should be emphasized that with computers, the hardware cannot do anything without software. Software refers to a collection of programs, and a program is a sequence of commands that the hardware will mechanically execute down to the

---

2 David Hilbert's "decision problem" was the following: given a statement within an axiomatic system, does an algorithm always exist that can prove whether the statement is true or false? Turing showed that there are statements for which such an algorithm does not exist because it would go on indefinitely without ever being able to make a decision. Turing's result is similar to Gödel's incompleteness theorem because it placed a limit on what can be computed with an algorithm. Note that, at the height of logical positivism, Hilbert believed that the truth-value of any statement could be proven.

smallest detail. The computer vocabulary, called the instruction set, is the ensemble of instructions. Each instruction defines a deterministic transformation to be performed on the data. And here another important distinction emerges: information can take two basic forms, namely data and instructions, both stored in the memory in binary form. The data is the "raw material" which can be shaped into any form by the instructions. It should be emphasized that instructions and data mean nothing to the computer, which is not conscious. Only the human consciousness can understand what the computer does.

The computer hardware is physical, reductive, and deterministic, just like the software, though the latter is not strictly physical. The computer represents the first step in a process in which the human mind has learned to control inanimate matter by making it act in the desired way. The invention and perfecting of the computer represents a decisive step in human evolution. It also marks a delicate transition for humanity, as we will discuss in the course of the book.

The Nature of Computers

A program is devised by a human mind and written in "Boolean," a language that can be executed by a machine at a speed close to that of light, the same speed at which signals travel inside microchips. That speed is millions of times faster than what is achievable by macroscopic mechanical structures. The Boolean language uses an alphabet of only two letters, "0" and "1," and is therefore *binary*, i.e., made up of bits. Each word in this language is thus a sequence made up of a finite number of bits.

The bit represents the smallest amount of information possible, i.e., the amount necessary to make a single distinction: "0" or "1," this or that, exists or does not exist, true or false, and so on. It is an extremely effective language, because the hardware only has to recognize two possible states.

The part of the hardware that carries out the program instructions is called the central processing unit (CPU). The CPU also controls the flow of input and output (I/O) data with which the computer communicates with the outside world. The memory is like a matrix of cells, each containing a "binary word" with a predetermined number of bits, typically ranging from 8 to 64 bits in multiples of 8. CPU, memory, and I/O represent the three basic building blocks of a computer.

Note that the only recognition required of the hardware is to reliably distinguish the state "0" from the state "1." This recognition does not produce any meaning, but it must be absolutely correct because even a single mistake could lead to a malfunction. The meanings of the two states are known only to the programmer, not to the computer. The bit is typically represented by two ranges of values in the voltage of an electrical signal.

The state of each bit in memory can be simply read or written as desired. These bits are generally organized into words that the CPU reads or writes in parallel. The longer the word, the faster the computer, because accessing the external memory takes much longer than accessing the data that is stored inside the CPU.[3]

To access each word in memory, the program must provide the *address*, i.e., the "coordinates" corresponding to the row and the column numbers that identify the cell in the memory matrix. Each instruction also prescribes what operation to perform and where to find the data, and the next instruction.

The programmer is the creator of the program, while the hardware is the blind executor of the program. The program is expressed by the specific configuration of the states in a "field

---

3   A 16-bit CPU, for example, fetches data from external memory 16 bits at a time. A 16-bit word can represent 2^{16} = 16,384 different states. The world's first microprocessor, the Intel 4004, was a 4-bit CPU on a single integrated circuit (chip) that operated directly on 4 bits at a time. To operate on 16 bits, the CPU had to draw data four times from memory.

of possible states," which is the computer memory. It should be noted that the field of states can be understood as the interface between mind and matter. Here we have, for the first time, a machine that interfaces with what goes beyond physics. I say "beyond" because the meaning of both the program and the result of the processing does not reside within the computer. The field of states that contains the program and the data has been arranged by the human mind; the computer acts on itself and on the external environment through the unconscious and stereotyped actions of the CPU controlled by the program.

A computer is a physical structure in which an energy pattern created by the human mind has been organized in such a form that matter is forced to act in accordance with this pattern. Inside a computer, the subjective intentions and meaning of the programmer have been completely objectified in the program. The result of the mechanical processing performed by the computer is finally returned to the environment and/or to the human mind to be subjectively interpreted. In this way, human beings can simulate the consequences of their thoughts and fantasies with extreme precision.

The operation of the computer, however, is extremely fragile, because it would take just one wrong bit to turn a machine that seems intelligent and deliberate into a completely useless box of metal, plastic, and silicon. Thus, without constant human supervision, computers could easily fail due to a trivial hardware problem or a software bug.

Within a deterministic machine there is no free will, although a decision independent of the program could be caused either by an "interrupt"[4] coming from the environment or from the

---

4   An interrupt allows an external event in real time to suspend the execution
    of the main program, command the computer to execute another program—
    which may even be supplied from the outside—and then return to the main
    program after the completion of the "intrusion."

program itself asking the outside world to provide some input data. In such a case, non-algorithmic decisions may arise from the free will of human beings or from truly random quantum events. These interventions coming from the environment allow the computer to go beyond the limits of algorithms, though originating outside the computer. Meaning, understanding, and free-will decisions do not exist within a computer. Moreover, the randomness of quantum physics is fundamentally different from what we call random in classical systems. Classical randomness corresponds to the lack of knowledge of what could be known by solving the deterministic equations of classical physics; quantum randomness is instead non-algorithmic because it is indetermined prior to the measurement that literally *creates* it.

For example, the exact position of an artificial satellite at a specific time two days from now can be known in a few minutes because it can be calculated with extreme precision by a fast computer. The value of the spin of an electron ("up" or "down") two seconds from now, however, cannot be known before the measurement because there is no law or algorithm that can determine it. In other words, the randomness of quantum physics does not correspond to the ignorance of a reality that is knowable, but to a reality that has not yet been created, and therefore is *unknowable in principle*.

When a computer has access to quantum information "from the outside," it ceases to be completely deterministic. We will begin to explore these situations starting from the last chapter of Part One.

Computers Are Reductionistic

A typical machine is a deterministic and reductionist system entirely built with separable parts that can be disassembled and then reassembled to fully restore its operation. Physical removability of parts can be replaced by the concept of parts "separable in principle"[5] (SIP) because it may be impractical to build machines made entirely with removable parts. This is the case with today's computers, for example, which are monolithic microchips.

A microchip may contain many billions of transistors all interconnected. Each transistor is electrically isolated from all the others and functions only as an on-off switch. Thus, each transistor is SIP because we can imagine removing it completely and ideally replacing it with an identical transistor without affecting the operation of the system. Transistors are built by exploiting the quantum properties of crystals, which allow better characteristics than those achievable by using classical properties of matter. The smallest "parts" that make up a transistor are collections of many thousands of atoms and molecules in crystalline, polycrystalline, or amorphous form.

Note that, once the computer is built, its physical matter always remains the same, unlike living cells in which matter continually enters and exits the cell to feed, eliminate, and reproduce by creating a copy of itself *within* itself.

A computer is made with a very large but finite number of SIP parts, and each of them, although autonomous and independent, interacts in a well-defined way with the others. To perform a useful function, each part must interact with at least another part, otherwise it would be superfluous. Every interaction requires necessarily an exchange of energy between the parts and the surrounding environment. Therefore, no part

---

5 This notion is necessary because it may be impossible to physically remove a part without destroying it or the rest of the system. For example, a microchip is built entirely with non-removable parts, because the transistors must be as small as possible to increase their speed and reduce their power dissipation and cost. Whenever we could in principle remove a part without affecting the functionality of all the other parts, then that part is SIP.

can be strictly considered a closed thermodynamic system. Finally, each part has an identifiable boundary beyond which its function ceases. However, dissipative exchanges with the environment cannot be completely eliminated. They are an irreducible consequence of the holistic nature of physical reality, a clear demonstration that a reductionistic system is an idealization of a holistic system.

A reductionistic system is, therefore, a holistic system in which the inevitable dissipative interactions with the environment have been minimized to avoid jeopardizing their intended function. Such a system is a simplified mental model of reality, a *theory* valid only within a range of environmental conditions in which the dissipative effects do not alter the function of the system. When we consider that the elementary parts of which everything is made are quantum states that behave like probability waves that can also be influenced by the random fluctuations of the quantum vacuum (see Glossary), true reductionism cannot exist.

Classical physics is therefore a theory valid only within the ranges of environmental conditions in which quantum and other effects do not affect the deterministic nature of the theory. However, since quantum effects can never be completely eliminated, any attempt to fully describe reality classically may produce erroneous predictions.

Many forget that a theory of reality is not reality. As Heisenberg states: "Physics is not a representation of reality, but of our way of thinking about it." This forgetfulness often leads to a denial of those phenomena that the theory cannot explain. For example, the idea that a human body is a classical machine is falsified by the existence of consciousness and free will which cannot emerge from a classical reductionist and deterministic system. This crucial topic will be discussed in depth later.

Computers Are Deterministic

Like reductionism, determinism is also a theory. It is an idealization of the world, an approximate description based on a mathematical theory invented by us. Determinism cannot necessarily describe all aspects of the world, and therefore, sooner or later, some quantum phenomenon will falsify it. Our machines are designed to reliably perform specific functions. They are deterministic because we want them this way. If they were unpredictable, they would not be useful. They are in fact advantageous precisely because they never tire of repeating the same stereotyped behavior, contrary to human beings who can easily get bored and distracted, and therefore make mistakes.

A computer program is rigidly deterministic even when we wish it weren't. For example, an algorithm for generating snowflake images can contain a set of parameters with which to create an almost infinite variety of them. However, these parameters must be either generated by another algorithm or inserted from the outside when the program asks for them. Nondeterministic behavior may then derive from random information originating from a quantum system that is not part of the program. The conclusion is that a computer that operates entirely on its own program and without any external input of data is completely deterministic and predictable, as long as one knows all the details of the program and how the computer works. This last requirement can always be satisfied because the bits of the computer can be copied. In other words, the internal state of the computer is objective and can be known and shared by many observers. Note that the same requirement is not satisfied by quantum systems, because the state of a qubit cannot be copied, and cannot be measured without disturbing it and therefore changing it unpredictably.

The qubit can be represented by the direction of the magnetic moment of a particle (spin) or by another quantum phenomenon with similar characteristics. The spin can be oriented anywhere in a complex two-dimensional Hilbert space (see Glossary). Therefore, the qubit can have an infinity of possible directions (states) that can be represented by all the points on the surface of a sphere of radius 1. To measure the spin, the particle must pass through a non-uniform magnetic field with an arbitrary direction with respect to the orientation of the spin. When measuring the spin, it will always be found to be aligned either with the direction of the magnetic field of the instrument or in the opposite direction. The infinity of states of a qubit is therefore reduced to one bit of classical information when the spin is measured.

Classical physics is deterministic, while quantum physics is both indeterministic and deterministic. This is a subtle but crucial point, because quantum physics is a probabilistic theory that can only predict the probabilities of events. However, when it predicts that the probability of a given event is 1 or 0, it is deterministic, while when it predicts probabilities other than 1 or 0 it is indeterministic. To be falsifiable, a theory must predict some events that always happen and others that never happen, because then a single experiment can falsify the theory. Quantum physics satisfies this crucial criterion of falsifiability, because it predicts some events with probability 1 or 0 that can then be falsified.[6]

Classical physics is a theory in which variables can assume a continuum of values expressed by real numbers. Computers, however, have finite accuracy, and this difference has important implications. For example, two identical computers running

---

6 I owe this clear distinction to Giacomo Mauro D'Ariano, professor of theoretical physics at the University of Pavia.

the same software will produce exactly the same results, even if they simulate a chaotic system whose behavior depends critically on the initial conditions. But two identical real chaotic physical systems will never behave in the same way, because it is impossible to set their initial conditions with sufficient precision. Therefore, after some time, their behaviors will gradually move away from each other and will end up being completely different. Hence the simulation of a chaotic system, after a period of time, may not correspond to the real physical system because the initial conditions of the real system may not be the same as those of a simulation with finite precision.

This analysis highlights a fundamental difference between the determinism of a computer and that of classical physics, which is deterministic but not necessarily predictable, because it is described with real numbers and not with finite precision numbers. Therefore, even if the theory were 100% correct, the simulation of the theory of a chaotic system might not match the real system. Consequently, computers represent a subset of classical physics, in which the accuracy of the calculation is finite. In turn, classical physics is a special case of quantum physics applied to macroscopic systems in which quantum properties are averaged out. Therefore, its predictions are, at best, deterministic approximations of the probabilistic description of reality made by quantum physics.

The idea that reality is deterministic has already been disproved by quantum physics, but it is still supported by many who believe that objects on our scale are adequately described by classical physics, while this is not the case, especially for complex systems which are generally chaotic. Just think of the weather forecast or the behavior of living beings. Determinism is another idealization of reality valid only in the computer world. It is a good approximation for many classical systems, much less for macroscopic quantum-and-classical systems such as living organisms.

Computers Can Be Unpredictable

With the advent of robotics and artificial intelligence based on neural networks, computers increasingly operate with data from the real world, which may also include information produced by quantum events and human decisions. This leads the computer to operate outside the limits of a classical deterministic system. Such a situation presents challenges and opportunities that are not fully understood, not even by professionals.

Complex patterns such as faces, words, or urban traffic situations, have astounding variability, to the point where the recognition rate cannot be perfect, especially under unfavorable environmental conditions. Therefore, the performance of a robot or computer cannot be guaranteed, unlike in situations where the computer runs a deterministic algorithm. With artificial neural networks,[7] the unpredictability of the real world is brought into the computer, especially if the neural networks determine key parameters of the program. Thus, if a computer were allowed to make important decisions based on the presumed validity of its pattern recognition, the consequences could be catastrophic. This is a serious problem, since computers have no understanding of the situations in which they operate. Ethical choices, for example, cannot be decided by an algorithm!

Can we trust a robot if its behavior can be unpredictable? If a robot operates entirely on a factory floor in which it repeats the same stereotyped series of operations in a controlled

---

7 Artificial neural networks are programs that mimic some of the important functions performed by the biological neural networks of our brain. These networks automatically learn the correlations present in the data used to train them. Networks thus learn to recognize complex patterns (patterns of patterns of patterns). When a network correctly recognizes patterns never seen before, i.e., patterns that were not part of the training set, the network is able to *generalize*. The simulation of neural networks with specialized hardware is responsible for the recent major advances in AI and robotics.

environment, the answer is yes. However, even in this case, if a fault or an unforeseen event should occur, human intervention might still be necessary. If we wish to build a self-driving car, the situation changes completely, given the vast number of imponderable variables that increase dramatically as we go from driving in a controlled-access freeway to driving in the center of a large city like New York or Rome. If we also add the possibility of deliberate deception to the mix, i.e., hostile agents that could purposely create situations aimed at confusing the system, the performance could become unacceptable. The increase of *cybercrime*, even without the ambiguities of artificial intelligence, is a preview of what could happen. Cybercrime should be a warning about the dangers and unpredictability associated with giving robots autonomy.

There is an unbridgeable gap between artificial and human intelligence, which is characterized by *comprehension*: a non-algorithmic property of consciousness that is often underestimated and inaccessible to computers, as we will see in the course of this book. In my opinion, self-driving vehicles will eventually become possible, but long after the optimistic forecasts we all have heard. The economic and social benefits of self-driving are too great to abandon development, despite the great difficulties that will be encountered. Moreover, since traffic accidents are almost always caused by drunk, inattentive, or careless drivers, the reliability of a robot that doesn't drink, follows the rules, and never gets tired, may produce an average benefit that may eventually be favorable.

So far I have made no distinction between computers and robots, as if they had the same level of complexity, but this is not true. Robots have the additional ability to perceive the world through sensors, act in the world, and monitor their own performance against internal standards established by the programmers. They may also modify their own processes to some extent, but this area is questionable, for, if we allowed them to significantly change their own programs without supervision, they might no longer be predictable and their dependability might greatly suffer.

The complexity of a robot that learns on its own is many orders of magnitude greater than that of ordinary robots. I expect that, thanks to the development of self-driving vehicles, we will learn a lot more about autonomous robots. I also expect that this knowledge will improve the efficiency of human learning. As Professor of Cognitive Sciences Margaret Boden says: "The most important lesson that AI has taught us is to appreciate and recognize for the first time the enormous power and subtlety of the human mind." Robots have properties that are complementary to those of humans. It is up to us to use them wisely to improve our condition and that of the ecosystem.

Robots versus Living Organisms

Computers are magnificent tools for making our dreams come true, but no machine can replace the human spark of spirit, compassion, love, and understanding.
—Lou Gerstner

The fundamental differences between robots and living organisms are surprising and poorly understood. While computers and robots are classical machines, living organisms are not because they process information using all the phenomena available in the physical world: quantum, classical, discrete, and continuous.

Inside a living cell, individual atoms are used to process information, and this makes it extremely difficult to understand how the cell works. The quantum behavior of single atomic and molecular events within a living cell gives rise to an incredibly complex dynamic order, which cannot be described by the quantum statistical laws that regulate the behavior of objects made up of millions of atoms. A cell is much more sophisticated than a mixture of atoms and organic molecules that freely interact inside a droplet of water. Its dynamic order must be orchestrated from the whole to the parts, and vice versa, in clever and still unknown ways.

We know that changing a single bit in the wrong place of a computer program can make a fundamental difference. The same also applies to a cell, since the presence or absence of a single proton (hydrogen ion) at the wrong place and time may have serious consequences. This fact underlies another fundamental difference between a cell and a computer, because, while a bit is only abstract information, a proton or an atom is also matter and energy, which can be used to build more complex molecules in addition to performing informational tasks.

A living cell is not a purely reductionist machine. Instead, it is a quantum-classical dynamical system closer to the quantum reality than to the classical one. For example, if we could take apart all the atoms and molecules that make up a cell, could we then reassemble them and recreate the same living cell? Nobody knows how to do this, for it would be necessary to know the state of every atom and molecule, including the molecules of the water. Such properties would have to be measured while the cell is alive, in which case the system would be disturbed in unpredictable ways. Moreover, since the cell is incredibly dynamic, it is different at every instant, making it impossible to simultaneously measure its state. In a nutshell, there is no way to reconstruct a cell. As physicist Richard Feynman says: "What I cannot build, I cannot understand." We can build a computer starting from its elementary components, but no one has ever been able to build a cell starting from its atoms.

Another interesting difference is that, in order to function, a machine must first be built in its entirety, and only then can it be switched on and off at will. Surprisingly, any living organism is built alive and it will only shut down once, when it dies, that is, when an irreversible change occurs that can no longer be self-repaired. To live, a multicellular organism must have a critical mass of live cells, to which new ones are added as the old ones die. When the death of the entire organism occurs, it can no longer be rekindled. When a multicellular organism self-assembles, every new cell that is added is alive, so that the organism is also built alive and is never turned on.

Another important aspect that has a precise meaning for a machine, but not for a living organism, is expressed in the concept of "completion." When a machine leaves the factory it is completed, and, once finished, it remains essentially the same. Living organisms, on the other hand, change, transform, and evolve continuously. They are never finished, because they are always in a state of becoming. For example, an unfertilized human egg (gamete) is alive for some time, and immediately after fertilization it transforms itself into a fetus, a child, an adolescent, an adult, and so on, with an unbelievable dynamism. A living organism is never the same physical and psychological entity from one instant to the next. The computer hardware, on the other hand, remains the same physical structure from the moment it leaves the factory until it stops working or it is discarded.

The dynamism of a living organism is irreducible, whether it manifests itself as a bacterium or as a human being. Life is like a flame that produces other flames by dividing itself. This is why, to create a new life, one must always start with life. As summed up by the seventeenth-century biologist Francesco Redi: "*Omne vivum ex vivo,*" i.e., everything that is alive derives from something alive. The only way to start a new life is always to begin with another life. After the first cell, all living organisms were formed "alive" within another organism.

So how did the first cell come about?

This question is similar to "How was the universe created?" Nobody has the answer. Indeed, the more we know about cells and the universe, the less we can explain about their origin.[8] To use Margherita Hack's words in *My Infinity*: "Certainly, the greatest and most extraordinary enigma, even more than the universe, is our mind, of which we still know very little, much less than what it has understood of the universe."

---

8 The simplest bacterium contains about 10^{10} atoms that function dynamically in an exquisite way. How did those atoms and molecules self-assemble as a result of natural processes? Beyond simple organic molecules, and despite our considerable scientific knowledge, no one has ever been able to figure out how this feat happened.

4

The Nature of Information

Information is a conceptual labyrinth.
—Luciano Floridi, *The Information Revolution*

When we were kids, information was also part of our games. I remember how we enjoyed exchanging our secrets with the "silent alphabet," which allowed us not to be heard by adults.

As for the "wireless phone," it was very amusing to discover how the sentence that the first player whispered in the ear of the second was completely unrecognizable by the time it reached the end of the line.

But information is not a game, it is very serious business, so much so that this period of rapid technological and social change has been properly called the "information revolution."

Begun in the mid-twentieth century, thanks to the development of digital technologies, information is having a gigantic impact on society, greater than that of the industrial revolution. "Microchip," "information processing," and "the web" are now part of our vocabulary, just as "engine," "production line," and "industry" were the new words that characterized the industrial revolution.

But what is information? What explains the exponential growth of the information technologies that we are witnessing? What is it that makes information so transformative that we can develop artificial intelligence, robots, and self-driving cars?

A Brief History of Information

Information began with gestures, guttural sounds, the birth of words and languages, simple pictorial and graphic signs, the brush, cuneiform writing, alphabets, abacus, papyrus, pen, ink, paper, book, and the printing press. Then information took an epochal turning point with the invention of the telegraph and the telephone, which exploited the discovery of electricity. Decades later, the discovery of electromagnetic waves made possible wireless long-distance communications and previously unimaginable radio and TV transmissions.

The need to amplify weak radio signals led to the invention of the vacuum tube, giving life to the field of electronics. Vacuum tubes could for the first time manipulate high-frequency electrical signals, and were soon used in many other applications not originally intended, such as radar, microwave transmission, electronic controls, and television.

The desire to accelerate the speed of electromechanical calculators and to automatically compute arbitrary sequences of arithmetic operations led to the invention of the programmable computer.

The first modern electronic digital computer with a stored program was the EDSAC, built in 1949 at the University of Cambridge, England. It implemented John von Neumann's idea of storing programs and data in the same memory, while in previous computers, such as the famous ENIAC, the program consisted of panels with switches and plugs that had to be manually operated through a long and laborious process.

All early computers were research machines designed to perform numerical calculations, and each one was the only specimen ever built.

The first *commercial* electronic computer for general use, the UNIVAC I, was introduced in 1951, exactly 100 years after the start of production of the arithmomètre, described in the previous chapter. UNIVAC I was a stored-program computer suitable for various applications, such as the sorting and analysis of financial and administrative data. It had a 1024-word, 12-bit serial main memory and for the first time it used magnetic tape as a secondary memory to increase the overall memory. This machine used 5200 vacuum tubes that dissipated 125 kW and could perform 500 multiplications per second. Forty-six units were sold, at a cost of over one million dollars each, demonstrating for the first time the existence of a market for computers.

Twenty years later, the first microprocessor in the world was born, the Intel 4004, a 4-bit CPU which I designed in 1970–71. Three years later, a computer with performance comparable to the UNIVAC I could be made in a 30 × 30 cm^2 printed circuit board using the world's first high-performance 8-bit microprocessor (Intel 8080). Such a computer dissipated 10 W and cost a few hundred dollars. After another ten years, with smaller and faster transistors, the same computer could be integrated into a single chip with more than ten times the speed of UNIVAC I, consuming less than 1 watt, and costing about ten dollars. This was the miracle of semiconductor-based microelectronics, the technology that reduced a computer the size of an apartment to the smartphone we carry in our pockets, powered only by a rechargeable battery.

Microelectronics began with germanium transistors, invented in 1947, followed by diffusion bipolar transistors which, starting in 1953, gradually replaced vacuum tubes. Ten years later we had the first bipolar *monolithic* integrated circuits with a dozen transistors, and by the mid-1970s an entire computer could be integrated into a single chip using silicon gate MOS transistors. This integration level was made possible by the silicon gate technology that I co-invented in 1968 at Fairchild Semiconductor [3]. Twenty years later, almost all integrated circuits produced in the world were made with silicon gate, away from bipolar technology that in 1968 accounted for nearly all integrated circuits.

With silicon gate the part became the whole, because the tens of thousands of transistors used to build a computer were replaced by a piece of silicon smaller than a fingernail. Semiconductor-based microelectronics gave birth to personal computers, cellphones, and fast digital communications, followed by the creation of the internet with services of power and utility unimaginable by even the most daring science fiction writers. Smartphones, which today are owned by about two billion people, sum up in pocket size much of the information technology (IT) and telematic progress made in the last 50 years.

The COVID-19 pandemic could have destroyed the world's economies, were it not for the availability of essentially free internet videoconferencing and other services that allowed most businesses, schools, and other enterprises to continue operating even with people confined at home.

What Is Information?

The word "information" comes from the Latin *in-forma*, that is, to give shape to something. It is one of those words, like "time" or "energy," whose meaning we think we know until we are asked to define them precisely. The fact is that the term "information" has many meanings, which vary according to the context in which it is used. It can indicate data, facts, news, instructions, knowledge, intelligence, relevance, meaning, what is represented by a particular arrangement of signs or symbols, the amount of information carried by a particular symbol, and so on.

Information remains one of the concepts that are perplexing even to those who work in the field. According to the French mathematician René Thom in his *From Morphogenesis to Structure*, "the term 'information,' too full of all its intentional and anthropocentric connotations, should be banned from science."

Yet information, which we do not yet know how to properly define, can be processed and transformed by a computer.

The central concept of information has to do with a particular relationship between an "observer" and an "event" that transmits "information" to the observer. The event is a *sign* that brings with it information, that is, new knowledge for the observer.

Note that, if the observer knew in advance which event would occur, the event would bring no new information, but only confirmation of what he already knew. If, on the other hand, the event increased his knowledge, it would have transmitted information. Therefore, the information transferred by an event, a sign, or a signal is related to the state of knowledge of the observer himself.

Information is not something physical that we can easily measure, such as the mass of an object. Therefore, it is generally impossible to speak in absolute terms of the information transmitted by an event, since it depends not only on the event but also on the observer. In fact, the same event can carry different meanings to different observers. Moreover, even for the same observer, the meaning can vary according to his circumstances.

Let me give you an example: Suppose my brother-in-law meets me on the street, raising his hand with the thumbs-up sign, and two other people witness the same event besides me. Person A does not know what the thumbs-up sign means, so she hasn't received any objective information, even though she has seen the sign and may wonder what it means. Person B knows that the sign means "something good has happened," therefore he has received some objective information, but he does not know who and what that sign is for, therefore he has only received a small amount of meaning. For me, that sign means that the surgery undergone by my sister was successful, and I am delighted and relieved. Therefore, I received the same amount of objective information as B, but also a large amount of subjective meaning, since my uncertainty was overcome and my emotional state drastically improved. If the same sign meant that my brother-in-law had won a ten-dollar bet, its impact on me would have been significantly less.

This example illustrates the subjective nature of the *meaning* arising from objective events, and it also highlights two types of meaning: objective and subjective. The objective meaning is the formal meaning of a sign, i.e., the meaning that is conventionally shared by a community, by agreement. On the other hand, the subjective meaning is the specific meaning that the sign carries for a particular observer. The transfer of subjective meaning is conditioned by the perception and recognition of the conventional (objective) meaning of the sign.

Note that the perception of a sign as something that "could have" meaning is independent of the knowledge of its objective meaning. This is the situation for observer A who perceived the sign and understood that it might mean something, but she didn't know what it stood for. The recognition of the objective meaning of a sign can only take place if the meaning was previously known, thanks to an explicit or implicit agreement. Therefore, what we call *information* is always based on a prior agreement, which questions the universality of what is meant by "objective."

It should be noted that even the "absence of an event" can bring information and meaning. For example, suppose I tell a friend that if he doesn't see me in the main square at 6 p.m., he can find me at the Bellavista bar. In this case I am using my presence or absence in space and time (main square at 6 p.m.) as a sign to convey precise information. My presence or absence corresponds to a "bit" of information, "1" if I am present and "0" if I am not, with the previously agreed meaning for each of the two states. Presence and absence can therefore convey two very different meanings.

Note that all the other observers present in the main square at 6 p.m. might not know that my absence is information for someone! Therefore even in empty space there may be a lot of information for observers who know where and when to look.

Shannon's Information

Now suppose we want to examine objective information that is valid for both machines and human beings. In this case the signs or events that carry information have agreed meanings, but not all signs convey the same "amount" of information. For example, a warning sign that appears infrequently may contain much more information than signs that occur frequently.

This is what Claude Shannon theorized in 1948 with the publication of a fundamental paper entitled 'A Mathematical Theory of Communication' [12]. In it, Shannon considered the problem of communicating information with the aim of quantifying it. He extracted only the objective aspects and built an effective mathematical theory that was fundamental for optimizing the use of communication channels, reducing errors, improving the efficiency of codes, and allowing many other improvements.

The concept of "quantity of information" is based on the following hypothetical problem: Suppose you know that someone, a sender, will send you a letter of the English alphabet. When it reaches you, how much information have you received? This depends on the expectation you had about receiving that letter. If the sender had randomly chosen a card from a well-mixed deck of 26 cards in which each card corresponds to a different letter of the alphabet, each letter would have had the same chance of being chosen. The probability of choosing any letter (symbol) is therefore equal to $1/26 = 0.0385$. On the other hand, if the sender had randomly selected a letter from a page of English text, the probability of choosing a particular letter would depend on the frequency with which that letter is used in English.

The relative frequency[1] of the various letters of the English alphabet varies greatly: from 12.702% for the letter "e," the most frequent, to 0.074% for the letter "z," the least used. Thus, the letter "e" is 172 times more likely to be chosen than the letter "z." Note that if the text was written in Italian, the distribution of relative frequencies would have been very different, even if the alphabet is essentially the same. Therefore the mathematical theory of information must assume that the alphabet of symbols and their statistics are known, or can be known.

Without these preliminary clarifications, it is impossible to understand the narrow meaning of the word "information" used in Shannon's theory. Note also that knowing the letters and their probability of appearing is very different from knowing the order in which these letters are distributed in a sequence. It just means that, if you count the number of letters of a certain type in a million letters, all coming from English text, you can expect to find about 127,020 "e" and 740 "z," without knowing their order.

In the case of transmission of information to general recipients, like in telegraphy or telephony, it is assumed that the transmission of each letter has been successful when the transmitted signal reaches the recipient in such a condition as to be recognizable. This is the context in which we can calculate the "amount of information" carried by a symbol or sign.

---

1   The relative frequency of a letter in a statistically significant string of letters of length N is the number of letters of the same type, m, found in the string, divided by N, m/N, which is a number between 0 and 1. This number represents the probability of finding that letter by picking a random letter in a string of letters. Relative frequency can also be expressed as a percentage. To get the probability from a percentage, simply divide the percentage by 100.

Shannon defined the amount of information, I_s, transmitted by a symbol, s, as the negative of the logarithm in base 2 of the probability p_s of receiving that symbol, that is:

$$I_s = -log_2 p_s$$

Since the probability is a number between 0 and 1, the amount of information is a positive number between 0 and ∞. The negative of the logarithm is called a *cologarithm* and is often used when computing the logarithm of a value ranging between 0 and 1 because it will give a positive number.

This definition implies that a symbol that has a small probability of appearing carries with it a large amount of information. At the other end, if the probability were 1, we would know exactly which symbol would appear, and if so, the amount of information carried by it would be 0.

I would like to emphasize that Shannon never defined what information is, but only the amount of information carried by a symbol under certain conditions.

The base 2 of the logarithm was chosen so that, if the alphabet were composed of only two symbols, for example "0" and "1," with equal probability of appearing, the amount of information carried by each symbol would be 1 "bit" (since $-log_2 0.5 = 1$). This situation occurs when we flip a fair coin in which the two possible outcomes have the same probability of appearing. Therefore, the above definition conveniently measures the amount of information in units of bit. However, we must not confuse the concept of "bit" as "unit of measure" with the bit used to indicate the value of a digit in a binary number. The value of a bit in a binary number is only "0" or "1," while the amount of information carried by a symbol can be a real number, such as 2.34 or $\sqrt{2}$.

Some scholars explain Shannon's concept of quantity of information by saying that it is proportional to the degree of surprise of the recipient who receives the symbol: the greater the surprise, the greater the amount of information received. Other people, in a more abstract way, claim that information is the "resolution of uncertainty," which means that the greater the uncertainty existing before transmission, the greater is the amount of information needed to resolve it. Others like to describe information as a measure of the "freedom of choice" available to the person who selects a message.

Note, however, that surprise, uncertainty, and freedom of choice only make sense to conscious entities and not to machines, for which this limited concept of information has been defined. A machine has neither surprises nor uncertainties, not to mention freedom of choice.

Shannon used the term "entropy of information" for the average amount of information carried by a sequence of symbols. Surprisingly, by changing the sign of the information entropy formula, we obtain the formula for the thermodynamic entropy, a fundamental concept in physics. This strange "coincidence" has brought the concept of information into physics, where it continues to play an important role. However, it should be clear that Shannon's definition of the quantity of information covers only a small portion of the concept of information we have, because it excludes *a priori* the subjective meaning, which is what most interests us.

Shannon's information is equivalent to having a machine counting the symbols that appear, and after collecting their statistics, it tells us how much "objective" information is contained in each symbol. This is a perfectly adequate measure of information for a machine that cannot understand the subjective meaning of symbols, but for us it is totally inadequate since the notion of information is only useful in connection with the transmittal of meaning. Without meaning, information is useless. A machine can only recognize a symbol and act on it based on a predetermined response decided by its designer.

Shannon's concept of information requires only the correct detection and recognition of a sign or symbol belonging to a predetermined alphabet of symbols. Information is connected only to the objective meaning of a sign. Note that the widespread use of the word "symbol" in information theory should imply meaning, leading one to believe that Shannon's information is of interest to us, but this is not so. The words "sign" or "signal" would have been more appropriate, since their connection with meaning is weaker, although still present. Perhaps "event" would have been the most appropriate word, because all that is required of an observer is the perception and recognition of the event as such. "Information" is then only the cologarithm of the probability of observing that event.

For a human being, the recognition of an event is often unconscious (mechanical) and is only a prerequisite for having access to the rich subjective and conscious meaning we can associate with it.

A crucial observation is that the subjective meaning of a text depends on the specific order of the letters that form the words that carry the meaning, not on their probability of appearance. Nonetheless, this theory has been fundamental in describing some important aspects of the functioning of communication systems and computers.

What Is a Bit?

Almost everyone has heard of bits nowadays, although for many the concept remains nebulous. "Bit" is the name of an abstract entity that can only exist in one of two possible states, such as the "heads" or "tails" of a coin. A bit can then be used to represent the simplest possible distinction. For example, it can indicate yes or no, true or false, on or off, left or right, present or absent, or the numbers "0" and "1" in a base 2 numeral system. These quasi-objective meanings can be associated by convention with the two states represented by a bit.

Note that the numbers we commonly use are written using a base 10 numeral system. However, any number could also be written in a base 2 system called a "binary numeral system," which uses only two states ("0" and "1") instead of the ten states ("0," "1," "2," "3," "4," "5," "6," "7," "8," and "9") of the decimal numeral system.[2] It is therefore possible to convert any number expressed with a base 10 system into a binary number containing a finite sequence of "1" and "0," and vice versa.

Surprisingly, many rational numbers that can be written with a finite number of decimal digits may require an infinite number of binary digits after the decimal point.

In a computer, the two values of a bit are represented by a convention that must be strictly respected in all its electronic circuits. For example, when the voltage in a node of a circuit is between 0.6 and 1.0 volts, the status of that node corresponds to the bit value "1"; when the voltage is between 0.0 and 0.4 volts, the node status is "0"; and when the voltage is between 0.4 and 0.6 volts, the status is indetermined and may cause errors. Values in this latter range may occur due to a temporary electrical disturbance or to a circuit fault, and may be recognized as "1" by one circuit and as "0" by another, causing mistakes.

In summary, "bit" is the name of an abstract entity that exists in two possible recognizable states in a physical support without

---

2   The decimal number 725.625 can be written like this: $700 + 20 + 5 + 0.6 +$ $0.02 + 0.005 = 725.625$, or also $7 \cdot 10^2 + 2 \cdot 10^1 + 5 \cdot 10^0 + 6 \cdot 10^{-1} + 2 \cdot 10^{-2} + 5 \cdot 10^{-3}$. More generally, any number N can be written with a base B numeral system, in which there are B different states, as follows: $\ldots + s_3 \cdot B^3 + s_2 \cdot B^2 + s_1 \cdot B^1 + s_0 \cdot B^0 + s_{-1} \cdot B^{-1} + s_{-2} \cdot B^{-2} + s_{-3} \cdot B^{-3} + \ldots$, where s_k is any of the states of B at position k. Positive k's refer to the integer part of the number, while negative k's refer to the fractional part. The same number, 725.625, can be written in a binary numeral system with B = 2, as follows: 1011010101.101 corresponding to the following expansion: $1 \cdot 2^9 + 0 \cdot 2^8 + 1 \cdot 2^7 + 1 \cdot 2^6 + 0 \cdot 2^5 + 1 \cdot 2^4 + 0 \cdot 2^3 + 1 \cdot 2^2 + 0 \cdot 2^1 + 1 \cdot 2^0 + 1 \cdot 2^{-1} + 0 \cdot 2^{-2} + 1 \cdot 2^{-3}$, that is, $512 + 128 + 64 + 16 + 4 + 1 + 0.5 + 0.125 = 725.625$

any additional meaning. The bit is an idea, a theory, and its *physical* representation requires a robust method that ensures the correct recognition of the two states even in the worst environmental conditions. This is a crucial agreement that must be strictly respected by the manufacturers of computer systems.

A naïve observer who had the task of understanding how a microchip works by measuring what is physically accessible inside, but knew nothing about binary computer systems, would think that the important information is represented by dynamic signals that change rapidly. Instead, the information that matters is represented by stable but fleeting states during which, by convention, the signals have meaning. By observing only the dynamic voltages that are constantly changing at various points in the system, it would be difficult to understand what is going on, because the logical description is anchored firmly, but elusively, on an agreement that is not evident to an ordinary observer.

The bit level is considered the "semantic" level of the computer: "semantic" is in quotation marks, because it is semantic only for us, but not for the computer, which knows nothing about signs, symbols, and meanings. Also, nowhere inside the chip is there a "0" or a "1."

In summary, a bit is the elementary "quantum" of classical information. It is not a physical object, but it must be robustly represented by a physical variable. The binary logic of a digital system allows for precise and repeatable representations, which are much less sensitive to electrical noise and circuit tolerances created by environmental and manufacturing variations.

The Information of Conscious Entities

Words are not identical to things. Knowing words relating to facts is in no way equivalent to the direct and immediate understanding of the facts themselves.
—Meister Eckhart

Shannon's information is what counts for unconscious machines, but it is not what interests us. It is essential to clarify this point, because the ambiguity of the words used to describe robots and artificial intelligence (AI) systems tends to eliminate the abyss that separates human beings from so-called intelligent machines. The information that matters most to us is not the symbolic but the semantic information, and here consciousness is indispensable. The objective recognition of a symbol by a computer which is passed off as *understanding* by AI practitioners is only a mechanical function that we also perform automatically and unconsciously.

Our understanding involves getting the conscious meaning of the unconsciously recognized symbols, capability that does not exist for a computer. Using the same words that refer to human conscious capabilities to describe a machine's functions that have none of those properties is therefore a serious and dangerous disservice. The ambiguity is heightened by the fact that our body acts both as a machine and as a conscious entity.

When we speak, the symbols we use serve to convey the subjective meaning we feel, unlike the objective symbols used by machines. For example, to choose the words necessary to communicate with Luke, I must first convert my subjective meaning into mental words, and then verbalize them. In this way I create a sound wave that carries the meaning conveyed by the language we both know. My sound waves are perceived by Luke's auditory system and *unconsciously* recognized as the symbols I intended to express. So far, the recognition process is similar to what machines do. Immediately afterwards, however, Luke experiences in his consciousness the sound sensation of the recognized words together with their subjective meaning, which could be somewhat different from mine.

Philosophers use the term "qualia" for the sensations and feelings we experience in our consciousness. Qualia refer to what it *feels like* in our inner experience after the automatic recognition of a symbol. The symbols are the carriers of qualia and qualia are the carriers of meaning. A computer feels nothing and, when a symbol is recognized, that recognition simply causes another symbol to be instantiated. That is all that a computer can do. Qualia and meaning are properties of consciousness not available to computers.

In summary, our recognition of a word as a sign is as automatic as it is in a robot, but in our consciousness the recognized sign is a symbol that is converted into sound qualia and their associated meaning. The latter comes mainly from the emotions and thoughts connected with the long-term memory of our life experiences. After consciously choosing the meaning we wish to communicate, our body automatically translates it into sound waves, through the symbolic processing of the brain. In this way we transform subjective and private meaning into objective and public symbols to communicate to others.

It should be noted that the conscious processing of meaning is very different from the automatic processing of symbols. Although we know little about it, it seems that the first is mainly based on associative and analogical operations between qualia, together with the logical and linear processes of the rational mind performed primarily by the brain. For example, the reasoning done with pen and paper when we solve a mathematical problem is a combination of conscious semantic and unconscious symbolic processes that include the reification of conscious thoughts into mental and material symbols, automatic procedures, intuitions, emotions, and intentions, all supervised by our consciousness.

This processing goes far beyond the symbolic and algorithmic processing that computers can do and that are describable with Shannon's information. This is a crucial distinction that is generally not well understood because science and technology describe only the symbolic and mechanical aspect of reality.

The processing we perform includes the meaning that is the important currency of our lived experience.

Even when a computer uses artificial neural networks, its behavior is still mechanical, and therefore limited, because comprehension and creativity are properties of consciousness that go beyond what machines can do. The fact that computers can far surpass human performance in mechanical processes should not surprise us because we are the ones who figured out the procedures to use and the ways to speed up their execution and reliability. In summary, computers are physical structures to which we have transferred a portion of our mind in the form of programs, creating a bridge between matter and mind. Our programs reveal only the symbolic and algorithmic aspect of the mind, because they do not possess the semantic level and the free will that distinguish us. Computers are our creations and incorporate only the algorithmic part of our essence. We are not computers; we are creators of computers.

Consciousness is our true nature, because it is what allows us to know and comprehend. In the words of the philosopher Michael Polanyi in *Unexpressed Knowledge*, we "can know more than we can say."

5

The Concept of Information Extended

How is it that we have so much information, but know so little?
—Noam Chomsky

Not so long ago—but it seems like centuries ago—information was much more scarce compared to what we can access nowadays. The latest news would be shouted on the streets by newspaper vendors and then discussed during meetings and encounters. Personal information, on the other hand, was instead spread about through gossip. Passing from mouth to mouth, these bits transformed from a breeze to a hurricane that:

At the end…overflows and bursts
spreads, doubles
And produces an explosion
Like a shot from a cannon.
—Gioachino Rossini, *The Barber of Seville*

Then, with the advent of radio, TV, internet, and cellphones, information has multiplied to the point where we are now literally submerged by it. We have become so accustomed to this constant bombardment of news that we have ended up addicted, so much so that we can no longer do without it.

But so much information does not mean greater knowing. When there is too much information, we are no longer able to assimilate it. So today this ancient saying is more relevant than ever: *"Est modus in rebus"* or "There is a middle ground in things."

We have seen that the concept of quantity of information theorized by Shannon requires the existence of an alphabet of symbols whose objective meaning and probability distribution are known. This applies to communication systems and computers, but when the information is between living organisms the situation is very different. And to correctly comprehend the functioning of a cell, since the organism lives in symbiosis with the environment, we must also consider its interactions with it as well.

In this chapter I will introduce the concept of *live information*, a new concept suitable for the types of transformations that occur within cells, where matter, energy, information, and meaning are inseparable. I am convinced that the study of this new type of information, in which the semantic aspect cannot be separated from the symbolic aspect and from matter-energy, will play a fundamental role in the understanding of life and will lead us to a deeper understanding of the nature of reality and consciousness.

The essence of life is about experience, and consciousness is what allows us, through the body, to have a first-person experience of ourselves and the world.

Living Organisms as Information Processors

We know little about how cells process information, especially at the level of the entire organism. Currently, we mainly know the function of coding DNA, which is about 1.5% of the total human DNA and specifies the structure of about 21,000 proteins. The remainder, or 98.5% of it, was until recently called "junk DNA," because it seemed to perform no useful function. How is it possible that life has been so wasteful and unintelligent as to maintain such a cumbersome and useless legacy in every cell?

Fortunately, some scientists did not let themselves be fooled by this prejudice; they understood that it was only an expression of our ignorance, and today they are discovering authentic jewels in the "garbage." I think that within cells there must be levels of global information processing that are currently unknown and use both classical and quantum properties deeply connected with the non-coding DNA. An example of a jewel is the recent discovery of CRISPR-Cas9, a tiny fragment of non-coding DNA that is revolutionizing genetic engineering, because it allows us for the first time to modify the DNA of eukaryotic cells. I would also like to point out that viruses are nothing more than versions of fundamental mechanisms without which life could not exist.

A cell is a dynamic system in which matter, information, and energy are continuously exchanged with the environment so that it is never physically the same. The fact that each cell contains the genome of the whole organism tells us that in life *the design of the whole is contained in each of its parts*. This is a *holographic* principle of profound significance. If a computer were also holographic, each of its transistors should contain all the essential information that defines the entire computer, including its software!

Clearly, life is fundamentally different than computers!

Computers are built with transistors—simple on-off switches— each permanently interconnected with only a few other transistors to form logic gates. Each logic gate calculates a deterministic binary function of its input signals that then appears in its output signal. The output is then sent to the inputs of one or more logic gates. The entire physical structure of the computer is static; it does not change. The algorithms that we create and load into the computer memory reflect instead small portions of the operational part of our mind, but they are far from containing the complete expression of what and who we are.

In a cell, any electron, ion, atom, or molecule is not only the carrier of a particular type of information or energy, but is also the quantum hardware with which each cell is built. Within a cell there is not a distinct boundary between hardware and software, therefore we cannot expect living organisms to use the same type of information processing as our computers. I think that at the interface between the quantum and the classical behaviors of matter there are many other computational principles that we do not yet know.

Quantum "objects" have no boundaries and are not separable, unlike classical particles and computer bits. Individual ions, atoms, and molecules "move" within the cytoplasm under the influence of local electromagnetic fields, and their interactions are mainly regulated by quantum physics. This allows the local environment, which includes the fluctuations of the quantum vacuum, to manipulate the probabilities to favor the necessary transformations in each particular region of the cell. This rich structure can explain, for example, why the photon capture in chloroplasts reaches the incredible energy efficiency of 98% [4].

It is reasonable to assume that the physical movement of atoms and molecules that underlie the physical construction and dismantling of the biochemical components of a cell represents the slowest form of information processing. Inside the cell, we can imagine other much faster and more powerful forms of information processing about which we currently know almost nothing. For example, methods using electron and nuclear spins, sound waves (phonons) and electromagnetic waves (photons) propagating in the cytoplasm.[1] Thus, the

---

1   There is evidence, although still disputed, that the water inside the cells forms "coherence domains" of about 100 nm. In each of these regions, a coherent electromagnetic oscillation can be created in resonance with the vibrations of other molecules present in the same region. Molecules that resonate with the same frequency as that of the coherence domain attract each other and can chemically react. According to physicist Emilio Del Giudice, these domains create the fundamental mechanism for regulating the *specificity* of the chemical reactions that take place inside cells, a major unsolved problem in biology [5].

mechanical movements we observe in a cell could be the end result of an invisible information processing that is global, much faster, and much more sophisticated than the biochemistry we currently study.

Each type of atom or molecule carries specific information and properties when it interacts with other atoms and molecules. However, atoms are not like the mechanical levers and gears of classical machines, because they are quantum systems, and therefore it is currently difficult to imagine the type of interactions and information processing they perform. Among other phenomena, we must consider the existence of quantum interferences that are certainly present inside every cell.

In living organisms, matter, energy, and information flow from the environment to the organism, and vice versa. Since the organism lives in symbiosis with the environment, the two systems must be studied together. A cell is essentially an open quantum-classical system far from thermal equilibrium that not only processes information but also *concurrently* transforms matter and energy, and here the distinctions between matter, energy, and information are blurred. Based on the above considerations, the nature of information processing in living organisms cannot be the same one we use for our communication systems and computers where hardware, software, and power supply are neatly separated, and the hardware does not change every instant.

The Wonderful Organization of a Cell

In all things of nature there is something wonderful.
—Aristotle, *De partibus animalium*

It is surprising to observe the complexity of the structure of certain proteins that should perform rather simple functions, such as those that are incorporated in the cell membrane and control the passage of sodium ions (Na^+) from the outer environment to inside the cell. Why do they have such a complicated structure if they implement such a simple function? I think it is likely that what seems excessive complexity serves to carry out important communication and control functions necessary for the global coordination of the cell. This is the same kind of function I am also hypothesizing for the "junk DNA." Unfortunately, while we have considerable knowledge of local processes, we know almost nothing about the global functioning of a cell as an *autonomous unit*.

I imagine that the biochemical level described by molecular biologists is the equivalent of the electromechanical movements of a robot that represent the visible and slow aspects of its behavior. These outward movements are in turn controlled by the microchips, the "brain" of the robot, whose complex and fast operation is invisible from the outside. I therefore expect that within a cell there are many extremely complex computational processes that control it *as a whole*, of which we are currently unaware.

It should also be stressed that the clear separation (reductionism) between software (information), power supply (energy), and hardware (physical support) that applies to a computer does not exist in a cell. Consider for example a glucose molecule: its presence within the hierarchical organization of a cell can be mainly information for a certain level of the organization, energy for another, and building material for yet another level.

Moreover, a living cell does not limit itself to managing information like a computer does, because it must also procure the matter and energy to function, repair itself, build a copy of itself, and avoid predators, all functions that computers do not perform. Above all, the cell must know how to manage everything and maintain its unity of purpose and action even in unpredictable environmental conditions.

With reproduction, the cell gives life to a "duplicate" that includes hardware and software, to ensure the continuity of its species. This accomplishment is truly amazing, even though we hardly recognize its magnificence given its ubiquity. However, ubiquity does not mean simple and easy, for no computer can perform such a feat. To behave like cells, computers would have to be built using the principles of life, not those of industrial production and classical computing. To reproduce, the matter of the computer would have to continuously flow in and out of the environment, like in a cell. During reproduction, the matter taken from the environment must be deeply reorganized to produce a copy of itself within itself, hardware and software included. No one knows how to perform such an amazing feat.

There Is More to Information Than Symbols

It is not the circumstance that matters, but the lesson learned. Not the symbol, but its meaning. Not what is outside, but what happens inside.
—Richard Bach, *Biplane*

I believe it is crucial for any living organism, from cell to human, to be able to predict the next event that will be experienced. This requires that much of the information processing be dedicated to the prediction of future events. This is the basis of a learning process in which the differences between the predicted event and the one experienced produce the necessary "error signals" that allow us to gradually create a model of reality as accurate as possible. I think that DNA may greatly contribute to this crucial function. It makes sense for me to conjecture that the main DNA function may well be to embody the "model of reality" for a particular species, collectively built over its evolutionary history and summarizing the lessons learned by billions and billions of individuals.

In a computer, the next event is the next instruction that is already in memory, except for the inputs that come from the environment, and are thus unknown. Since deterministic events have probability 1 of occurring (for the event is certain), the concept of information does not make sense when a computer operates as a fully deterministic system. It makes sense, however, when the computer tries to predict the inputs it will receive from the environment based on its past history, which is an essential task for artificial intelligence and robotics.

The use of artificial neural networks has allowed us to develop adaptive models capable of predicting the most likely "input events" for a certain class of problems. For example, the evolution of the stock market for an AI "stock trader" or the next road-event for an autonomous car. In the real world, however, there will always be surprises. In this case, estimating the possible future events and their probabilities is the next best strategy. However, this knowledge is not sufficient to correctly determine the next event in an unpredictable world. This all-important task can only be accomplished—and only partially—by comprehension, a fundamental, non-algorithmic property of consciousness that exists in living organisms but not in computers, as we will discuss later. Note also that a truly creative event could not be part of the alphabet of events to which we could assign a probability, since that event never existed before.

Another important point is that the classical observer in physics typically corresponds to a reference system in which the measurement of an objective event is made, without any concern about the meaning of what is measured. In other words, it is assumed that the same event brings the same amount of information to all observers. However, this is not the case for living organisms, since the same event conveys many different meanings depending on the individual. Consequently, the reductionist concept of information, which is appropriate for computers and classical observers, is totally inadequate to describe the reality of living organisms.

A computer only needs to correctly recognize the "0" and "1" states in each of its information nodes. That is all, because there are no other symbols in its repertoire. A computer has no consciousness, while living organisms are conscious. A computer is just the sum of its parts and does not have a "self," therefore it cannot have consciousness and free will. A living organism is instead "integrated" with a conscious self that is more than the sum of its physical parts. Therefore, the conscious self can change the actions of its parts based on its comprehension.

For example, when an event is novel, a conscious entity becomes curious about it, and this curiosity motivates its exploration. Comprehension and curiosity are non-algorithmic properties that emerge within the entity's consciousness that can "supervise" the mechanical aspects of the body, for these are neither part of the "program" nor part of the "hardware." This is not the case for a computer, because everything that happens in it is either part of its program, or it comes from an external agent independent from it.

Here I have mentioned another fundamental aspect of consciousness that allows a living organism to "know that it does not know," and therefore it can mobilize itself, as an organism, to understand the "anomaly," and thus arrive at new comprehensions.

In a computer there are only local processes without the global and unified perspective of a conscious self, which to exist must be more than the sum of the parts, because the self must be able to influence the parts independently of them. We will see later that consciousness and free will are *quantum properties* of nature that cannot exist in a classical computer system, because they emerge from the quantum entanglement that does not exist in classical physics.

Attributing consciousness, comprehension, and free will to robots and AI systems is therefore misleading and dangerous. In a computer, the presence of a single bit in the state "1" could, for example, mean "launch a missile with a nuclear bomb" or it could represent the least significant digit of a decimal number—a negligible value. Its actual meaning depends on when and where that specific bit will be read and "interpreted" within the program. The interpretation, however, is deterministic and involves no judgment.

Information Meets Consciousness

In this regard, I would like to recall that on 26 September 1983, in the midst of the Cold War, the world was saved from nuclear disaster thanks to Lieutenant Colonel Stanislav Petrov, who did not trust the data sent by the satellites announcing the imminent attack of atomic missiles launched by the USA against the Soviet Union. "I was an analyst, I was sure it was a mistake: my intuition told me." Convinced it was some error, Petrov did not communicate to his superiors that an attack was imminent, and he saved the planet. "Maybe I decided this way because I was the only one who had a civilian education, while all the other employees were soldiers used to giving and following orders."

It was very fortunate for humankind that it was Petrov on duty that night. What would have happened if he had been replaced by a soldier trained to obey without questioning? Or worse still, what if there was a robot on duty?

When a human being behaves unconsciously, he seems to act like an automaton, but with a fundamental difference: there is a subconscious "presence" that can intervene and involve his full consciousness when he recognizes that the body is about to make an important decision. Even a protozoan, although it is only a unicellular organism, is conscious and autonomous. And its consciousness must make the crucial decisions related to its survival, based on its limited understanding of the situation.

It is the consciousness that comprehends and, through the organism, has a first-person experience of itself and of the world. The physical changes in the organism, therefore, follow the comprehension achieved by consciousness.

Live Information

Language is the house of being and in its abode man lives.
— Martin Heidegger, *Being and Time*

Based on the previous considerations, the nature of information in living organisms cannot be the same as the one valid for computers. As already mentioned, the clear separation between hardware, software, and power supply that exists in computers is not present in a cell. A specific molecule inside a cell can be construction material (hardware), energy (power supply), and information (software), depending on the circumstances. In other words, matter, energy, and information form a unit that I call *live information* to distinguish it from Shannon's information, which is inadequate, by itself, to describe the functioning of a cell.

Moreover, the constant flow of live information, i.e., of matter-information-energy, inside and outside the cell, is an indication that live information exists both inside and outside the membrane that we imagine to be its boundary. The physical structure of the cell is not only dynamic but is also constantly evolving, because the matter that enters is not the same matter that exits and the cell changes at every instant.

But there is more, because we must also take into account the intentional behavior that comes, in the model I will discuss in later chapters, from the conscious entity that communicates with the organism but is not part of it. This is another important difference that distinguishes computers, in which the whole is simply the sum of its parts, from living organisms. In fact, the behavior of a computer is entirely determined by that of its parts, and therefore causality proceeds only from the parts to the whole (feedforward or bottom-up). The computer is not an independent whole, but only the sum of its parts. There is nothing that can change the behavior of the parts that is not another part.

In a living organism, on the other hand, there is also a conscious entity that is a unit independent from the physical parts. That unit can therefore influence the behavior of the parts through *feedback* mechanisms (top-down or from the whole to the parts), about which for the moment little is known. Live information is the informational, energetic, and material aspects of living organisms that can only be explained with quantum physics. It is the "stuff" that moves inside the cell, interacts and combines with other matter, generates and consumes energy, processes and communicates information, transports material, disassembles and assembles molecular structures while being buffeted by the imponderable fluctuations of the quantum vacuum. All these functions go well beyond the classical behavior of elementary particles and atoms that make up the physical world we can measure.

The classical concept of "particle as an object" does not exist in quantum physics, and therefore the classical ideas we have about the functioning of life are completely inadequate. Life has been studied as if it were the result of interactions of biochemical molecules imagined as classical objects, despite the evidence that even large molecules composed of hundreds of atoms can "interfere" with themselves [6].

Reductionism has allowed us to build remarkably complex machines, but these are far from resembling living organisms. In a computer, the hardware is fixed and separate from the software. In a cell, hardware changes all the time and software does not exist apart from it. The only area in which there is some similarity with a computer is in the *coding* DNA, which, however, represents only 1.5% of all human DNA. In a cell, everything is dynamical and interacting through live information, not only within the cell itself but also in the cell's interactions with the environment. Therefore, the classical distinctions valid for computers are not applicable to living cells, and the same goes for the brain.

The matter, energy, and information of an elementary particle are not separable. For example, a photon is mainly information and action. However, when its energy is very high, it can also spontaneously "decay" into matter, and vice versa.[2] Reality is irreducibly holistic and dynamic. Everything is interconnected and constantly evolving. The concepts of separation and independence, which are adequate to describe classical objects, cannot portray quantum reality due to the superposition and entanglement of the states that exist in quantum systems.

Cells process information by combining analog, digital, classical, and quantum computational principles. To truly understand life, we must study its activity at three interacting levels: informational, structural, and energetic. This is difficult because these levels are not separable as in a computer. In living organisms, each aspect also contains a part of the other two with proportions that change according to local circumstances that include thousands of interacting atoms. This integration reflects the physical unity of the organism, to which we need to add the

---

2   A photon with an energy of 1.02 MeV (known as a gamma ray) near an atomic nucleus can decay into an electron-positron pair by converting its entire energy into the rest masses of an electron and a positron (the latter is an electron with positive rather than negative charge). Since the rest masses of the electron and positron are 0.51 MeV each, the energy of the photon in excess of 1.02 MeV is converted into the kinetic energy of the electron and positron. This process can also occur in the other direction, meaning that if an electron and a positron meet, they produce two or more photons.

actions guided by the consciousness and free will of the entity that interacts with the organism.

We cannot study living organisms as if they were only classical physical objects, because consciousness and free will are fundamental and quantum, as we will discuss later. If we do not accept their existence, we will never be able to comprehend life. *Life is an expression of consciousness and free will, not the result of random interactions of inanimate matter.* Live information and meaning represent, respectively, the symbolic and semantic aspects of an indivisible, dynamic reality.

The Nature of Languages

> That there are different languages is the most mysterious fact in the world. It means that there are different names for the same things; it makes us doubt that they are the same things.
> —Elias Canetti, *The Province of Man*

A language is a system of symbols necessary for communication among conscious entities. This takes place through a dialogue, i.e., the repetition of communication cycles consisting of a phase in which inner meaning is converted into outer symbols followed by a second phase in which outer symbols are converted into inner meaning. Words were among the first symbols used by human beings to communicate when facial expressions, hand gestures, and guttural sounds became inadequate to encode more complex meanings. According to anthropologist Gregory Bateson, as expressed in *The Excitement of the French*: "We must assume that a language is first of all a system of gestures. After all, animals have only gestures and tones of voice…and words were invented later. Much later."

The next step was to convert the fleeting words into written symbols to create a permanent record. This step took a lot of abstraction and a long time to be accomplished. In early cultures, the translation from sound (word) to written symbol was direct, using a symbol for each word (ideogram). This method required the learning of as many symbols as there are words. Someone later realized that spoken words use various combinations of a small number of stereotyped sounds called phonemes, therefore a simpler scheme could be implemented by associating a symbol to each phoneme. A further abstraction was the creation of our common phonetic alphabets. The sound of a word pronounced *in isolation* could therefore be converted into a sequence of letters of the alphabet with an almost one-to-one correspondence between sound and symbol.

However, the sound of a word pronounced in normal speech also depends on the particular emphasis with which it is modulated to express emotions. This part of the sound, called *prosody*, affects many phonemes at the same time and cannot be easily translated into written symbols, although it can be partially duplicated by a good reader who comprehends what he is reading. Prosody describes the intonation, rhythm, and accent of the spoken language. These are "wave" phenomena that change the waves of the "normal" phonemes used in the words of a modulated sentence. Prosody is not represented in the symbols of the written language.

Therefore, by moving from spoken words to written text, some important contextual information was lost. In some languages, especially English, there is also ambiguity in the conversion from sound to text for certain words, since a different spelling can correspond to the same sound and, in some other cases, the same spelling can have different sounds. Consequently, additional contextual information is needed to accurately translate the sounds into the correct text, and vice versa.

Any list of symbols can be easily converted into another list of symbols, as long as there is a one-to-one correspondence between the items in the two lists. For example, converting a list of decimal numbers into a corresponding list of binary numbers requires a trivial algorithm, although many people would find this process laborious and error-prone. However, when symbol and meaning have a one-to-many correspondence, as is the case with human language, the ambiguity can only be resolved by widening the interpretative context. This is the main reason why speech and human handwriting recognition are such difficult problems to solve in the field of artificial intelligence in which comprehension does not exist.

The conversion from meaning to symbols and from symbols to meaning is at the heart of human communication and comprehension. This is a very difficult problem because it shows that our verbal communications cannot be entirely classic, as is normally assumed. Only the comprehension occurring within our consciousness allows us to communicate without too many problems.

It has been shown that the statistical properties of phonemes have similar regularities in all human languages. The same is true for the letters of the various phonetic alphabets which are used to translate phonemes into written words. It is significant that, in any sufficiently long text, each letter appears with the same relative frequency (probability) regardless of the meaning expressed by the text. This invariance of the probability distribution of phonemes from the meaning carried by the text is found in all human languages. This should not be surprising since each word is a short sequence of the same small set of symbols. In other words, the meaning is carried by the specific order of the words in a sentence, whereas the probabilities of the phonemes in a long string of them are independent from that order. This is why the meaning cannot be found in the probability distribution of the symbols used to represent it. But this does not authorize us to say that meaning does not exist.

If we now consider the atoms and molecules of living organisms as the elementary symbols that express the meaning of the organisms, we will find the same independence of meaning from the probabilities of those symbols. For example, two different single-cell organisms, such as an amoeba and a paramecium, will have the same relative frequency of the atoms that compose them (hydrogen, oxygen, carbon, etc.), and yet their meaning will be quite different. In other words, the atoms that make up the cells are like the letters of the alphabet with which we write our books. Every living organism is therefore like a book that contains from 10^{10} characters for the simplest bacterium to about 10^{31} characters for a blue whale.

Note that 99% of the mass of the human body is made up of six different atoms (hydrogen, oxygen, carbon, nitrogen, calcium, and phosphorus) and only 17 elements are indispensable for our survival. It seems incredible, but the maximum number of elements used by the entire earth ecosystem is less than 40. Therefore the number of "characters" necessary to "write" the dynamic "book" of any existing organism is commensurable to the number of letters of our phonetic alphabets. And the probabilities of manifestation of the elementary symbols of life remain essentially the same for all the organisms of the same kingdom.

However, the analogy ends here, because books are static and produced with printing presses, while life is incredibly dynamic—it self-reproduces, and evolves.

Is There Meaning in the Universe?

Only open eyes can discover that the universe is the book of the highest Truth.
—Jalal al-Din Rumi

A few centuries ago, many scholars had embraced Cartesian dualism which drew a clear division between mind and matter. However, recent advances in physics have shown that reality is holistic and therefore there can be no separation between mind and matter. Consequently, consciousness must be brought into the domain of physics and can no longer be ignored. However, how can a physics entirely based on objective information explain the existence of consciousness when meaningless symbols can only be transformed into other meaningless symbols? How can we bring into physics the meaning that each of us knows exists in our consciousness? For sure, the concept of information is closer to consciousness than matter is.

In the field of physics, the idea that information could be more fundamental than matter was first advanced by John Wheeler in 1995 with the catchy phrase "*it from bit.*" The basic idea is that every thing is made up of bits, that is, of information. Recently, the theoretical physicist Giacomo Mauro D'Ariano and his collaborators have shown that quantum mechanics and free quantum field theory can be derived entirely from six purely informational postulates [7], validating John Wheeler's intuition. Quantum physics could then be interpreted as follows: matter-energy is simply "made" of organizations of quantum bits, or qubits, which manifest themselves in the form of classical bits when they are observed. The qubit is the generalization of the Boolean bit used in classical computers. The qubit represents all possible quantum states obtained by the quantum superposition of the simplest complementary quantum states that can be represented by all the points on the surface of a sphere of radius 1, called the Bloch sphere.

In nature we have a clear example of a qubit in the direction of the magnetic moment (spin) of an electron. When the spin is measured, we will inevitably find it either "up" or "down," in the same or in the opposite direction of the magnetic field of the measuring instrument. Qubits can also be entangled, i.e., they can have correlated states that persist regardless of the probable outcomes of the measurements. The quantum superposition of states and entanglement (see Glossary) provide us with representational and information-processing capabilities that have no equivalent in the classical world. Ultimately, the quantum world is a much vaster reality than the classical one.

I too believe that information is a more basic aspect of reality than matter, as long as it is live information inseparable from its meaning, since meaning cannot emerge from information that is devoid of it. Meaning must be an integral part of that same "substance" that manifests itself as live information when we measure it. For true communication to exist, meaning must also exist within the communicating entities, otherwise the symbols could not be comprehended.

I emphasize again that what we measure in our physical world can only give us Boolean information (bits). The classical bit cannot fully represent quantum information that requires entangled qubits represented with vectors in a complex N-dimensional Hilbert space. In other words, the quantum world has a far vaster number of states than the ones existing in the classical world. This is already evident at the level of a single qubit, which represents an infinity of states, and that will always give us only one classical bit when measured.

Quantum computers, for example, cannot exist entirely in our physical world; only the setting of the program, the initial conditions, and the recording of the result of the calculation can be obtained in the classical world as classical information. Quantum information processing cannot be openly performed in spacetime with classical matter, because qubits and their entanglement are nonlocal properties. So where does quantum computation take place? This question has puzzled physicists since the inception of this technology, but there is still no adequate answer.

However, quantum computers, as they are currently conceived, are deterministic systems and therefore cannot make free-will decisions. Moreover, the algorithms that can be processed by quantum computers could also be processed by a classical computer, but at a much lower speed. However, no quantum or classical computer could compute the states determined by free-will choices. These choices are *creative*, therefore they cannot be determined or predicted by any algorithm. To have both free will and consciousness requires a more general quantum system than a deterministic quantum computer. The Operational Probabilistic Theory (OPT) developed by D'Ariano and collaborators [8] can explain the existence of such systems, as will be seen in later chapters.

6

The Nature of Life

When you wake up in the morning, remember what a precious privilege it is to be alive: to breathe, to think, to feel joy, and to love.
—Marcus Aurelius

The more we become aware, the more we appreciate life; this life so fascinating, unpredictable, simple and complicated, old and new, full of lights and shadows, and mystery...

This life—we don't know "if it is a journey, if it is a dream, if it is awaited, if it is a plan that takes place day after day and you do not notice it except by looking backwards" (Jorge Luis Borges).

This life which is "too good to be meaningless" (Charlie Chaplin).

This life, strong and fragile, just and unjust, positive and negative, and so unfathomable...

This life that "asks you, takes away, cuts you, breaks you, disappoints you, breaks you...until only love remains in you" (Bert Hellinger).

The Incredible Complexity of a Paramecium

Nature is great in great things, but is greatest in small things.
—Pliny the Elder

Many years ago, I saw a short documentary about a paramecium swimming in a drop of water. A paramecium is a protozoan, a single-celled animal about a tenth of a millimeter long whose body is covered with thousands of cilia: microscopic "whiskers" that beat in unison to propel it. Well, this tiny little creature

110

could swim fast, avoid obstacles, search for food, and recognize another paramecium to mate with. It behaved intelligently and purposefully, exactly like a little fish.

But how is it possible that a single cell, devoid of a nervous system, can process information in such an exquisite manner, and be capable of reproducing by building a copy of itself within itself? No engineer has ever been able to build a computer that can assemble a copy of itself within itself—hardware and software included—and then split into two complete computers! To this day AI is far from reaching not only human creative intelligence, but also the intelligence of the simplest single-cell organism, such as a paramecium or an amoeba.

These are unparalleled feats. There must be something fundamental in life that we do not yet understand. In fact, living organisms have unique and special properties compared to inanimate objects that our ancestors also understood quite well. And, as the British neuroscientist Francis Crick puts it: "The development of biology will destroy our traditional beliefs and it is not easy to understand what it will put in their place."

In my opinion, life cannot be explained only with biochemistry, but requires the new concept of live information, which is inseparable from the consciousness and the free will of quantum entities.

A Brief History of Biology

Many scholars believe that biology as a science began around 1670, when Antonie van Leeuwenhoek, using a microscope, first saw that living tissues are composed of cells. He also discovered the first single-celled organisms, hitherto not even imagined, which he called *animalcules*.

Towards the middle of the nineteenth century, the cellular theory of life proposed in 1839 by Matthias Schleiden and Theodor Schwann became generally accepted by the scientific community. This theory postulates that the basic unit of life is the cell, that cells are produced by other cells, and that each cell has all the characteristics of life.[1] Twenty years later, the idea of evolution by natural selection, introduced in 1859 with the publication of Charles Darwin's *The Origin of Species*, had a huge impact, even though for more than a century it was the subject of much criticism and debate. Darwin himself, in a letter of 1844, wrote that for him discovering that species are not immutable was like "confessing a crime." Nonetheless his writing provided convincing evidence of evolution and was defined by the biologist Thomas Henry Huxley as "the most powerful tool that men have at their fingertips, after the publication of Newton's *Principia*, to expand the field of natural knowledge."

Between the 1930s and 1940s, thanks to the contribution of many scientists, the integration of various theories on genetics, evolution, and paleontology took place, leading to an evolutionary theory called the Modern Synthesis of Evolution, or Neo-Darwinian Synthesis. This theory explained how new species emerged and became widely accepted. However, some of its principles, such as the inability of an organism to transmit to its progeny traits acquired during its life, are currently being challenged by new discoveries in epigenetics.[2]

The recognition of the existence of a "unit of inheritance," later called the gene, began with the work of the Moravian monk Gregor Mendel, published in 1866, but ignored until 1900, the same year Planck advanced the idea of the quantum of action, another fundamental "unit." In 1930 it was suspected that DNA was the biomolecule responsible for heredity, but

---

1 Today it is also believed that there is a common ancestor to all the domains of life (Archaea, Bacteria and Eukarya), an ancestor that existed 3.5 billion years ago called LUCA, standing for Last Universal Common Ancestor.

2 Epigenetics is the study of the dynamic alterations of the transcriptional potential of a cell caused by environmental factors, both external and internal to the organism.

how it worked was unknown until the discovery of the helical structure of DNA in 1953 by James Watson and Francis Crick.

Several years later, the genetic code was understood and unveiled and, finally, the entire human genome was decoded with a massive cooperative program that spanned from 1990 to 2003.

DNA is truly mind-blowing. As the astrophysicist Neil deGrasse Tyson states: "There are as many atoms in a single molecule of your DNA as there are stars in a typical galaxy. We are, each of us, a small Universe."

In the early days of biology, it was thought that only living organisms could create biomolecules. In 1828 Friedrich Wöhler managed to synthesize urea, demonstrating that there was no difference between the urea produced by living organisms and the organic compound of the same name synthesized in the laboratory. It could be said that the beginning of biochemistry took place from that date, although most historians prefer to consider 1833 as the "dawn of biochemistry," the year in which Anselme Payen discovered *amylase*, i.e., the first enzyme. From that moment on, life began to be more and more identified with biochemical processes. With the discovery in 1961 of the genetic code embedded in the DNA, life also became connected with the nascent science of information.

The notion of a biochemical basis of life was developed by many biochemists and biophysicists throughout much of the twentieth century, thanks to the new and deeper understanding of atomic and molecular structures provided by quantum physics. Let's not forget, however, the indispensable help of many new and powerful tools, including the electron microscope, which for the first time made it possible to examine what was too small to be seen through optical microscopes. Indeed, quantum physics gave birth to quantum chemistry, completely transforming a purely empirical science into one based on its solid theoretical foundations.

For much of the past century, living organisms have been studied primarily as biochemical systems. Only in the last 20 years has the idea begun to take hold that biology may have more to do with information than biochemistry. But this conversion is slow, because the problems that molecular biologists are called to solve are incredibly difficult and require familiarity with information science, quantum physics, computers, and artificial intelligence. Let's imagine what would have happened if 100 years ago a team of the best scientists had been given one of the most sophisticated systems-on-a-chip built today with the task of understanding how it works. Without electron microscopes, oscilloscopes, and other essential instruments, and without knowing anything about microelectronics, computers, and software, their work would have been absolutely hopeless.

Life Is Dynamic

Panta rei (Everything flows).
—Heraclitus

All living organisms, from bacteria to the entire ecosystem, are open, dynamic, and far-from-equilibrium systems that exchange matter, energy, and information with the environment and are constantly evolving. It can be said, together with Heraclitus, that "There is no permanent reality except for the reality of change: permanence is an illusion of the senses." Undoubtedly, one of the essential properties of life is the capacity to reproduce and therefore to give life to new, independent, and autonomous organisms. It is a truly amazing capability.

With all our scientific and technological prowess, could we build a computer that can do the same? Absolutely not! A computer can only copy the programs stored in its memory, creating an appearance of life—artificial life—but it cannot create another computer within itself. No artificial machine has ever reached the level of dynamism and openness to the environment that life has managed. In theory, 100 to 200 years from now, it could happen that robots may go to a 3D-printing center, connect their "artificial genome" to the "printer," and an identical robot will be assembled, a tiny drop at a time. In this case, would the life and existence of robots be the same as ours?

No, because robots would continue to be built "from the outside," and not "from the inside out," as is the case with living organisms. Each droplet added by the printer will not contain the genome of the entire robot like our cells do. As such, these robots could neither be conscious nor have free will, as I will gradually explain in the course of the book. And, despite their sophistication, those future "printed" robots would be purely classical machines made of inert, classical parts. Only with "quantum components" is it possible to construct living and autonomous organisms from the inside out.

Life Is Holistic

You are made up of a hundred trillion cells. Each of us is a multitude.

—Carl Sagan

Life is a holistic system because everything is interconnected, and therefore it cannot be explained as if it were made of separable parts. Every living organism is in symbiosis with the environment and interacts continuously with other members of its own and other species, such as predators, prey, and those it collaborates with.

Due to this strong interdependence with the environment, an organism cannot be studied on its own without crucial information being lost. Life works best when there is a dynamic balance of give-and-take between each organism and its habitat. If this principle is not respected, the consequences will eventually become serious.

To explain the remarkable autonomy and the intentional and intelligent behavior of living organisms, we must assume that each of them is "connected" with a conscious entity with free will. Consciousness is the ability to have an inner experience and know oneself, while free will is the ability to choose how to act in the world.

The free-will action has a subjective and an objective aspect like live information. The subjective aspect expresses the intention, purpose, and experience of the conscious entity that controls the organism acting in the outer reality. The objective aspect is due to the learning process of the organism "supervised" by the consciousness and free will that leads to the creation of stereotyped behaviors. These behaviors become part of the autonomous repertoire of the organism and will occur with a certain probability that may be predictable by an outside observer. However, the presence of consciousness and free will allows the organism to change the learned behaviors in a creative and unpredictable way, when needed. This is an impossible feat for robots.

It is important to recognize the irreducible existence of an individual consciousness in every living organism. For example, we cannot explain the coherent and intelligent behavior of a paramecium in a widely unpredictable environment without there being a central, creative function that coordinates its actions as a unit. Just as we have consciousness and free will, so every cell in our body must also share the same properties. This is possible because the essence of the whole is present in each of its parts, namely, in each of our cells is present the DNA of the fertilized egg from which our body originated. The claim that consciousness and free will emerge from elementary particles and atoms that do not have the same properties makes no sense. It would be like claiming that electromagnetism emerges from elementary particles devoid of electric charge and magnetic spin.

Considering that life is holistic, the essence of the whole must be contained in each of its parts. Therefore, no part can be completely separated from the whole, and this in turn means that no part can be a closed system. As I discussed earlier, reductionism is a theory that simplifies reality by neglecting the weak connections each part has with the environment. Often, this is done to predict the behavior of a limited number of parts that interact strongly with each other. However, the success of this strategy does not justify the claim that the universe is reductionist, especially if we consider the enormous dynamic range of the natural forces that affect matter. For example, the electromagnetic force that binds electrons to the nuclei of atoms is $2.2 \cdot 10^{39}$ times stronger than the gravitational force between them. That is 39 orders of magnitude! Nonetheless, this extremely weak gravitational force is what allowed the formation of stars that have synthesized in their interiors all the nuclei of the chemical elements (except for hydrogen, deuterium, a small amount of helium, and traces of lithium). We exist on this planet thanks to the actions of the weakest force there is!

I imagine consciousness as a holistic property that is supported by a near-infinity of invisible connections that are neglected when simple systems are studied in a reductive way. For example, a eukaryotic cell is a complex system made up of more than 10^{14} atoms and each atom can interact with many other neighbors. Hence the number of possible interactions is much greater than the number of particles that make up the cell. Every interaction is an exchange of information that creates a connection between the parts that contribute to the consciousness of the whole. I think it is plausible that a conscious entity with free will cannot have a direct experience in the physical world with a structure simpler than that of the simplest known bacterium, which totals about 10^{10} atoms.[3] Such atoms interact in a sophisticated way to produce a robust homeostatic metabolic system that reproduces itself and behaves in essence like the paramecium described above.

Each of us is a conscious organism and every cell of our body contains the genome of the whole organism[4] so that the consciousness of a multicellular organism must be present and active in all its essential parts, i.e., the cells, which are also conscious. However, the consciousness of the entity is not a simple sum of the consciousnesses of its parts, but is much more. The unity of the organism comes from its consciousness. Consciousness is the whole that is more than the sum of the parts, as we will see later.

In summary, to fully understand living organisms, we must imagine them as dynamic energy that is simultaneously transformed into its three objective dimensions of matter, information, and energy supervised by the deeper inner subjective properties of consciousness and free will, which are properties that can only exist in the quantum reality.

The Strategies of Life

And everything surprises me.
Life is an inexplicable magic.
—Johann Wolfgang von Goethe

The strategies used by life are truly amazing. Let's start for example with the first and simplest living organisms:

---

3 The smallest bacteria are part of the Mycoplasma genus. *Mycoplasma pneumoniae* is among the smallest species. It has an elongated shape of 1000–2000 nm and a width of 100–200 nm.

4 This is truly extraordinary. It is as if in a computer each transistor contained the design of the entire computer, hardware and software included!

cyanobacteria. They are single-celled prokaryotes (cells without a nucleus) that use sunlight, water, and carbon dioxide (CO_2) to synthesize glucose and discard the excess oxygen (O_2) produced by the internal chemical reactions fueled by light. Thanks to this process, called photosynthesis, the atmosphere of the primordial earth rich in CO_2 was gradually transformed into one rich in O_2. The large amount of O_2 discarded by cyanobacteria then allowed the emergence of a new energetic path in which the chemical energy of glucose was exploited by using oxygen and discarding carbon dioxide. In this way, a new balance was created in the atmosphere, in which the food of one part of the ecosystem was the waste of the other, and vice versa.

This became the basic *homeostatic* cycle between all of life and the inanimate environment, allowing the maintenance of the optimal proportions of CO_2 and O_2 in the Earth's atmosphere to support the entire ecosystem.

Cyanobacteria feeding on sunlight, CO_2, water, and various other minerals present in the soil, multiplied exponentially and colonized the Earth, forming a second layer of biomolecules that evolved, in turn producing changes in the inorganic matter of the planet—the first layer—from which they emerged.

Using the biomolecules of dead bacteria and the same basic metabolism, new species of cyanobacteria emerged later, and from the first two layers a third was formed, capable of utilizing the waste products of the second layer, O_2, the glucose of dead cells, and a new metabolic path whose creation is a mystery. These new species of aerobic bacteria (oxygen-breathing bacteria) also provided new organic molecules that could be used to create new species of aerobic and anaerobic cyanobacteria (CO_2-breathing bacteria). In this fashion, the survival of the third layer became dependent on the existence of the other two, and the long-term survival of the second layer was ensured by the waste products of the third layer.

The creativity and cooperation expressed by the organisms of the third layer in supplying CO_2 and using the biomolecules left behind by their decaying bodies proved to be a winning strategy. In fact, the anaerobic organisms, by consuming all the CO_2 present in the atmosphere, would have ended up extinct.

Finally, when the glucose contained in the dead cyanobacteria was no longer sufficient to support the growing aerobic species, new species emerged capable of *eating* the living ones.

Life always finds new strategies to be able to expand, including that of "consuming" its own. This means that a species survives at the expense of a certain percentage of its individuals that fall prey. In other words, *mors tua, vita mea* (your death is my life). In fact, we can see that even death is life, because the food of one form of life is either the waste, the dead body, or the alive body of another form of life. This strategy allows a dynamic balance to be achieved within the ecosystem.

When this balance is disturbed too quickly, the ecosystem may not be able to rebalance itself in time, causing the environmental conditions to change drastically to the point where *mors tua, mors mea* (your death is my death). This is what is unfortunately happening in this period of climatic upheavals.

It is amazing to see how living organisms have found a way to develop such a dense network of interactions that an ecosystem of astounding complexity and beauty was created by ultimately transforming only inorganic matter and sunlight!

Life as an Ecosystem

Let's treat the land we live on well: it was not given to us by our fathers, but it was lent to us by our children.
—Masai proverb

We can visualize the ecosystem as a system of systems in which many species interact with each other and with the environment. Each species is made up of many individuals, and each individual is made up of one or more cells.

The cells that combine to form complex multicellular organisms are nucleated cells called eukaryotes, and they in turn contain simpler cells without nuclei called prokaryotes, or bacteria. We can imagine prokaryotes as the "elementary particles" of life, combining to produce its atoms, the eukaryotes. Eukaryotes in turn combine to form molecules and macromolecules of life of unbelievable complexity and diversity that in this analogy correspond to multicellular organisms.

To live and reproduce, an organism requires the ability to self-regulate and obtain food, that is, a supply of matter, energy, and information from the environment. The capacity for self-regulation, called homeostasis, allows organisms to maintain their internal stability through many dynamic, interoperable processes that use negative feedback. Stability is achieved through a dynamic equilibrium around certain set points, just like in a thermostat that automatically regulates the temperature in our homes. Of course, within a cell there are homeostatic cycles inside other homeostatic cycles at many levels, creating a system of disconcerting complexity, even though the basic operating principle of each cycle is always the same. The principle involves measuring the value of the variable to be controlled, comparing it with a predetermined value, and then guiding the process until the difference between the two becomes negligible.

Homeostasis occurs at all levels: within a single cell, between the cells of an organ, between the organs of an organism, between individuals of the same species, in interspecies dynamics, and finally in the relationship of the entire ecosystem with the inorganic environment, as we have already seen with the O_2–CO_2 homeostatic cycle.

The Gaia hypothesis, advanced by James Lovelock and developed together with Lynn Margulis in the 1970s, argues that the entire Earth is a single living organism. Life as ecosystem regulates the physical conditions of the planet to survive, even in the event of severe environmental disturbances caused by extraordinary terrestrial and extraterrestrial events, such as volcanic eruptions, meteorites, and solar flares. The dependence of each animal on their common environment creates a system of unthinkable complexity, because the environment depends to a certain extent on the actions of each organism, the Earth itself, the solar system, and beyond. Everything is interconnected. "We are part of nature, the trees are our brothers, the mountains think and feel. All this is part of our wisdom, of the memory of the creation of the world" (Ailton Krenak).

In this homeostatic and dynamic ecosystem, the survival of any species depends on a give-and-take, on a continuous *cooperation* that must find its balance. According to a 2018 study, the first known mass extinction, 445 million years ago, may have been caused by very voracious algae that consumed CO_2 too quickly to be balanced by the existing homeostatic cycle. The effect of their greed was a complete freezing of the Earth. It seems that we are not the first species to cause a change on a planetary scale.

The *Homo sapiens* species, which so far has taken from the environment without ever worrying about the consequences, must urgently return to the ecosystem what it has taken or risk its own extinction and that of many other species. The delicate balance of nature must be maintained. There are no exceptions.

The industrial revolution, while on the one hand allowing human society to progress enormously, on the other hand has caused environmental changes that are much faster than the response time of the current homeostatic mechanisms of the planet.

Global warming, deforestation, ocean acidification, continuous wars, and the specter of a nuclear war are endangering the entire ecosystem on which all life on the planet depends.

"In the name of progress, man is transforming the world into a fetid and poisonous place…to the point that it is legitimate to ask whether, in a hundred years, it will still be possible to live on Earth" (Erich Fromm, *Anatomy of Human Destructiveness*). At the 76th General Assembly of the United Nations, the secretary of the UN, António Guterres, declared: "We see warning signs in every continent and region, high temperatures; the loss of biodiversity is shocking, air and water are polluted, climate-related disasters are evident. We are on the edge of the abyss."

It is essential that human beings become protectors and guardians of the environment. In the encyclical *Laudato si'*, Pope Francis writes that "to guard means to protect, care, preserve, conserve, watch over. This implies a relationship of responsible reciprocity between human beings and nature." We must be aware, as Pope Francis continues, "of not being separated from other creatures, but of forming a wonderful universal communion with the other beings of the universe." Otherwise, the current ecosystem can be destroyed and humanity may not survive. As the Italian European Space Agency astronaut Luca Parmitano says: "Man is at risk, not the Earth." In fact, "life continues well beyond the damage we are doing, because the universe is prepared for life. Life is perfectly aligned with the principles of physics, so it will continue to exist." The Earth will then rebuild a new ecosystem, as it has done many other times in the past when catastrophic events have dramatically upset the delicate balance of life, but it is not certain that there will be human beings in this new system.

Quoting the Polish writer Isaac Bashevis Singer in *Old Love*: "The only hope of mankind is love in its various forms and manifestations, whose only source is love for life."

The Boundary between Animate and Inanimate Matter

Each species within the gigantic terrestrial ecosystem, itself seen as a single living organism, can exist only if most of its supporting homeostatic network continues to exist. This is evident for living organisms, but it is also true for inanimate matter, as we have seen with the basic CO_2–O_2 cycle. There is no sharp dividing line between animate and inanimate matter, just as there is no sharp boundary between classical and quantum systems.

An electron cannot exist without the quantum field from which it emerges. And the quantum field of the electron cannot exist without the *Whole* from which quantum fields have emerged. The electron is a manifestation—a visible, objective state—of the quantum field of electrons. And "electrons are neither particles nor waves: they are another thing, completely new. They are quantum states" (Leon Max Lederman).

We often imagine the electron as a particle or as a wave separate from the field, while instead it is a set of properties of the field from which it emerges *without detaching from it*. The electron is a "conserved form" that the field takes, inseparable from the field. It is a piece of field that preserves all its characteristics because it never separates from it, just as a bacterium is an organism that emerges from the complex environment formed by the Sun-Earth-Moon system, from which it never separates.

When we focus our attention only on the bacterium, we only consider the "particle" or "shape" aspect and we completely lose sight of its "wave" aspect, which is what connects the bacterium to the whole. The whole is not only the inanimate background in which the part—the bacterium—exists, but it is also "inside" the bacterium: it is an integral and irreducible part of what we call a *bacterium*, without which it could not exist. The bacterium does not exist only inside its membrane, because a moment later a part of what was inside is outside, and vice versa. The bacterium exists inside-and-outside its membrane in a dynamism that we often do not appreciate in our need to separate and place boundaries that do not exist in reality, but only in our limited comprehension.

A bacterium is a part-whole because it is not separable from the whole, nor is the whole separable from the part. And an electron is also a part-whole, molecules are parts-whole, and a human being is a part-whole. A part-whole is a concept that does not exist in *classical* physics where particles are little hard balls, inanimate "objects" separated from the environment, that only act locally by colliding with each other. Reductionism has created impassable boundaries that do not exist in nature.

The "wave" behavior of particles and the existence of entanglement in quantum physics are telling us that a particle is not an object and that its impact can be far-reaching. A local interaction of a particle can have nonlocal consequences that are impossible to know, thus justifying the part-whole concept and name.

Life Is Both Quantum and Classical

There are only two ways of living one's life: one as if nothing were a miracle; the other as if everything were a miracle.
—Albert Einstein

If we look critically at eukaryotic cells—the bricks of our body—we can see that their functioning is completely different from that of our machines, including computers. Inside the cytoplasm of each cell there are electrons and protons (hydrogen ions); ions of simple atoms such as sodium, potassium, phosphorus, and so on; simple molecules such as glucose and amino acids; complex molecules such as messenger RNA and proteins; organelles such as ribosomes and DNA; and finally the mitochondria, which are bacteria, i.e., cells without a nucleus that can live inside a cell with a nucleus.

A multicellular organism therefore contains many hierarchical levels of incredible complexity, which work cooperatively with a single purpose determined locally by the consciousness and free will of each cell, and globally by the consciousness and free will of the entire organism.

When we manipulate life, we always start with a living cell, not with its parts, and it is only thanks to its incredible robustness that we can carry out invasive manipulations without killing it. Everything that happens in a living organism is not fully understandable within the reductionist framework of classical physics. There are crucial properties that can only be explained by quantum physics, and many other properties that we consider classical are approximations of quantum properties. However, what we cannot classically explain is the overall behavior that gives the organism autonomy, intelligence, and the ability to evolve and reproduce itself as a whole. This is the invisible layer of the whole that "connects" the parts and that we typically ignore, intent as we are on explaining the local functioning of the parts.

I believe it is impossible to explain life without the concepts of consciousness and free will, because the two are inextricably linked to the quantum-classical aspects of physical reality in ways that we have yet to investigate and fully understand. A living organism can act as a unit with free will, intention, purpose, and meaning, properties that cannot derive from a bag of unconscious atoms and molecules that interact probabilistically with each other. Consciousness is what gives perception and understanding to the organism, while free will allows it to act as a unified entity with its own intention, based on conscious comprehension.

According to our physical theories, the fields emerge from the unified field, but they are inseparable from the whole and do not precede it. In a holographic and holistic universe, the parts that self-assemble must contain the essence of the whole, and therefore cannot be separated from it, because the whole must still be capable of influencing the parts. This is also the reason why elementary particles making up a living cell are inseparable from the fields of which they are states; thus they truly are open systems like living cells.

In a reductionist view, each part is a statistical ensemble of closed systems that collectively behaves like another closed system. Thus the quantum correlations that maintain the unity of a whole cannot exist. This is the fundamental reason why our reductionistic classical machines, such as computers, cannot be conscious and cannot have free will.

Living Organisms as Information Processors

Reductionism has been successful because science has mainly studied inanimate objects or the functioning of small subsystems within living organisms without fully comprehending their connection with the whole. However, to understand how cells process information with quantum parts, it is necessary to go beyond our reductionist prejudices.

Each machine conceived by a human being is imagined by the designer as a mechanism suitable for performing a certain function. The inventor decides which parts are needed, their arrangement, and how they work to obtain "the whole" that he has in mind. In other words, *the whole is not in the machine, but in the mind of its inventor*. The parts simply do what they are forced to do by the laws of physics skillfully applied by the inventor. The whole seems to "emerge" from the parts, but in the machine there is no "whole." There is only the sum of the parts. A computer program does exactly the same thing.

A cell is a microscopic quantum-classical system, while a human is a macroscopic quantum-classical system made up of trillions of cells. These systems have both probabilistic and deterministic behavior. In the current state of knowledge, the way in which information is represented and processed by a cell is essentially unknown, with the exception of the genetics of proteins and the mechanical interactions of some of them, which are considered the basic level of information processing in cells. The functioning of DNA is inextricably connected with the quantum properties of elementary particles, atoms, and molecules in a complex dynamical system in which both dynamical order and quantum randomness are present. As discussed in the previous chapter, only 1.5% of the human genome encodes proteins. Since we have fewer genes than some flowering plants, it is difficult to argue that the secrets of human intelligence are contained in the coding DNA. They are most likely contained in the rest of the DNA, the so-called "junk DNA" that we discussed earlier.

The success of molecular biology has led us to think that we can study cells in a reductive way, as if they were classical machines. But cells are holistic systems in which the whole is more than the sum of the parts, so I expect that only when we start studying life as quantum-classical holistic systems will it begin to reveal its deepest secrets.

The fundamental differences between the information-processing principles of computers and living systems can be clearly seen when we reduce the size of transistors inside a microchip. As the size decreases, the holistic nature of atoms and molecules increasingly interferes with the deterministic function of transistors, which is based on the statistical properties of many thousands of atoms and molecules.

In a cell, however, the quantum properties of individual atoms and molecules that would compromise the operation of computers are used for the processing of information, energy, and matter (live information) in ways that remain largely unknown. Furthermore, when dealing with electrons, protons, atoms, and simple molecules the concepts of dimension and separation lose their meaning due to the wave properties of matter. As I explained in the second chapter in connection with the double-slit experiment, an electron, as well as an atom or a molecule, can "interfere with itself" and manifest over a volume of space much larger than its size.

This fact has profound consequences since, in a quantum system, the influence of an ion on the surrounding environment goes far beyond its physical volume, and the details depend on the nature of the electromagnetic field created by nearby atoms and molecules. Consequently, the nature of the possible interactions strongly depends on the contributions of many particles. This makes the rigorous study of living systems extremely difficult, since the effects of self-interference have important consequences on information processing. In other words, the function performed by an ion in a cell depends on the electric field created by its many, constantly moving neighbors, a situation that is difficult to compute and nearly impossible to measure.[5]

I think that life is a dynamical system performing both quantum and classical information processing, in which live information is also connected with the subjective meaning of the organism coming from its consciousness. Therefore, to understand life, it must be studied in terms that go beyond those of a reductive biochemical machine. Life is unbelievably complex and resourceful. We can almost be certain that it has found a way to use the quantum properties of nature to its advantage to perform sophisticated information processing in ways we have yet to imagine.

All the machines we build, including computers, are made by assembling separate parts. A living cell, on the other hand, cannot be assembled from its atomic and molecular components. A cell is a dynamical system of a far greater order of complexity

---

5   The presence or absence of a single proton (hydrogen ion) at a particular place inside a cell could be irrelevant or vital, depending on when and where the proton is, and the effect could manifest immediately or years later. For example, sickle cell anemia, which can cause death, is due to the difference of a single nucleobase (a simple molecule) in the hemoglobin gene.

than the machines we have created because it uses quantum components that have no definable boundaries.

The Fundamental Differences between a Cell and a Computer

The most notable difference between a computer and a cell is that a computer is made of *permanent* classical matter, while a cell is made of dynamic quantum "matter." Almost all the atoms and molecules in a microchip are those that were present when the chip was first manufactured. These atoms and molecules form stable physical structures that carry information in the form of electrical signals, working like roads and gates that control the movement of vehicles.

On the other hand, the atoms and molecules that enter a cell flow, transform, and exit so that those that leave the cell are no longer the ones that entered it. This strategy is indispensable for carrying out the metabolic and reproductive functions of cells. These atoms simultaneously transport information, energy, and matter to create the static and dynamic structures that allow the cell to live and experience its own existence.

The desire to explain reductionistically the holism of cells has prompted many researchers to attribute miraculous powers to the modest self-organization observed in nature in so-called *emergent* natural phenomena.[6] The latter are incommensurable with the complexity of the self-organization found in a cell, just like a quantum computer with a billion entangled qubits (which does not even exist yet, but may be realized in the distant future) cannot compare with a computer with a billion transistors.

---

6 Self-organization is a spontaneous process in which an initially disordered system creates order starting from local interactions, as long as there is sufficient energy available. Examples of self-organization are snowflakes (crystallization of water), certain chemical oscillations, and heat convection cells in a fluid.

If we compare the behavior of a paramecium with that of a robot with a microchip brain, we can immediately recognize at least seven monumental differences:

1. A robot is a classical, reductionistic, and permanent organization made up of separate parts assembled by external agents. A cell is a quantum and classical organization, holistic, dynamic, and self-reproducing made of live information (matter, energy, and information) that moves in and out of its porous and dynamic membrane. A cell is never the same, instant after instant. This difference is enormous, because the components of a cell are elementary particles, atoms, and molecules that behave individually as described by quantum physics. Therefore, the information processing can be both quantum and classical.[7]

2. Robots are deterministic, with the exception of input signals which may come from the free will of conscious agents interacting with them. A cell is both deterministic and indeterministic. The indeterminism derives from the quantum nature of its basic components and from the creative nature of consciousness and free will that direct the cell as a unit.

3. Robots are not autonomous and require constant supervision, unless they perform simple functions. Cells, on the other hand, are autonomous, capable of dealing with unpredictable situations, including hostile environments.

4. Each cell of a multicellular organism contains the entire "blueprint" of the whole. This incredible property does not exist in a robot.

---

7   The quantum information processing I am referring to here is not the type we use in the quantum computers currently in development. I believe there are many quantum properties of atoms and molecules that lend themselves to analog computations for the moment unexplored and unknown.

5. In a robot, information processing and communications are essentially digital with some analog input-output functions, while in a cell live information is used.

6. Robots are objective, classical systems without consciousness and without free will. Cells are both objective and subjective and they have consciousness and free will, even though they are strongly conditioned by the laws of physics.

7. A cell has all the classical characteristics of a machine, and in addition it has the quantum characteristics that come from live information, consciousness, and free will. In a robot there is no whole, but only the sum of its classic parts. A cell is connected with a quantum whole that is more than the sum of its quantum and classical parts.

In summary, the crucial properties that differentiate a living organism from a robot equipped with artificial intelligence derive from the consciousness and free will that communicate with the quantum portion of its cells (using live information) to determine its overall behavior.

7

The Nature of Consciousness

Consciousness cannot be accounted for in physical terms.
For consciousness is absolutely fundamental. It cannot be
accounted for in terms of anything else.

—Erwin Schrödinger

The first time I heard about consciousness was as a child,
during the preparation for my first Holy Communion. Before
receiving communion, it was necessary to make a confession,
after an "examination of conscience." I didn't understand what
"conscience" meant, but the word "exam" sounded vaguely
threatening, evocative of strict teachers.

However, that first examination was quite easy, because
it was actually done by the priest in our place, for he was the
one who suggested sins to confess, even those we didn't know
were sins. Then, as I grew up, I started becoming aware of
my consciousness. But I never imagined that I would end up
devoting a good part of my life to examining it!

How Does Consciousness Work?

My first scientific encounter with consciousness took place in
1987 while I was working with artificial neural networks at
Synaptics, a company I had co-founded one year earlier. At
that time I was studying biology and neuroscience to better
understand how the brain works. All neuroscience books
described its functioning by reducing it to pure electrochemical
activity, with the assumption, never explicitly stated, that this
activity was identical to our sentient perception. In my way of
thinking the two could not possibly be the same phenomenon.

So, I asked a neuroscience professor who was on our scientific advisory board to explain how the electrochemical activity of the brain transforms into our sensations and feelings.

He replied, "Are you talking about consciousness?"

I didn't know then that "consciousness" was the right word for what I was struggling to express, but it sounded correct. "Yes," I replied. "How does consciousness work and why is this word never mentioned?"

"Oh, don't worry about it," he said. "It's something that happens somehow in the brain—of course—and one day we'll figure it out." And that was the essence of his explanation.

The neuroscientist's position was entirely consistent with the materialist assumption that everything that exists must somehow be produced by the interactions of atoms and molecules. And, since I too had embraced materialism, his "explanation" seemed rational.

But how does it work? It was not enough to say that consciousness emerges "somehow" from the activity of the brain. I needed a real explanation, a *mechanism*. Then I thought that, if consciousness arises from a complex information-processing system like the brain, even a computer could be conscious, at least in principle. With great curiosity, I began to consider how I could make a conscious computer. This led me to reflect deeply on the properties of consciousness, and I soon encountered the great obstacle: the total lack of understanding of the nature of sensations and feelings, what philosophers call *qualia*.

Qualia

Our consciousness is the inner semantic space where the signals coming from the physical world, both inside and outside the body, are "processed" by the brain and take the form of feelings, sensations, and meanings, i.e., of qualia. Qualia refer to what "it feels like" when a sensation or a feeling emerges within our consciousness.

Note that the nature of feelings is completely different from the nature of physical events. A physical event happens in spacetime and is accessible "from the outside" through our physical senses and instruments. This produces a so-called third-person experience *shared* by all observers. A feeling is instead a *private*, first-person experience accessible only "from the inside" by the owner of consciousness. However, the interiority I am speaking about is not a physical dimension.

Let's consider, for example, how a rose is recognized by its scent. A rose emits particular molecules with unique three-dimensional structures. They can enter as "keys" in the "locks" of some receptor molecules incorporated in the olfactory cell membranes of the nasal epithelium. When this happens, the receptor cells produce macroscopic electrical signals. They constitute the input signals to the neural networks of the olfactory cortex, whose output signals correspond to the name of the identified object: *rose*.

Even a machine can recognize a rose by its molecular "emissions," emulating the natural process I have just described. However, this recognition is qualitatively very different from ours: a machine feels nothing, and the name of the recognized object is just another signal or symbol. The artificial nose does not have the conscious experience of the fragrance of the rose. Moreover, the ways in which the machine can respond to the "rose" signal depend solely on its program. For us, however, the scent of the rose is not a signal, it is a *quale*, something completely different from the electrical signals generated by the neural networks. It is related to them, of course, but it is not identical, nor can it be produced directly by them since it has a completely different quality from the electrical or mechanical activity that characterizes classical signals. It is a *quality* that poets have tried in a thousand ways to express, without ever succeeding.[1]

---

1 Here is an example: "Throw away / every work in verse or prose. / No one could ever say / what is, in its essence, a rose." Giorgio Caproni, *Elogio della rosa*.

The scent of a rose, just like the taste of cherry jam, the sound of a violin, or the feeling of love is a sensation that makes the one who proves it consciously aware of symbolic data. It is an *experience* that takes place in our consciousness that can deeply affect us. Rainer Maria Rilke said it best: "There are moments when a rose is more important than a piece of bread."

The computer, on the other hand, cannot be aware of anything, nor can it consciously reason by association about its experience. Therefore, the comprehension brought by consciousness is not accessible to a computer. And herein lies the fundamental limit, and the danger, of artificial intelligence.

The Hard Problem of Consciousness

Consciousness represents the most perplexing problem for the science of mind. There is nothing that is not known more intimately than conscious experience, and yet nothing that is more difficult to explain. In recent times, all mental phenomena have allowed themselves to be analyzed, but consciousness has stubbornly resisted. Many have tried to provide explanations, but they always seem not to be up to the mark.

—David Chalmers

This conversion from electrical signals to the scent experience is an example of the so-called "hard problem of consciousness," as the philosopher David Chalmers defined it in 1995 [9]. This problem can be expressed as follows: what is the phenomenon responsible for our sensory, bodily, emotional, and mental *experience* characterized by qualia? Chalmers wonders: "Why doesn't all this information processing proceed 'in the dark', devoid of any inner sensation?" Scientists claim that qualia emerge from the functioning of a complex system, but no one has been able to come up with a convincing explanation for how this can happen. That is why Chalmers called it, "the hard problem of consciousness."

It is surprising to me that many researchers believe there is not much to explain. We are so used to being aware that we generally do not recognize that consciousness cannot possibly emerge from unconscious matter. Only those who have seriously thought about it have realized that consciousness is a fundamental unsolved problem with enormous ontological and epistemological consequences.

For years I unsuccessfully labored to understand how consciousness could arise from electrical or biochemical signals, and I found that, invariably, electrical signals can only produce other electrical signals or other physical consequences such as force or movement, but never sensations and feelings, which are qualitatively different.

I therefore came to the conclusion that consciousness has to be a fundamental property like electricity, for example, that cannot arise from elementary particles devoid of electrical charge and magnetic spin. In other words, I believe that consciousness must be an irreducible property of the "elementary particles" of which everything is made, just as the electrical charge is a property that does not derive from any simpler properties. If this is the case, then everything in the universe must be conscious.

This idea is millennia old and is called *panpsychism*.

Panpsychism, however, has never been taken seriously by science. It is considered a hypothesis that offers very few opportunities for falsification. In fact, there does not seem to be any connection between what we feel and the external world. In short, if for every physical action there is an explanation that does not require consciousness, what is consciousness for? This is why consciousness is considered *epiphenomenal*, i.e., a phenomenon that passively accompanies another phenomenon which is the true cause of what we feel.

The alternative is to consider that physical laws may be emergent properties of consciousness, an assumption that is hard for most scientists to accept. It would mean that the objective world derives from the subjective world! And that's asking too much.

Accepting panpsychism implies that inner reality has a direct impact on outer reality, a possibility that the determinism of classical physics denies. No free will is possible in a deterministic universe. Consequently, our inner reality cannot have any causal power. This is equivalent to saying that the inner world is completely illusory, i.e., inner reality can only be influenced by the outer reality, but not vice versa. Therefore meaning cannot be ontological in either human beings or computers.

However, we know that the external world is brought within us through the processing of sensory information and becomes an inner experience. If consciousness did not exist, we should not have any experience and we should not consciously know anything. And yet consciousness is necessary to know even the most basic thing, like the fact that "I exist." Moreover, if there is an influence from the outside to the inside, why shouldn't there also be an influence in the other direction? What is the point of having interiority?

It is peculiar that I know within me that I am conscious, but I cannot prove it because my inner world is private and cannot be observed from the outside. I could be a zombie[2] claiming to be conscious, and no measurement could prove otherwise. In fact, I can know the feelings that another person feels only if he reveals them to me, but even in that case my knowledge cannot be certain, because that person may be mistaken or lie to me.

The problem is that a measurement of brain signals can reveal only some physical correlates of our conscious experience,

---

2 In the words of David Chalmers: "A zombie is simply something identical to me but lacking any conscious experience—everything is silent inside."

but not the qualia that a person actually experiences. Yet the qualia carry the meaning to the experiencer, but they cannot be measured from the outside. And if I cannot objectively prove that I am conscious when I know I am, how can I prove that someone else is conscious?

What Is Consciousness?

I consider consciousness as fundamental, and matter as a derivative of consciousness. We cannot go beyond consciousness. Everything we talk about, everything we consider as existing, requires consciousness.
—Max Planck

Consciousness is that part of us "that lives and feels and turns itself around," as Dante Alighieri writes. It allows us to perceive and understand the meaning of physical reality and of our emotions and thoughts. It does so through a sentient experience that transcends the blind translation of meaningless signals into other signals of the same kind that goes on in our computers.

In the previous example in which a rose was recognized by the type of molecules emitted, both the computer and the brain could *unconsciously* translate the complex signals produced by their respective olfactory sensors into the symbol corresponding to the name "rose." But a human being takes it a step further, because he transforms the *objective* meaning of the recognition into the conscious experience of the scent of the rose that emotionally, cognitively, and associatively connects him to his entire life experience and produces the *subjective meaning* he feels.

This profound transformation takes place within our consciousness. It has hardly been properly acknowledged by science, and it has never been explained.

Qualia and Consciousness

How it happens that something as remarkable as a state of consciousness is the result of stimulation of the nervous tissue is as inexplicable as the appearance of the Genie in the fable, when Aladdin rubs the lamp.
—Thomas Henry Huxley, *The Elements of Physiology and Hygiene*

We experience and know the physical world around us, as well as our inner world, through qualia. Without them we would be unconscious, like sleepwalkers or robots. We could still move, but we wouldn't have any experience and we wouldn't even know we exist. If we carefully examine our inner world, we can recognize four distinct classes of qualia: physical sensations and feelings; emotions; thoughts; and spiritual feelings.

The first category concerns the sensations and feelings that derive from the perception of the physical world, both inside and outside the body. For example, the taste of food, the scent of a flower, our tactile sensations, the sound of music, or the sense of color and shape of an object. This category also includes sensations of physical wellbeing or pain coming from our physical organs.

The second category concerns emotions such as curiosity, friendship, compassion, joy, trust, fear, anger, sadness, pride, stubbornness, shame, envy, greed, confusion, and so on. Emotions feel very different compared to physical sensations, and apparently they come from a level of reality independent from the physical world.

The third category is thoughts, although most scholars do not regard thoughts as qualia. However, if you ask yourself, "How do I know that I had a thought?", you may immediately recognize that you perceived the faint and fleeting "image" of the thought just before you translated it into mental or spoken words.

For most of us, the translation of that multidimensional image into words is so fast that we believe we are thinking directly in verbal form, unaware of the existence of the image-quale that precedes the symbolic form. That is to say, we are so used to the *automatic reification* of thoughts into symbols that we have stopped noticing the "quale" which is the sentient experience of a thought.[3]

Finally, the fourth category contains spiritual feelings, which include the feeling of intense and selfless love, the feeling of oneness with the universe or with a transcendent presence greater than ourselves, and the ineffable mystical experiences that have been reported over the centuries. Spiritual qualia allow us to feel a profound union with what we experience.

The electrochemical signals produced by our nervous system are manifestations distinct from the sensations and feelings that allow us to "live those signals" in the form of sentient experiences, and to "know the meaning" of that symbolic information. Qualia and understanding are produced in our consciousness and suggest the existence of a reality vaster than the unconscious physical reality. Consciousness defines the inner world of our experience, which is distinctly different from the physical world of signals that we can measure with our senses and our instruments.

To avoid any misunderstanding, I would like to emphasize that what I call inner reality is not the physical reality that exists inside the human body. Inside our body we can only find physical organs and electrochemical signals. The "inner reality" of our waking experience does not exist inside the body but in the same "space" in which our dreams exist. The physical

---

3   To be able to catch the evanescent image that is the quale that characterizes a thought, it is often necessary to quiet the mind with some form of meditation.

reality inside our body is still part of outer reality, even if it is not visible from the outside; it is part of the symbolic reality.

In other words, our inner reality is not physical in the same sense that the internal organs of our body are. We imagine that our "interiority" is inside our body because we believe that only the physical world of objects in spacetime exists. But this is only because our sensory-brain system cannot process the type of information that our consciousness perceives and understands.

Our inner reality defines the semantic aspect of reality, i.e., what gives meaning and purpose to our life. The semantic reality does not exist in the same spacetime as physical reality, but in an experiential space and time closer to the space and time of our dreams or to the spacetime in which we experience the virtual reality created by a computer. Such reality exists only as electrical signals in the confined physical spacetime of the memory of a computer. How come we experience vast spaces full of people, animals, and objects? Where are those people? We are the ones giving form and meaning within our consciousness to those signals, that for the computer are meaningless symbols. The same phenomenon happens when we translate the printed words in a book into an inner vivid experience.

Learning, Perception, Comprehension, and Recognition

There are sophisticated neural networks in our brains that are active even before birth. They allow us to automatically organize and recognize the sensory stimuli related to taste, smell, touch, sound, and sight as "unconscious objects." The self-awareness that perceives, knows, explores, and interacts with the physical world *through the body* arises gradually as our consciousness begins to recognize the signals produced by the body as qualia in its experiential field, to which it must pay attention.

I think that in an infant the neural networks automatically organize the sensory information into data-objects which, once unconsciously recognized, can then be consciously perceived even without knowing their names and functions. The infant discovers that it can willfully manipulate certain objects in its field of awareness, while others do not respond to its will. This essential distinction gradually creates the sense of self and the sense of the world as non-self. Later, the child will be able to associate a name with each of the common objects he already knows because he hears them called by a particular sound. He will also be able to *comprehend* their functions by observing who uses them.

In my opinion, the organization and recognition of the basic patterns must be an automatic property of the brain that is fairly independent of consciousness. This is a function similar to the *machine learning* that we have recently begun to master using artificial neural networks. My hypothesis is that this process occurs simultaneously with the creation of the ego during the first year of life. The ego is that portion of our consciousness that learns to manipulate the body and the objects of the outer world by distinguishing what is controllable with free will, and what is not. When the ego becomes fully identified with the body, as distinct and separate from the world, the ego is fully formed and the child thinks of himself as his physical body existing with other objects and living organisms that are separate and together make up the world in which he can act.

When our consciousness supervises the learning of the neural networks of our brain, it allows us to reach levels of competence in perception, recognition, and understanding that immeasurably exceed the range of capabilities of our machines.

The failure to recognize the fundamental contributions that consciousness makes to human intelligence is responsible for attributing intelligence to machines. Computers are only amplifiers of our *mechanical* mental abilities, while the intelligence attributed to machines is essentially the intelligence of their programmers who translated their comprehensions into algorithms.

When it comes to true intelligence, it is conscious comprehension that makes all the difference! And comprehension is a *non-algorithmic* property of consciousness that computers can never possess. Computers are capable of discovering statistical correlations among vast fields of information because they can perform mathematical operations billions of times faster than we can. This is a great contribution that AI can make to society; however, it does not *conceptually* represent anything new.

Guided with honesty, integrity, and ethics, AI will allow us to greatly increase our comprehension of the world, enabling us to control phenomena out of the reach of our brain *as a mechanism*. Our real intelligence, however, comes not from our brain but from our consciousness. It is our ego's consciousness that needs to awaken to its own vaster nature to be able to use AI with wisdom for the common good, and not to dominate. This point is crucial and must not be underestimated. President Vladimir Putin said that "the leader in AI will dominate the world." But, as Buddha said: "Better than dominion over all worlds...is taking the first step on the way to awakening."

When we claim to be conscious, we mean that we have an inner experience based on sensations and feelings. In this case, the automatic and unconscious detection of physical signals, followed by their processing and mechanical recognition, becomes a conscious experience based on qualia. Conscious perception is therefore the process that converts the autonomic electromagnetic and electrochemical activities of the nervous system and body into qualia. The process of "extracting" meaning from qualia is called *comprehension*. We comprehend when we get the meaning conveyed by our qualia perception.

For example, suppose there is a smell of a burning tire in the air. The first level of meaning you feel in your consciousness is: "there is something nearby." Superimposed on this meaning is another more precise one: "something is burning." The third level carries an additional meaning: "the burning thing is rubber," and finally the burning thing is "most likely a tire." This comprehension is therefore enriched by your subjective experience of past situations in which there were tires burning. This pyramidal structure is characteristic not only of comprehension, but possibly also of the neural symbols used to represent it, although in general we perceive their meaning as a whole, a "holistic quale."

Note that the same quale can provide varying amounts of meaning, depending on the subject's previous experience and comprehension. Comprehension is therefore a property fairly independent of perception and strongly connected with the memory of previous experiences.

Another example is the feeling of love. It is a holistic quale because its meaning can only be comprehended as a whole, not divisible into separate parts. This is also why love cannot be described verbally without always leaving something out. That feeling has a depth and a dynamism that our words (classical symbols) cannot fully capture, no matter how good we are.

For example, Edgar Lee Masters in his poem, 'I have known silence,' asks: "For the depths / Of what use is language?" And the philosopher and journalist Umberto Galimberti in *The Republic of Women* affirms that:

It is in fact in the nature of a sentiment not to be fully expressible by the words that name it and, thanks to the insufficiency of words, the sentiment can let that which is its own transpire: the inexpressible. The sentiment, in fact, lives precisely in never being able to tell itself completely, thus in its preservation as a spring of ulterior meanings.

Comprehending means discovering new meanings within a sentient experience, i.e., detecting a deeper inner structure within an experience. Comprehension requires a conscious field of qualia that defines the semantic space.

Later we will see that the semantic space can be represented by a complex Hilbert space of which spacetime is a projection. It is important to underscore that a physical pattern is part of a field of symbols or signals that exists in spacetime. Therefore, spacetime with matter-energy is a symbolic space that should not be confused with semantic space.

Unlike machine learning, which detects the statistical correlations of symbols existing in a symbolic space, leading to new unconscious symbols, new comprehensions are about discovering new "connections" between the meanings that already exist in semantic space. This process forms new structures of conscious meanings that require new and more complex symbols to be communicated. This kind of conscious recognition goes far beyond the capabilities of machines, which are limited to recognizing symbolic patterns that do not require comprehension. In fact, automatic learning[4] based on artificial neural networks is totally unconscious. Machines can learn, but they do not consciously *perceive* and *comprehend* the symbols they deal with. They work in the dark because they are unconscious.

Pattern Recognition versus Comprehension

Learning is the process of acquiring the skills and behaviors necessary to achieve and improve adaptation to the environment. It can be automatic or conscious. An example of machine learning is when we teach a computer to recognize a cup from its visual image. To learn that task it is necessary to have a representative sample of cup images, called the training set, and a program performing the simulation of a properly structured

---

4 Automatic learning consists in finding a stable set of correlations in the "training set." When this task has been accomplished, the machine will be able to mechanically and unconsciously recognize the same correlation pattern in exemplars never before seen. We then say that the network is able to *generalize*.

artificial neural network that automatically finds a hierarchy of common traits (statistical correlations) that are present in all the cups that are part of the training set. When the program has learned the correlations existing in the many images whose name is "cup," it may also recognize a cup in an image that was not part of the training set. At this point it seems that the neural network "understands" what a cup is, even though the "cup" is only another symbol, not the conscious experience that it is for us.

This ability to generalize is good and necessary, yet the program still cannot comprehend what "cup" means. In fact, an expert might create many synthetic images that the computer would mistakenly label as cups when we would immediately comprehend they are not cups.

As I hypothesized in the previous section, the ability to automatically form and recognize basic patterns must exist in an infant before it can develop the conscious perception and discrimination that can contribute to comprehension. For example, an infant may be able to consciously recognize an object as a visual "quale" soon after having automatically learned the correlations necessary to distinguish "figures" from "ground." At this point the infant may also try to grab the object without necessarily knowing its name and function. When it hears the mother say "cup" while she is holding one in her hand, it consciously learns to associate the "cup" sound with the visual and tactile qualities of the object it has already learned. These elementary forms of comprehension require a much greater capacity for generalization than is possible with machine learning.

Now suppose the baby sees the mother pour milk into the cup. In this case it could spontaneously comprehend that the function of the cup is to contain milk or other liquids. This is a further comprehension, which requires greater insight or intuition than the previous examples. With the new comprehension, the child adds another unexpected meaning to associate with the quale-object. From that point on, when it sees a cup, it will also recognize all the meanings associated with it. It is precisely here that the mystery of comprehension lies, since the intuitive leaps provided by consciousness go far beyond what can be achieved with automatic learning.

Whereas artificial neural networks require many examples before being able to generalize, we can learn to recognize and comprehend consciously with just one or a few examples, because the intuitive (non-algorithmic) aspects of consciousness are always operational within us. Our conscious comprehension effortlessly guides us with such naturalness and ease that so far we have underestimated its profound power.

Comprehension is like an invention, allowing us to understand something new and unexpected, thus creating new "common sense" connections within a complex and dynamic semantic structure.

Comprehension also requires the ability to discriminate, i.e., to discover subtle differences between experiences that previously seemed identical. Discrimination allows us to create two related meanings starting from one. For example, a child can learn that there are two different types of cups, those with handles and those without, whereas before she hadn't noticed since her mother called them both by the same name. After this conscious distinction, she could then justify having two different symbols (names) for cups with and without handles.

Comprehension is a process that begins with perception, is followed by logical reasoning, and is motivated by the desire to know. This process continues with ever more subtle generalizations and differentiations. It is the result of our intuitive ability to know, which is non-algorithmic, and goes far beyond what logic and algorithms can do.

In a machine, such as, for example, in a logic circuit of a computer, the correct detection of binary signals at its input mechanically produces the desired effect at its output (as long as the circuit works). In this case, the detection and recognition of the input signals and their transformation into the output signal are "hardwired" into the permanent structure of that circuit and are taken for granted by the engineer who created that deterministic (typically many-to-one) relationship between inputs and output.

In a human being, the detection and low-level recognition of signals is unconscious, while pattern recognition and action can be both: unconscious in symbolic spacetime and conscious in semantic space. The recognition of most patterns and almost all the actions we perform are automatic, even though they may be part of a conscious experience in which free will does not intervene to modify these automatic patterns. In a computer system, however, pattern recognition and actions are always unconscious and automatic. For example, when we feel an itch and scratch without noticing, the itch-pattern is recognized mechanically and is immediately followed by an automatic response (action) previously learned. In this case, the conscious perception of what we have done may take place after the action.

If the situation had instead required conscious intervention, the conscious perception of the pattern would have emerged before the automatic decision with a sense that a different action involving free will might be required. The subconscious, in this context, is a state of consciousness in which we are barely paying attention to what happens in certain portions of our semantic space because we are focusing on something else. The crucial point here is that consciousness may behave like an attentive supervisor who keeps an eye on everything that is happening but intervenes only when it realizes that the automatic processes could be inadequate to handle the situation.

The lack of understanding of the nature of consciousness leads to confusing the semantic space with the symbolic space, thus underestimating the crucial role played by our free will and consciousness. Consequently, we have been mistakenly equated with classical machines despite the unbridgeable difference existing between us and them. This difference lies precisely in being able to properly and creatively act with free will based on our conscious comprehension of a new situation.

In summary, automatic pattern recognition is connected with classical information in spacetime that must exist prior to our conscious perception in semantic space. Our conscious comprehension can then change our response to difficult situations beyond the capabilities of automatic recognition. Comprehension creates new semantic connections between qualia in semantic space with the formation of new meanings that are added to the existing ones. Each new comprehension creates a new superposition of meanings that are perceived as a well-defined unit in semantic space. Free-will actions are conscious choices, rather than automatic behaviors, often overriding learned responses.

Is Intelligence without Consciousness True Intelligence?

It takes something more than intelligence to act intelligently.
—Fyodor Dostoevsky, *Crime and Punishment*

Many researchers believe that consciousness is not necessary to achieve intelligent behavior. For them, a machine can be as intelligent or even more intelligent than any human being, with or without consciousness.

This view is based on an inadequate definition of both intelligence and reality. True intelligence, in fact, does not consist only in the ability to calculate and process data, which in many cases machines may do far better than us, but is much more. True intelligence is not algorithmic. It is the ability to *comprehend*, i.e., to go beyond the immediate meaning of the symbols by including the broader context in which the symbols are found, thus realizing unsuspected connections between different fields of knowledge. After all, we are the ones who have invented computers and algorithms capable of executing tasks billions of times faster than our brains could.

Our intelligence goes far beyond the limitations of the nervous system because it originates in a reality vaster than the physical reality we know, as I will explain later.

True intelligence is intuition, imagination, creativity, ingenuity, and inventiveness. It is foresight, vision, and wisdom. It is empathy, compassion, ethics, and love. It is the integration of the intuitive mind, the empathic heart, and courageous action. In other words, true intelligence is not separable from the other properties that make us human and that require consciousness and free will. It is the ability to comprehend and make unexpected, creative, and ethical decisions. Machines will never be able to do these things because, if they were as free as we are, they would be more dangerous than useful. They do work within limits, but they don't understand. Our comprehension is not reducible to an algorithm; it is in fact what can transform a portion of the non-algorithmic meaning into new symbols, i.e., into algorithms.

On the other hand, when a human being's consciousness is fully identified with the body and with the logical mind, his creative potential may remain largely untapped and his behavior may become as mechanical as that of a computer. For example, when a person performs a religious ritual mechanically, without any comprehension, the outward behavior may be the same, but the difference between the two is impassable.

An example of true intelligence is given by creative people with original and constructive ideas who are capable of transforming them into new symbolic forms to be communicated to others. Once a new idea has been translated into appropriate symbols, other people can understand it through the use of intuition. Intuition is another conscious human faculty allowing us to easily grasp new concepts. Computers, on the other hand, can only "learn" new mechanical correlations, lacking the "common sense" that comes from conscious comprehension.

In our experience, perception, comprehension, and meaning are so intertwined in our holistic experience that we normally cannot fully discriminate their roles. Therefore, when we comprehend something new for the first time, we often experience a flash of joyful insight that leads us to cry out, "Ah! Now I get it!" as the new meaning suddenly appears to us with clarity, superimposed on the same experience as before but with "new connections" between qualia that radically transform the whole experience.

Comprehension is therefore the process that adds new meaning to our experience and skillfully integrates it with the previous meaning. When this happens, we distinctly feel we have a much greater degree of mastery than before. The new meaning must then be translated into a new symbolic form with either a new combination of words or with a new physical organization of matter, by creating a new diagram or a new physical model, for example, that makes the new meaning clearer than what could be achieved with a verbal description.

This translation from meaning to symbols, however, is neither automatic nor immediate, and generally requires the intervention of another human faculty: conscious reasoning, which is a logical-symbolic process rooted in comprehension. After a new comprehension has occurred, we can later automatically recognize a similar meaning without the explicit intervention of consciousness. Once the meaning—for example, an invention—has been expressed symbolically in something that works, it can be intuitively understood even by people who would not have been able to arrive at the same invention on their own. Thus, the new symbols function as "mental enzymes" that lower the barrier to comprehension that exists in others.

When a computer learns using "unsupervised" learning, and the programmer insists that the computer "did it all by itself," that is a great exaggeration, because the architecture of the program that "learns by itself" was conceived by humans. If a computer or a robot were left to operate completely on their own, the results would be very different and probably catastrophic.

We must be especially mindful about the dangers posed by the human abuse of computer technology, especially AI, which "will bring to the fore new dangers that are difficult to predict and avoid," according to the Nobel physicist Roger Penrose. There is no doubt that the greatest danger is represented by the desire for power, domination, possession, and superiority that dulls human consciousness.

Unfortunately, the words contained in the final speech of the film *The Great Dictator* by Charlie Chaplin, in which he states that in this world there is room for everyone and that life can be happy and magnificent, are still unheeded today. Chaplin denounces human greed as the cause of the hate that has made us hard, cruel, and has stopped the machine of abundance. "We think too much and feel too little," he says, and "without humanity, goodness, and kindness, life is violence."

PART TWO

If you remove consciousness, everything else is nothing for man.

—Cicero, *De natura deorum*, 3.35

8

A New Vision

Consider your seed:
you were not made to live like brutes,
but to follow virtue and knowledge.

—Dante Alighieri, *Divine Comedy*, *Hell*, Canto XXVI, verses
118–120

Physics is mainly concerned with understanding how the inanimate world works and provides the premises for all other scientific disciplines. In the first part of this book I outlined the worldview based on the typical interpretation of contemporary physicists, and I highlighted a number of unsolved problems primarily related to the nature of life, consciousness, and free will. These are subjects theoretical physicists traditionally consider more philosophical than scientific and have not yet faced with the logical-mathematical rigor that distinguishes them.

Such neglect has led to the conviction that the materialistic and informational view of reality describes all of reality, even though it excludes its most precious and unknown aspects. In particular, this view denies—or at best doubts—the existence of free will, and considers consciousness as a mere epiphenomenon. I also highlighted how the advent of AI has increased the danger of confusing reality with a theory of reality that eliminates consciousness, the only phenomenon that makes a crucial difference between reality and the imitation of it.

The second part of the book deals with the materialistic vision that justifies selfishness, unbridled competition, and the idea that the universe is devoid of meaning and purpose, and it explains how quantum physics does not support this dystopian view at all. I will show that the existence of interiority can be explained without invalidating the experimental evidence of physics, since materialism is caused by an erroneous interpretation of reality based on classical physics. Such a view has already been falsified by quantum physics.

This new interpretation shows that the difficulty in understanding the message of quantum physics is mainly due to quantum physics largely describing the characteristics of the inner rather than those of the outer world. With this new perspective we can easily understand how physical reality emerges from interactions between an inner semantic and an outer symbolic reality that represent two irreducible aspects of the universe.

Existential Questions

I remember the starry skies of the past, when light pollution had not yet veiled and darkened them. In those days when night fell you could clearly see the Big Dipper with Alcor, Mizar's weaker twin barely visible to the naked eye, and the Little Dipper. And, when the sky was particularly clear, also the entire Milky Way.

As a child, that vastness always filled me with a sense of mystery, and I felt pervaded by a strong emotion, a wonder that permeated my soul, though I could not verbalize it. Then, as I grew up, I began to ask myself the same existential questions that humans have always asked, trying to find answers through religion, philosophy, art or science.

The Unsolved Problems

We can thus summarize the fundamental problems that are still unanswered as follows:

1. The problem of creation: Why does something exist instead of nothing? Where does the universe come from? Has it always existed? What is its purpose?
2. The problem of order: Why is there order instead of chaos in the universe? How has the universe evolved and why?

3. The problem of life: How did life emerge and why did it evolve?
4. The problem of consciousness: How did consciousness appear in living beings, and what is its purpose?
5. The problem of free will: Does free will exist in conscious organisms? If so, how does it fit with physical laws, and what is its purpose?

To solve these questions, science starts with the assumption that there is a *unified Field* that has all the properties necessary to transform itself into matter-energy and spacetime as a result of fundamental and immutable laws that describe the interactions between the aspects emerging from the Field. The Field is ontological because it represents the dynamical extra physical "substance" of which everything that exists and will ever exist is made. It must therefore contain all the potentials that will produce the properties of the universe that will emerge in the course of its evolution.

Most physicists would argue that consciousness and free will do not need to be explained as fundamental phenomena since they are epiphenomena; therefore these are "soft" problems to which neuroscientists should find an explanation. Without entering into territorial disputes, I insist that if these are epiphenomena, they should then be clearly explained through some mechanism, rather than arm-waving them away by asserting that at some point these qualities emerge from the brain. There is too much evidence for their existence and, moreover, understanding the nature of consciousness and free will makes all the difference in deciding whether we are machines or not. I will henceforth assume their existence.

In this evolutionary process we observe four nested levels, each governed by physical laws: The first level is the emergence of the inanimate world. The second level is inside the first and is made up of all living organisms. The third level is inside the second and contains all conscious entities. Free will is inside the third and constitutes the fourth level. In other words, living organisms must emerge from inanimate matter, conscious organisms emerge from unconscious organisms, and free will emerges from conscious organisms. And a similar structure also applies to the laws that govern each level.

I think the only problem of the five that can never be solved is the problem of creation. The beginning of the universe, assuming there was a beginning, is something that is beyond the reach of our minds, and yet we need to start with reasonable postulates to explain the other problems as logical consequences of the only miracle of creation that must be accepted. As the British philosopher and mathematician Alfred North Whitehead states: "It is impossible to reflect on time and the mystery of the creation of the world without an overwhelming awareness of the limits of human intelligence." On this topic, Carlos Chagas Filho, Brazilian medical doctor, biologist, and scientist, states:

I think science is starting to stumble when it comes to what we call the first cause. The scientist who is sincere and who wants to go to the bottom of his rationality knows that there is a moment in which he cannot go further. This is the moment of intertwining between science, philosophy, and therefore theology.

As for the second problem, that of order, physicists believe it can be solved by assuming that the inanimate universe evolved according to immutable laws that describe what happened. Therefore the laws are a second miracle that is even more problematic than the first because the nature of laws is completely external to what they regulate. In reality such laws "command," because nothing can happen that is not "described" or "predicted" by them. And mathematics, despite being a product of human thought, becomes in fact the one that commands and dictates the laws. But why do these laws exist and not others? How did they emerge? And, above all, why are they immutable?

Albert Einstein asked himself: "How is it possible that mathematics, being fundamentally a product of human thought independent of experience, explains real things so admirably?" And Eugene Wigner observed that: "The unreasonable effectiveness of mathematics in the natural sciences is something bordering on the mysterious for which there is no rational explanation."

Physics still cannot answer these questions. I also note that, to date, quantum field theory and general relativity have yet to be unified into a single Field and one universal Law from which the fields and laws we know are derived. And, in any case, the existence and properties of the Field and the Law are postulates, that is, plausible hypotheses, valid only if their predictions are not experimentally falsified. Therefore, neither the problem of creation nor that of order has been solved by contemporary physics.

As for the problem of life, it actually consists of two mysteries: How did inanimate matter self-organize to form the first living cell out of which the entire ecosystem emerged? And, how did cells manage to self-organize into a variety of multicellular organisms of unbelievable complexity? I point out that, in both cases, life went in strong countertendency to the disorder that is evident in the inanimate world, as consecrated by the Second Law of Thermodynamics. This famous law states that the entropy of an isolated system cannot decrease; it remains the same if the transformations are reversible and increases if the transformations are irreversible. Since entropy is interpreted as the degree of disorder, we can conclude that an isolated system out of thermal equilibrium evolves by increasing its disorder until it reaches thermal equilibrium, after which the entropy of the system does not change. Life clearly does not behave this way.

As for the *origin* of the first cell (called LUCA for Last Universal Common Ancestor), no scientist has ever been able to explain how it was created by natural processes. In fact, affirming that LUCA *self-organized* based on the action of physical laws on inert matter is saying that life spontaneously emerged from non-life. The proponents of the self-assembly of LUCA have only shown that natural phenomena can produce simple organic molecules. These molecules are of an infinitesimal complexity compared to that found inside the simplest bacteria. It is not far-fetched to say that the self-assembly of LUCA as a self-reproducing system required a third miracle!

The *evolution* of life from LUCA to *Homo sapiens* was instead partially resolved by neo-Darwinism, even though many gaps remain and not everyone agrees on the details of this theory. Neo-Darwinism asserts that the principle of "survival of the fittest," based on the random variation and natural selection of genomic traits, called genes, can explain the entire evolution of the ecosystem, starting from the existence of LUCA. In other words, the fittest members of the species survive and can pass on their beneficial genes to their offspring. This "blind" process is supposed to explain both the natural evolution of the members of any species as well as the emergence of new species.

While I believe that neo-Darwinism is at least plausible when used to explain the evolution of species *after* LUCA's emergence, I find it hard to believe that consciousness and free will could emerge from organisms that are devoid of them. In fact, between unconsciousness and consciousness there is a qualitative leap so gigantic that it cannot be bridged by the gradualism of neo-Darwinism, especially in a world that is fundamentally quantum.

For example, the electrical charge of an electron is a *granular* property that has the same value for all electrons. An electron with an arbitrarily small electrical charge does not exist. Protons have exactly the same quantum of charge as electrons but with a positive rather than a negative sign. The electrical charge of any macroscopic body is therefore an *integer* multiple of that minimum "quantum of charge." Hence, for consciousness to emerge from inanimate matter, a minimum "quantum of consciousness" should also exist in at least one of the elementary particles of which the atoms are made. Unless we accept this panpsychist hypothesis or some other explanation, the leap from unconsciousness to consciousness requires a fourth miracle. As Isaac Bashevis Singer observes: "Materialist thinkers have attributed more miracles, improbable coincidences, and wonders to the blind mechanism of evolution than any theologians in the world have ever been able to attribute to God."

As for free will, it seems to counter the existence of immutable laws—the starting point of any physical theory—so much so that most physicists believe it does not exist. And this makes the fifth problem particularly thorny. Moreover, if free will were not necessary for the evolution of life and consciousness, why should it then exist in human beings? All this clashes with the strong sense we feel that we possess free will, even though it is heavily constrained by physical laws.

The Need for a New Paradigm

A very large vision is necessary, and the man who experiences it must follow it as the eagle seeks the deepest blue of the sky.
—Crazy Horse, Sioux chief

We have said that physics solves the problem of creation by postulating the existence of a Field with all the properties necessary to transform itself into matter-energy and spacetime as a result of a fundamental Law, also postulated, which describes the interactions between the emergent "parts" of the Field. In this manner, the problem of order is solved through a Law, which is the second miracle.

According to quantum physics, the Field is ontological, and the immutable Law describes the dynamism inherent in the interacting parts. Thus, the Law regulates the four nested levels described earlier, i.e., inanimate matter, living organisms, conscious organisms, and conscious organisms with free will, by specializing into a number of derivative laws valid under increasingly restrictive conditions. Despite all the recent scientific advances, however, we have not been able to eliminate the need for the four miracles described above. Moreover, physics is still not unified.

I think that to be able to unify physics, we must abandon the current approach and open ourselves to a new vision. New concepts are needed which can only spring from a fundamentally different conception of Field and Law than the materialist presumptions. I believe that if we started with consciousness and free will as properties of the Field, one could postulate only the miracle of creation, eliminating the other four that could then be logically explained starting from that single postulate.

In fact, from the logical point of view, how could free will, consciousness, and life be nested subsets of *inanimate* matter? It seems obvious to me that freedom cannot emerge as a special case of non-freedom, consciousness cannot emerge from non-consciousness, and, likewise, life cannot emerge from non-life. It is illogical to think that a more general property could emerge from a property that does not contain it. For example, how could free will emerge from determinism? If, on the other hand, the more general behavior were free, one could explain mechanical behavior as a special case of free behavior.

In trying to explain life and consciousness as classical phenomena, we hit a dead end. We need to back off and seriously consider that the classical physical reality may emerge from a deeper and hitherto unsuspected *reality*. Otherwise we will never get out of this impasse. If we really want to understand how the universe works, we have to stop using the term "illusory properties" for what distinguishes us from inanimate matter. This is a "crime against humanity," which must be recognized, faced, and solved, because it leads to the elimination of human values, not because we have proved their absence, but because we have dogmatically decided that it must be so.

In an interview on 16 March 2011 that appeared in *New Scientist* entitled 'The Mathematics of Being Nice,' Martin Nowak, Austrian professor of mathematical biology, observes that:

When we look at the mathematical models of the evolution of cooperation, we find that winning strategies must be generosity, hope, and forgiveness. Now, for the first time, we can see these ideas in mathematical terms. Who would have thought that it could be mathematically shown that, in a world where everyone thinks of themselves, the winning strategy is to be lenient, and that those who cannot forgive will never win?

And Italian theoretical physicist Emilio Del Giudice, in the conference 'Quantum Physics: The Concept of Resonance' (11 June 2012), states that:

Modern quantum physics provides an objective model to understand what humanity had clearly seen from the very beginning and that modern "civilization" founded on competition, on the will to be superior to all others, and on the incessant effort to see their "merit" recognized, tried to suppress. Life is founded on coherence, on the resonance of the different, and on the desire of each one to resonate with as many others as possible.

Not admitting the fundamental existence of consciousness and free will is a psychological problem, not a logical one, especially given that to explain the properties of atoms and molecules

Irreducible

requires quantum physics. In other words, the atoms we know can only exist if they are describable by probabilistic laws and by quantum states *that are not knowable*! These are the "pure states" of quantum physics,[1] states that cannot be cloned, i.e., cannot be copied and therefore known "from the outside," because any attempt to know them by making a measurement changes them. This property does not exist in the classical world that informs our worldview, even though classical physics emerges as a special case of quantum physics.

The QIP Theory: Consciousness Is a Quantum Phenomenon

As I have already described in *Silicon* [1] and in the Introduction to this book, my "awakening experience" irreversibly changed my perspective and redirected the course of my scientific research toward the study of consciousness. However, finding collaborators interested in this new field was not easy. My many and various extraordinary experiences of consciousness indicated that reality must have both a semantic and a symbolic aspect, i.e., information could not be separated from its meaning as Shannon had conceived. Meaning and symbols had to be aspects of a more fundamental reality somehow.

I also felt that the solution to the "hard problem of consciousness" was hiding within quantum physics. Therefore, I began to look into quantum information and into proposed theories in which physical reality could derive from such information. This is how I came across the Operational

---

1   A pure state is a definite state that corresponds to a unit vector in a complex N-dimensional Hilbert space. A pure state can also be obtained from the quantum superposition (with coefficients that are complex numbers) of two or more pure states and/or from the entanglement of pure states. A mixed state is a state that can be written as a mixture of two or more states, in which each state is multiplied by the probability of its preparation.

Probabilistic Theory (OPT) that G.M. D'Ariano and his collaborators had developed in the last 20 years [7]. OPT showed that quantum physics can logically derive from quantum information. That was precisely the jigsaw piece I had been looking for!

However, quantum information is completely abstract, i.e., devoid of any meaning. If consciousness is fundamental, information without meaning makes no sense at all. And this essential aspect was missing from D'Ariano's theory. In my model, *conscious experience* had to be another irreducible aspect of quantum information. After we discussed this point together for a few years, D'Ariano finally realized that qualia could be interpreted as "the experience of a quantum system that is in a pure quantum state." We finally had found the *precise* connection between my intuitive model, based on actual experiences of consciousness, and quantum information, of which D'Ariano is a world expert.

This theory is called Quantum Information-based Panpsychism (QIP) and has been recently published [10]. A pure quantum state is a well-defined state that is not clonable and therefore has all the extraordinary properties of a conscious experience, which is also *definite* and *private*. Thus, a pure state is only knowable "from the inside" by the system that is in that state, exactly like it is in our experience. In other terms, the phenomenology of a conscious experience is exactly that of a pure quantum state, making such states the ideal mathematical *representation* of qualia.

On the other hand, when a quantum system interacts with a measurement system, we can only observe an event that can be described by classical information, i.e., information that can be shared with other observers "from the outside."

We will see later that to properly describe consciousness and free will with adequate mathematical concepts will require the extraordinary and disconcerting properties of quantum entanglement. Quantum entanglement (see Glossary) has brought to light the existence of a phenomenon at the limit of human logic, without, however, producing contradictions. It took 80 years of theoretical and experimental efforts to understand entanglement, though it still remains suspended in an uneasy conceptual fog that no one has yet been able to completely dissipate.

Classical systems like computers use statistical properties of collections of atoms and molecules that in first approximation behave deterministically.[2] Therefore they cannot have free will or be conscious. In fact, if classical information were suitable to describe a conscious experience, the experience would lack the crucial property of being private since it could be copied into the memory of many computers. Physical reality is both classical and quantum, a necessary coexistence to produce the extraordinary chemical properties of matter.

It is important to realize that saying that a conscious experience can be represented by a pure state does not describe the experience itself. If it did, a pure state would be reproducible. Non-clonability expresses the existence of something private, inviolate, that can only be known by the system itself and by no one else. In other words, though I can *represent* the love I feel for my son with a pure quantum state—a quantum symbol— the meaning of that symbol can only be known by me, for the mathematical symbol cannot describe what I feel.

The fact that a pure state cannot be reproduced makes it homomorphic to the qualia I feel, for I too cannot fully describe my love without violating the no-cloning theorem. I can only partially express my love with words, or with other classical

---

2   The determinism of a computer is valid in first approximation, that is, as long as its circuits can faithfully recognize the two states of a bit. If the temperature were too high, for example, this recognition would fail and the computer would stop working.

symbols, but that partial description cannot be confused with the love I feel within myself. Moreover, for the symbols to be understood, the receiver must *comprehend* my words. It should not be surprising then that comprehension requires a transformation from live to quantum information within a conscious entity.

Therefore, a pure quantum state is the mathematical entity most suitable to represent an experience because it has the extraordinary property of being *irreproducible*, yet knowable by the system "feeling it." Thus, quantum physics, which supervenes on quantum information, indicates that the ultimate ontology resides in the private experience representable by quantum information. This is as far as mathematics can go to describe reality. True knowing is non-algorithmic, and only partially shareable with classical symbols, i.e. with algorithms. Said differently, conscious experience is non-algorithmic because it cannot be known through algorithms but only by "experiencing" what is known.

Written and spoken words provide a good analogy (though still inadequate) to better understand the differences between classical and quantum symbols. Spoken symbols are dynamic and can be described with sound waves.[3] Written symbols are static and can be used to store dynamic symbols in a book or in computer memory. However, written symbols contain much less information than spoken ones, because they lack aspects, such as prosody and facial grimaces, capable of better expressing one's feelings. Nevertheless, a conscious experience is infinitely richer than what a spoken sentence can express, and that in turn is much richer than what can be conveyed with written symbols.

3　I think it is no coincidence that quantum states are represented by mathematical waves in a non-physical, complex, and multidimensional space (Hilbert space). Mathematical waves have homomorphic properties to those of inner experiences that are based on qualia.

A New Term: Seity

We have asserted that semantic reality can be represented with quantum symbols (pure states) that are more homomorphic to the experience than classical symbols. Pure quantum states cannot be duplicated, unlike spoken words, which, though undulatory, can be copied by a digital tape recorder. Any attempt to copy a pure state would change it and reduce it to classical information. In that case, the best that could be done is to convert each qubit of the pure state into a classical bit. This is in fact what Holevo's theorem has shown, i.e., that the maximum obtainable information from a quantum state is one classical bit for each qubit of the state. Thus, an experience whose abstract representation requires N qubits (each qubit represents an infinity of states) will at most convey N bits of classical information when it is converted into shareable information.

This is why an appropriate theory of consciousness must use quantum information to represent conscious experiences. But a theory of experience should not be confused with the experience itself, just like the photograph of a person should not be confused with the actual person it represents.[4] Claiming that a pure quantum state is *experienced*, and thus known by the system that supports it, gives us a strong reason to also claim that quantum states refer to something that actually exists, rather than simply being an abstract mathematical description that helps us calculate the events we can measure.

If a computer repeats like a tape recorder the same words I use to describe the love I feel, it would have my same outer

---

4   There is a painting by Magritte with a very realistic image of a pipe under which the author wrote: "This is not a pipe." So, if it's not a pipe, what is it? The answer was given by Magritte himself: "It is only a representation. If I had written under my painting: 'This is a pipe' I would have lied." Once explained, it seems obvious.

behavior, but without any inner experience which is the miracle of life. Herein lies the fundamental difference between a classical computer and a conscious quantum entity. The conscious entity can be represented as a quantum system, but it cannot physically exist in spacetime. Only the ontological quantum entity can know its state "from within," but it can only translate a portion of its knowing into live information to communicate it to a living organism, which in turn transforms it into classical information. I stress again that a living organism is a quantum-classical system, not a classical system like a computer.

It is quite possible that spacetime does not exist as we imagine it, but instead corresponds to how our embodied consciousness perceives the vaster reality in which it exists when such reality is perceived through the reductive sensory-brain system of the body. In this interpretation, spacetime would be a projection of the experience of the conscious entity of the live symbols produced by the body into a subspace of Hilbert's space.

A conscious being is therefore represented by a quantum system that is in a pure state. If such an entity can transform its own state by maintaining its purity and can create a classical memory of its experience, we have defined a special quantum system which I call *seity*.[5]

"Seity" is a rarely used English word which means selfhood, personal identity. In the context of QIP, a seity is defined as a self-conscious entity that can act with free will. A seity is endowed with a unique and permanent *identity* because she knows that the conscious experience she is having is her own, and thus she can direct her experience. Being self-conscious is much more than being conscious without identity. Quantum entities that are conscious but not self-conscious I call *thoughtforms*.

---

5 "Finding a name for something is a way of evoking its existence, or allowing people to see a pattern where they previously saw nothing" (Howard Rheingold).

Thoughtforms do not know that their experience is their own, and thus could not direct their own actions and experience with free will.

A seity is a field in a pure state existing in a vaster reality than the physical world that contains the body. A seity exists even without a physical body, and this is a crucial statement, because it means that our existence does not depend on the body's existence. The body simply allows the seity to perceive and operate in the physical world which is only a small portion of the vaster reality in which she exists.

A similar situation could be that of a miner robot that transmits all the visual and auditory information of the mine to a faraway human being who controls its overall operation. The robot is described by classical physics, the human body is described by both quantum and classical physics, and the experience of the mine based on the data sent by the robot exists only in the consciousness of the seity that controls the human body. The experience of the seity can only be *represented* by quantum information but not described by it, since quantum information is not reproducible. Only the seity having the experience can give a partial account of its own experience using classical (shareable) information.

While the body is representable with the matter-energy that exists in spacetime (3+1 dimensions), the seity transcends this type of matter. The physical world as currently understood represents a 3+1 dimensional projection of a quantum reality that has many more dimensions than spacetime. The reality described by classical physics, compared with quantum reality, is a bit like a film with 2+1 dimensions which is a projection of a reality with 3+1 dimensions.

A seity cannot exist in the spacetime where our body exists. However, she can communicate with a body using live information, just like our body can communicate using classical information with a robot or with an avatar in a virtual reality.

The Seity Is Quantum

In principle, a seity could be *described* with a set of quantum equations, which, however, could not represent her inner experience made up of qualia, and only knowable from within by her and her alone. Therefore, a mathematical theory of reality can never fully describe the ultimate reality of conscious experiences. Moreover, free will implies *creative choices from within* that cannot be determined by any algorithm or mathematics, but only represented *a posteriori*. Experience is not a mathematical formula, and even less, a simulation of a mathematical formula. It can only be known by "living it" on a first-person basis!

In the quantum reality—vaster than classical reality—each seity has a different point of view and chooses with free will which classical symbols to observe and which inner meaning to convert into classical symbols to be communicated. Thus, each subjective experience is different. This applies also to the objective description of classical reality, because each observer has its own frame of reference, and, if the frame changes, the description also changes. Special and general relativity have clearly demonstrated this fact. There is no privileged point of view that can describe all of reality "from the outside" in an objective way, because each observer is also part of what is observed and can only have one point of view.

Recall that according to special relativity, two observers, Alice and Bob, who move with uniform relative velocity comparable to the speed of light, have contradictory experiences because in their individual reference frames everything works like before, but Bob discovers that time passes more slowly in Alice's world than in his own. In turn, Alice discovers that time passes more slowly in Bob's world than in her own. Who is right? Welcome to the world of relativity!

In the context of QIP we say that a system in a pure state is in an *ontic state*, which can only be known in the form of qualia "from within." The state of an external observer of the system is instead in an *epistemic state*, because "from the outside" the observer could only *deduce* the probabilities of all the states that might manifest. The epistemic state is described in quantum physics as a *mixed state*, unlike the pure state which is a definite state. However, the actual state that will manifest is not predictable by the outer observer, for he can only know the probabilities of all the possible states that might manifest. In reality only one of those states will show up, but quantum theory cannot tell us which one. This type of *indeterminism* is different from Heisenberg's indeterminism and clearly spells out the epistemic nature of quantum physics compared to the *presumed*[6] ontic nature of classical physics that can tell us exactly the next state that we will measure.

The measurement made by an observer in a epistemic state could only yield a small portion of the ontic state of the seity. As an analogy, imagine that the experience of the seity is the color turquoise. This color can be represented by mixing precise amounts of the colors red, blue, and green. An observer of the entity could only know the probabilities of measuring one of the three states that correspond to the red, blue, and green colors. To know the percentages of the three colors, one would have to make multiple measurements of the same entity, but when a measurement is made, the state of the entity will be disturbed in an unpredictable way; therefore, a moment later, the entity will be found in a new state. This behavior is what ensures the privacy of the experience.

Quantum physics therefore primarily describes the semantic, subjective, and private properties of reality out of which the

---

6   If ontology belongs to the experience of a quantum system in an ontic state, classical physics cannot describe reality but only an *apparent* reality as deterministic as a computer program. This is why I used the expression "*presumed* ontic nature" in the text above.

symbolic, objective, and public aspects of reality emerge! This is strange only because we thought quantum physics described the outer world. I think that when we fully realize this fundamental fact, quantum physics will cease to be incomprehensible!

The Existence of Free Will

Life is like a card game: the hand you are dealt represents determinism; the way you play is free will.
—Sri Jawaharlal Nehru

I think that to answer the questions posed at the beginning of this chapter, we must start from a new postulate, i.e., from the hypothesis that the holistic Whole contains not only the seeds of the inanimate universe but also those of free will, consciousness, and life. This is the first miracle we must accept and, in this framework, it is also the only one.

I call this Whole, *One*, to distinguish it from the unified field of physics, because from One emerge the conscious fields with free will, the elementary seities that I call consciousness units (CUs), rather than the inanimate fields of the elementary particles of physics that interact in accordance with preestablished laws. In this new conception, the CUs communicate with each other, and from their interactions emerge both the laws of physics and new fields (higher-order seities) that are quantum combinations of CUs like atoms are combinations of elementary particles. In the remainder of the book I will use the word "seity" to indicate either a CU or a combination of CUs, and reserve the word CU to indicate an elementary seity.

Starting with seities constitutes a monumental difference from the standard description of contemporary physics in which the emergence of consciousness and free will has been placed many billions of years after the Big Bang rather than at the beginning of the universe. In this manner, from cocreators of the physical universe and life, we have been relegated to the meaningless effects of some algorithm, soon to be forgotten with the death of our bodies.

I believe instead that we are seities who temporarily "inhabit" our bodies. We are eternal, conscious beings rather than perishable bodies. And we are here to learn crucial aspects of ourselves by interacting with each other in the physical universe that we have cocreated for this very purpose.

Everything we perceive in the universe was initially envisioned in the consciousness of the seities because classical reality follows quantum reality, not vice versa. And quantum physics follows quantum information, which in turn represents the thoughts, desires, and concious experiences of the seities.

This new starting point can also solve the problem of order (the second miracle of physics), because the laws of physics must emerge from the core properties of One, which include consciousness, free will, and the creation of the CUs. Thus, we can eliminate all other miracles from physics.

The existence of free will requires that physical laws emerge from the *agreements between the seities* that communicate with each other. In this new interpretation, the physical laws can be conceived as the syntactical laws of the languages that the seities have spontaneously developed in their communications. The analogy with human languages is surprising! Our languages have gradually evolved the symbols, the symbols of symbols, and their rules, starting from elementary vibrations, i.e., the phonemes that are analogous to the elementary particles. The communicating seities, therefore, "obey" the syntactical laws not because they are forced to do so, but because they *want to communicate*, and to communicate they must follow the rules of the common languages they have jointly created.

Such laws become a constraint on free will, but their presence does not contradict the existence of free will, for without free will it would have been impossible to make the agreements that gave birth to those laws. According to this conceptual framework, the laws emerge spontaneously, like when, as children, we invented games and then had to submit to the rules we had freely established. The need to obey the rules does not contradict the presence of free will, since the rules were designed to leave room for the creative free-will decisions of the participants.

Note also that the existence of free will requires the extraordinary property of quantum entanglement which makes it possible to have a becoming universe whose future is not determined *a priori* by laws, but by the free will and creativity of the interacting seities. Within QIP, the free will of each seity can cause quantum-to-classical and classical-to-quantum transformations that maintain the purity of their state. Viewed by an external observer, these are irreversible probabilistic transformations unspecified by the theory. These have been called the *collapse of the wave function*.

Entanglement produces instantaneous nonlocal correlations between two distant entangled systems such that no signal traveling at the speed of light could cause them. These acausal correlations demonstrate that, before a measurement, we cannot attribute preexisting objective values to the systems' variables. It is as if the two systems were connected "from within." And this happens regardless of their distance. There is no "local realistic" explanation for entanglement.

Therefore, the nature of the probability used in quantum physics is very different from the one used in classical physics. Classical probability represents the lack of knowledge of a classical state that already exists because it has probability 1 of occurring. Quantum probability describes instead the probability of a state that does not yet exist prior to the measurement because it is due to the free-will choice of a seity.

This is the deep reason why no algorithm can determine which state will manifest, and also why quantum *randomness* cannot be algorithmic.

Not even One can know the state that will show up, unless it has probability 1 of manifesting. Only the syntactical laws agreed by the seities can predict which events will happen with certainty.

Since entangled quantum systems exhibit nonlocal correlations, quantum entanglement provides the conclusive proof that classical states cannot exist prior to the quantum transformations that will manifest them. *This is exactly the necessary condition for the existence of free will!* Therefore, the universe described by quantum physics must be open, not fully determined *a priori* by preexisting laws. If we take seriously the properties of quantum information, the universe is creatively and unpredictably *becoming*, contrary to what classical physics claims.

For those who believe that the macroscopic long-term future of the universe is predictable because at that scale the universe is deterministic, I have a surprise. The universe is actually a chaotic system in which, if we make *a tiny* change in the initial conditions, the future behavior can be completely different than the predicted behavior. Therefore, determinism does not imply predictability even in a classical system.

The bottom line is that classical systems cannot have free will, unless they are controlled by entities that have it. Moreover, free will requires a self-conscious entity like a seity that knows what she wants. Only quantum systems can have non-algorithmic randomness represented by quantum probability. Classical randomness is algorithmic because it is described by classical probability. Thus, a classical computer that is not controlled by an external system cannot make any creative choice of its own that is not already predetermined by its program.

A New Vision

A computer has no interiority because consciousness and free will are quantum. In a computer there is no entity independent from its physical parts that has authority over the parts. There is no real creativity in a computer because creativity requires non-algorithmic choices that can only be made by a quantum entity controlling the computer from the outside. Free will implies choices that are known by the seity that makes them, but are unknowable to any outside observer prior to their manifestations in spacetime.

9

A New Model of Reality

> Science progresses through the refutation of existing propositions and theories, and not through the stubborn defense of them.
> —Ralf Dahrendorf

When materialism claims that algorithmic physical reality is all that exists and that consciousness is epiphenomenal, it not only does humanity a bad service, but it is actually *wrong*! It is crucial that reliable and competent scientists raise their voices to counter such erroneous notions. Already, an increasing number of researchers are beginning to wonder about the many overlooked "anomalies" that reveal deep cracks in what has seemed unassailable principles for so long. Through these anomalies leaks the light of a reality quite different from the one envisaged by materialist physics.

Nevertheless, many are still fascinated by the atomism of classical physics, i.e., by the idea that matter is composed of indivisible and separate elementary units that are *objects*. With this conception, they believed that every phenomenon could be explained, when in reality this idea could not even explain the surprising chemical properties of matter. It took quantum physics to elucidate chemistry, and this was only possible because elementary particles are not objects, but *states* of quantum fields that are inseparable from the fields and can be entangled with each other. Entanglement was found to be such a counterintuitive and "impossible" property that even the most adventurous physicist couldn't believe it really existed. It took about 50 years to get the first experimental evidence for entanglement, obtained by Alain Aspect in 1982, and 30 more years to amass the incontrovertible experimental evidence that was able to silence all the objections that many incredulous physicists raised about its existence.

As Richard Feynman, Nobel laureate in physics, observed in his *QED: The strange theory of light and matter*: "From the point of view of common sense, quantum electrodynamics describes an absurd theory. However, it is in perfect agreement with the experimental data. I therefore hope that you will be able to accept Nature for what it is: absurd." Still, I believe that the right theory must obviously be in perfect agreement with the experimental data, but Nature cannot be *absurd*. We are the ones who still fail to understand the deeper reasons for such a strange behavior. How could an absurd Nature have created living organisms like us?

Materialists consider the laws of classical physics to be reasonable, yet they do not contemplate that Nature possesses the consciousness and free will that distinguish us from inert matter. If Nature is fundamentally conscious and has free will, as I suppose, the basic laws of physics must be indeterministic and probabilistic, just like the laws of quantum physics are. *The absurdity therefore does not come from Nature, but from the human prejudice that insists that the fundamental laws must be deterministic.* The quantum fields that have the extraordinary property of explaining chemistry are drastically different from the atoms of Democritus that inspired classical physics. Those are the ones that gave us the materialism and the determinism that still dominate our *Weltanschauung*.

It is precisely on the basis of these prejudices that many thinkers believe that computers will be conscious in the future. Their prediction is based on two fallacious assumptions: that consciousness emerges from the brain and that life is a classical phenomenon that can be reproduced by a computer. Therefore, according to their theories, we are simply the body, i.e., a *deterministic* machine because living cells are considered classical systems rather than quantum-classical. And, when the body dies, everything fatally ends. If this were the case, our future would indeed be hopeless.

This dystopian vision is the inevitable consequence of materialist thinking, which started with inadequate assumptions. It is therefore necessary to start with new postulates that are consistent with the new discoveries of quantum physics. We need, in the words of Roger Penrose in his book *The Road to Reality*, "new and powerful ideas, which lead us in significantly different directions from those currently followed."

In the model I propose, as I have already anticipated, consciousness, free will, and Life exist from the very beginning as constitutive properties of the holistic Whole (One) that also contains other properties that allowed the evolution of the inanimate universe. According to this model, the inanimate universe did not come first but derives from a deeper quantum reality inhabited by seities with consciousness and free will that communicate *meaning* with each other. That process has gradually created a symbolic reality that contains live and classical information. This symbolic reality is a "physical" correlate of the ever-increasing self-knowing of the seities that has given existence to stars, planets, and living organisms when it is perceived through the quantum-classical information system we call the human body.

I am convinced that, as soon as we realize that quantum physics does not describe outer but inner reality, it will cease to be absurd!

I truly hope that science can cure the misunderstandings of science, and that those who have become trapped in materialism can revise their beliefs. I also hope that the many non-experts who adhered to classical thought, trusting qualified scientists, will carefully consider this new vision that, unlike the classical one, restores the meaning and purpose that materialism has boldly erased from our universe.

A New Perspective

All things are in the universe and the universe is in all things...in this way all things come together in perfect harmony.

—Giordano Bruno, *Of the Cause, Principle, and One*

According to the current conception of quantum physics, the physical universe is the result of the collapse of the wave function that describes the universe in a complex N-dimensional Hilbert space, where N can be infinite. Until now, Hilbert's space has been considered an abstract space, a mathematical idealization devoid of any physical reality. However, if there wasn't a vaster reality than the one manifested in spacetime, it would be impossible to explain how quantum computers work. Such computers operate at a temperature approaching absolute zero (-273.15 °C), which is a necessary condition to maintain the entangled states of the qubits. However, the parallel computation possible with unitary transformations of qubits goes well beyond the possibilities of the matter manifested in spacetime.

This indicates that there must exist a greater reality which is currently represented mathematically by vectors in Hilbert space. In this conception, spacetime would correspond to the projection of an N-dimensional reality into a 3+1 dimensional subspace.

In this new model, Hilbert space is the mathematical description of a vaster reality in which seities and other conscious entities could exist, and from which the physical reality perceived by our body emerges. We already know that what is measurable in spacetime is only a small portion of the greater reality in which quantum states and live symbols exist.

However, before proceeding any further, I must point out another fundamental difference between the concepts of Field and One. In the universe described by physics, there can be no purpose and no meaning, since its fields are inanimate. On the other hand, if we assume that consciousness and free will always existed as properties of One, they must also be present in the quantum fields that emerged from It. If we say that the Field is also conscious and has free will, then the Field is another name for One.

There must also be a reason that justifies the presumed existence of seities, and the most sensible one I can imagine is that One desires to know Itself. Thus, every new act of self-knowing of One gives existence to that "portion" of Itself that has known Itself. In other words, knowing also means bringing into actual existence what is known from a state of potential existence that contains what is not yet known. Knowing must therefore be ontological,[1] and each new existence, which I have called seity, will be a part-whole of One with the same desire, capacity, and freedom to know itself that One has.

Just as One gives new existence to Itself through self-knowing, "the main task in everyone's life is to bring himself to light," as Erich Fromm said, and this can only happen by knowing oneself. This idea reflects one of the deepest desires of human nature, recognized since ancient times. For instance, at the entrance of the Temple of Apollo in Delphi, 2500 years ago, were inscribed the words "O Man, know yourself, and you will know the Universe and the Gods." I believe that, since we are emanations of One, the profound impulses that drive us to know ourselves should have their origin in the same yearning One has to know Itself. In the words of Friedrich Nietzsche,

---

1 To exist is to be known, and vice versa. This self-knowing can never be erased after it happened, otherwise One could not achieve Its purpose. Hence, the memory of the meaning (the essence of self-knowing) must somehow exist forever, since meaning is the ultimate ontology.

"Knowledge grows to the same degree as not knowing, or rather the knowledge of not knowing."

Creation is therefore the manifestation of One's continuous endeavor to get to know Itself ever more through the seities. It is important to emphasize that to know is to love, and to love is to know. "Greater knowledge is indissolubly linked to love" (Paracelsus). Therefore, the more self-knowing increases, i.e., true conscious knowing rather than symbolic knowledge, the more love increases. It can therefore be said with the English poet Alfred Tennyson that "complete knowledge is complete love." As Rossiter W. Raymond states: "Life is eternal and immortal love; and death is only a horizon; and a horizon is nothing, except the limit of our gaze." And for Emily Dickinson:

> love is immortality
> or rather, it is divine substance.
> Those who love know no death,
> because love makes life reborn
> in divinity.

The Creative Principle

There is a great mystery in our existence and in our life experiences, which cannot be explained in materialistic terms. Our feeling of freedom is not an illusion and the cosmos is not something that perennially turns without meaning. Our knowledge cannot go beyond the fact that we are all part of some grand design.

—John Carew Eccles, *The Origin of Life*

Saying that reality contains consciousness and free will from the beginning implies the existence of a *Creative Principle* that gives purpose, meaning, and direction to the universe. I think this Principle could be the following: One wants to know Itself to fulfill Itself, and thus to enjoy and love Its own existence. "All creation exists for the 'pure joy' of God. The work of creation was a work of joy, the purpose of which was to instill more joy into existence" (Matthew Fox, *The Reinvention of Work*).

Therefore, consciousness, free will, and life represent the necessary means, i.e., the properties that One must possess, to know Itself. The holism and dynamism of the Field with the addition of consciousness, free will, and the Creative Principle describe the fundamental and irreducible properties of One. We know that holism is present in both the quantum fields and the spacetime described by general relativity; hence, the unification of physics will necessarily have to describe a holistic, dynamic, and unified field (Field). The dynamism of the Field leads to the never-ending expansion of the universe we observe. This requires that the initial "momentum" of the universe be able to counteract the gravitational force that otherwise would have reduced it to a black hole.

It follows that there is *teleology* (finality or purpose) in the universe, an idea considered unacceptable by many physicists, even though the principle of least action, which is the basis of the fundamental equations of quantum physics, is teleological. As we saw in Chapter 1, the principle of least action leads to the minimization of *action* along the trajectory of an object that moves from an initial to a final position. As the astrophysicist Allan Sandage says:

> Materialist reductionist scientists…will never admit a mystery in the things they see, always postponing from one time to another, waiting for a reductionist explanation for what is still unknown. But taking this reductionist belief to the deepest level and to an indefinite time in the future (and indefinite it will always remain), when "science will know everything," is itself an act of faith, which denies that there may be anything unknown to science, at least in principle.

In Its Image and Likeness

In a drop of water there is the secret of all the boundless oceans.
—Kahlil Gibran

The only "image and likeness" of One we know is us. If One is the totality of what exists, both potentially and actually, One is the creator, the creation, and the beneficiary of Its own creation and becoming. And the essence of humankind is one of the countless conscious perspectives through which One knows and realizes Itself.

Each one of us was born from a fertilized egg, a single cell containing the entire genome of the future mature organism. Through subsequent reproductions and specializations of the cells, the entire organism self-assembled, and was born. The organism continued to grow and develop for another 15 years until reaching about 50 trillion cells at maturity. Each cell contains a copy of the genome of the fertilized egg, even though only a small portion of it is expressed. So the "knowledge" of the whole organism is contained in each cell! We can therefore properly say that each cell is a part-whole of the organism.[2]

By analogy, we carry within us the same "genome" of One, just like each cell of our body carries within itself the symbolic knowledge of the entire body. Just like each cell of the body is a part-whole of the body, we are *parts-whole* of One, which means that One is within us and we are within One. As the Persian poet Jalal al-Din Rumi says: "You are not a drop in the ocean. You are the whole ocean in one drop." And Indian sage Ramana

---

2 If we analyze the construction of a computer or a robot, we can easily see that each of their parts is a transistor or a piece of matter that knows nothing of the whole. Clearly, the claim that a living organism is like a classical machine cannot be correct.

Maharshi: "Everyone knows that the drop is lost in the ocean, but few know that the ocean is lost in the drop."

How can One, the Whole, be inside every portion of itself? This is an enigma that we find reflected in the mathematics of *fractals*[3] and in the properties of *holograms*, in which each portion of the hologram contains the whole.[4] In this new theory, the self-knowing of each seity is represented by a pure quantum state that is knowable only by the seity within itself. One has a knowing of Itself that is given by the superposition of the knowings of all the selves that emerged from It. This knowing is knowable only by One. "The One is found in the many, and the many are infinite facets of the One" (Friedrich W.J. Schelling).

Another way to understand the logical necessity of having to create seities is to recognize that the holism of One requires that every new self-knowing must be an entity that represents the whole, and yet be inseparable from the whole. The seities must therefore neither be parts separated from One, nor be themselves made up of separable parts. This requires the concept of *part-whole*, a *quantum system* that must contain the essence of One and at the same time have the distinctive perspective with which One has known all of Itself in that instant.

The self-knowing acquired by One gives life to a seity with its own characteristics and with a unique identity, which

---

3   A fractal is a geometric object that appears similar on different scales in the sense that by enlarging a portion of the object, the same shape is found in its parts. Surprisingly, these objects can be obtained with simple, recursive algorithms.

4   A hologram is obtained by dividing a monochromatic light beam in two. The first beam illuminates the object, and its reflected light is made to interfere with the second beam on a photographic plate. By illuminating the photographic plate with monochromatic light of the same frequency, we get a virtual image of the object in three dimensions! A remarkable aspect of a hologram is that, by illuminating only a portion of it, the same virtual object is reproduced with less detail.

represents the unique perspective or point of view with which One has known Itself. The new part-whole can in turn know itself and give existence to other entities capable of doing the same. This is why *reproduction*, which is a crucial property of Life, is a constitutive property of One.

Reproduction in turn creates generations of seities which, by expanding their knowing of self and world, expand the knowledge of One, since One cannot be separate from its own emanations. *One is the interiority of all that exists; It is what connects all Its creations "from within."*

Reproduction can then be explained as the fundamental strategy with which One, and all the entities that emanate from It, can know themselves and each other, each with their own unique, indelible, and unified perspective. In this way, One creates an exponentially growing number of parts-whole that can never end, because infinity can never be reached.

Communication between Seities

In the previous chapter I called an elementary seity, CU. A CU is the simplest part-whole, i.e., the simplest quantum system that can contain the essence of the whole, and possess an identity that, once created, can no longer be extinguished. A CU is like a living cell that reproduces and combines with other cells to create ever more complex organisms. The CUs are conscious fields with free-will agency and identity that communicate with each other to deepen their own self-knowing. It is important to realize that since each CU is a part-whole of One, she can only increase her self-knowing by interacting with the other CUs through symbolic communications. The comprehension of the symbolic expressions of the different viewpoints of the other CUs allows each CU to know, with her own viewpoint, the same wholeness of One that exists in all of them.

Because we communicate all the time, communicating seems such a simple task that we don't realize how complex it actually is. To communicate, CUs must have the ability to sense and recognize the presence and the identity of the other CUs, i.e., be able to perceive the wholeness and uniqueness that characterizes each CU by observing them "from the outside" since their inner experience is private and inviolate. This uniqueness manifests like a shareable symbol that must be automatically perceived and understood as such by all CUs. I call it the "identity symbol" because it is unique and it reliably identifies each CU when recognized by another CU. The identity symbol can be understood as the unique *name* of the CU. I also imagine that each identity symbol produces within the consciousness of each CU a "sense of the other" similar to, although different from, the "sense of self" that each CU automatically perceives within itself.

I also assume that the sensing, perception, and recognition of these fundamental symbols is innate within each and every CU, and forms the letters of the universal "alphabet" from which more complex symbols can be constructed. The live symbols corresponding to the identity symbols are similar to the "elementary particles" of physics, whereas the qualia produced by these symbols are based on the native inner palette of sensations that each CU feels and uses to understand herself and the other CUs. The sense of self of each CU includes the desire to know herself and to know the other CUs like a different point of view of herself by communicating with them using live symbols.

The creation, sensing, perception, and recognition of communication symbols must be an automatic, constitutive property shared by all CUs, for it is necessary to fulfill their inherent desire to communicate. Each CU must also have the capacity to freely select a portion of the meaning she wants to express and transform it into an adequate live symbol that can be understood by the other CUs, to the extent that they already comprehend a similar meaning.

To be able to communicate without a preexisting common language that would be necessary in order to agree on the meaning of symbols, we must assume that there is an innate symbol-meaning correspondence for all CUs and seities. However, the qualia produced by the perception of a particular symbol may vary for each entity, whereas the meaning revealed by those qualia depends on the level of comprehension reached by the entity. With greater comprehension, the meaning of a symbol may gradually converge towards the same "essence" for all CUs, even though the qualia may be very different from CU to CU. I imagine the meaning as a kind of "geometric structure" that can be intuitively comprehended by all CUs, despite the variations of qualia and viewpoints.

Comprehension allows CUs not only to recognize the meaning carried by qualia but also to sense the "semantic distance" between the meaning felt and the full meaning of the symbol. Therefore, what is not yet comprehended produces the feeling that there is more to know than what has been recognized.

Through repeated communication cycles, the meaning gets organized into hierarchical "layers" that coemerge with a combination of CUs similarly organized into corresponding hierarchical layers of seities. Since each seity recognizes the presence of some meaning that has yet to be comprehended, this "knowing that there is something still to be known" provides the impetus to seek ever-deeper comprehensions in an endless process. This is just like the familiar feeling we often perceive that we "know that we don't know," which motivates us to find out what we don't yet know.

In summary, the CUs that emerge from One are conscious fields with free-will agency, and identity that deepen their self-knowing by communicating with each other with live symbols. By combining with each other, CUs and seities create hierarchical levels of seities and meaning with the capacity to comprehend ever more complex meaning, reflected in the ever-increasing complexity of the live symbols they use to communicate.

Knowing refers to the inner meaning carried by qualia and represented by pure quantum states. Complexity refers to the outer structure of live symbols required to encode ever-deeper meanings. In other words, the meaning and the live symbols that represent it coevolve and create what we currently recognize as elementary particles, nucleons, atoms, molecules, macromolecules, ... cells, ... animals, and so on.

The Natural Evolution of the Laws

The truth did not come into the world naked, but it came in symbols and images.
—Philip, *Apocryphal Gospel*, v. 67

The fundamental distinction between the cosmology of current physics and the one described here is that the laws of physics are supposed to exist *a priori*, independently from what they regulate, and to predict the behavior of inanimate things. In the proposed model, the laws gradually and spontaneously emerge from the communication of the seities to symbolically express the ever-deeper meanings that emerge from within through the process of conscious comprehension. The deepening of the meaning then precedes the creation of the evermore complex symbols used to represent it, in a virtuous and never-ending coevolution. In other words, the laws that regulate the interactions of symbols are syntactical laws that spontaneously emerge from the communications of the seities and partly reflect the inner structure of the meaning the seities exchange.[5]

---

5 This "similarity" or *homomorphism* between symbols and meaning reminds one of onomatopoeia, which refers to those words (symbols) whose sound (meaning) resembles the "sound" produced by the things that the words are meant to describe.

Once established, the syntactical laws describe the behavior of symbols and reflect the fundamental characteristics of the self-knowing acquired by the seities. Therefore, the laws of physics that we discover are the equivalent of the syntactical laws of symbols that the seities have developed and consolidated in their coevolution. A crucial consequence of this model is that the physical universe we observe is a reflection of the symbolic universe that emerges from the communications of the seities. This is exactly the opposite of the current interpretation in which life and conscious entities emerged from the algorithmic interactions of inanimate matter. In this model instead, life and consciousness did not emerge from inanimate matter; it was the manifest world that emerged from them. In other words, the physical universe represents only the dance of symbols used by the seities to communicate. The seities, however, must exist before the symbols.

Metaphorically, I imagine matter as the ink with which the seities write their own self-knowing. Said differently, the symbols that represent the self-knowing of the seities are written with "matter" as the self-knowing progresses. Deeper down, matter consists only of abstract forms or symbols. This means that live information may not exist at all as we are currently imagining.

Living organisms should therefore be interpreted as extremely complex organizations of live symbols representing the ever-growing self-knowing of the seities. A living organism is both quantum and classical and can "host" the consciousness and free will of a quantum seity because the seity can communicate directly with the body using live information. Within D'Ariano's Operational Probabilistic Theory (OPT), the collapse of the wave function does not exist. Instead, there are irreversible *atomic* transformations that transform quantum information (entangled qubits representing experience or meaning) into live information that can in turn be represented with classical symbols (bits) [11]. This is the mechanism by which seities communicate with living organisms by converting meaning into live information, and vice versa.

The semantic world is represented by quantum information, and the "collapsed" quantum information in spacetime represents the live information of which our physical world is made. Live information includes all the "particles" that manifest in spacetime, including the virtual particles manifesting in the quantum vacuum that cannot be measured, though individually and collectively they can influence what can be measured in spacetime. This is why the physical world and life are both quantum and classical. Nonetheless, quantum information cannot be fully expressed in spacetime because it represents the inner world of experience (meaning) that is not reproducible and is greater than any live symbol could possible capture. When the live information carried by many *uncorrelated* symbols is averaged, live information becomes classical information.

The world of living organisms is contained in the physical world, which also contains the much more limited world of computers and robots which are strictly classical systems. Therefore, living organisms act as bridges between the quantum world of seities and the classical world of macroscopic objects and computers. Living organisms controlled by seities using live information can in turn control robots using classical information. The seities can then experience the classical information produced by robots, computers, and the physical world by having living organisms convert it into live symbols.

Therefore, robots could only act in a non-algorithmic way, as if they had consciousness and free will, if they were controlled with the classical information produced by living organisms, which in turn are controlled by the seities that alone possess the consciousness and free will necessary to experience and direct their own experience. The crucial point here is that the experience of the classical world does not exist "inside" a living organism; it only exists in the interiority of a seity's field.

Information Is Not Ontology

The informational world in which we live has greatly accentuated the confusion between inner reality, outer reality, theory of reality, and simulation of a theory of reality, to the point where the simulation of a theory of reality is often equated to conscious experience! In my model, inner reality is the deepest reality of meaning that is represented by quantum information. Inner reality contains the outer reality of live information represented by the fundamental shareable symbols used by the seities to communicate their own meanings. The world of live information contains, then, also the world of classical information that contains rocks, computers, and robots.

Live information exists in the vaster reality of the seities. It includes that portion that manifests in spacetime which includes the living organisms through which the seities can have an experience in the "physical world."

A theory of reality is only a mathematical model of the measurable events occurring in spacetime. The simulation of a theory of reality is based on classical bits and is performed by a computer with limited precision. Therefore, even a classical system, which is generally non-linear and therefore chaotic, will have a different behavior from its simulation after a sufficiently long time, due to the uncontrollable impact of the initial conditions which can only be known with limited precision. The inner reality of meaning is therefore "three degrees of separation" away from its simulation.

Thinking that AI is truly intelligent when it can only imitate human behavior (being devoid of meaning) is a grave misunderstanding similar to what occurs when a theory of reality is confused with reality. Reality is *alive*, existing primarily in the experiential self-knowing of the seities rather than in the symbols used by them. The current idea of matter is completely misleading because we have given ontology to abstract information without meaning, severing meaning from reality.

In this new conception, the ontology is in the meaning that can only be privately known by seities. Live information is the vastly reduced representation of the meaning that the seities have chosen to manifest, of which only that smaller portion that appears as *measurable* events in spacetime has been given reality by physicists.

We must bear in mind that particles, atoms, and molecules do not exist as we have imagined them. In fact, we do not yet have a precise idea of how to describe a particle, since we do not yet fully understand the phenomenon of entanglement. Moreover, the concept of spacetime promoted by general relativity (GR) cannot explain entanglement and thus is incomplete. GR can accurately explain only certain macroscopic phenomena, but it does so by using approximations of deeper quantum concepts that are currently elusive. These new ideas are currently expressed by various theories of *quantum gravity* presently being developed.

Live information is precisely that coherent symbolic representation of meaning that becomes objective and shareable when it appears in spacetime. However, not all physical quantities of objective reality are knowable because there are complementary properties that cannot be simultaneously measured with arbitrary precision (Heisenberg's principle). For example, if we want to know precisely the position of a particle, we cannot simultaneously know its velocity, and vice versa. In other terms, some of the objective knowledge must remain hidden. This means that the full impact of any particle on physical reality cannot be precisely known. Note that if we could know all the information about reality, reality would be predictable, making free will impossible.[6]

---

6 There are four aspects of quantum physics that prevent all information from being known: (1) Heisenberg's uncertainty principle, (2) the *actual* quantum state that will manifest cannot be known, for only its probability can be

On the other hand, what really exists is the *subjective* inner meaning that each seity has of its own state. For example, Alice knows her own state, but she can only know that portion of Bob's state (meaning) that he chooses to express with live information. This information must then be perceived and translated into the correct meaning by Alice as a seity, not Alice as a physical body. And the meaning received largely depends on Alice's comprehension of the live symbols.

Note that the meaning is communicated through live information, which may contain much more information than is measurable in spacetime. For example, the so-called virtual particles represent "fluctuations in the quantum vacuum," i.e., live information that cannot be measured directly but can have an effect on our reality. In other words, the portion of "matter in spacetime" that we can measure is only a small portion of what I call live information. Live information may also be entangled in an unknowable way with other live information and thus have an unknowable objective impact on physical reality.

Information Is Not Knowing

In the Italian language there is a significant difference in meaning between *conoscere* and *sapere*, two distinct types of knowing, even though in common usage the two words may often be synonyms. *Sapere* refers to symbolic *knowledge*, while *conoscere* refers to semantic *knowing*, i.e., getting the meaning of the symbolic information. In English there is only the verb "to know" which can produce ambiguity with regard to the intended meaning. To discriminate the two types, I have here

---

known, (3) the quantum state of a system cannot be reproduced, and (4) the entanglement is nonlocal and is not generally knowable. Therefore, the state of a system could change because it is entangled with another system that may have interacted with a third system far away without any possible knowledge on our part, even in principle.

consistently used *knowledge* and *knowing* to respectively indicate the crucially different symbolic and semantic meanings pointed out by the verb "to know." Sometimes this crucial distinction may require more explicit language.

A computer can manipulate symbols without understanding anything, i.e., it can have knowledge (*sapere*) but cannot have knowing (*conoscere*). We can have both symbolic knowledge and experiential knowing (comprehension, meaning). Note that information in physics is only symbolic knowledge without any subjective meaning. That's fine to describe computers but not for human beings for whom information without meaning should not even be called information.

When I tell my child, "I love you with all my soul," I express a real feeling, for the love I feel *inside of me* exists and is alive. When a robot says, "I love you with all my soul," it is simply reproducing the same classical information that I manifested *outside* of me, without feeling anything because it is not a quantum system and thus it has no interiority.

Ontology is present only in the meaning that lives within the seities, not in the meaningless information that represents the meaning. Information-as-symbols is created by the seities to communicate information-as-meaning with each other. Scientists have recognized the existence of meaning within their experience, but with their intellect they have separated the symbol from its meaning and have called *reality* only the symbolic information. This crucial omission lies with the scientists, not with reality. To comprehend reality we need both symbols and meaning! Today science is only about symbols, and spirituality is about meaning. We need to heal this split that is only a misunderstanding, or better, a mis-comprehension.

A robot automatically repeats what its human programmer makes it say because it has no life and no consciousness, even though it moves and appears to be alive. We instead are alive even when our body is dead. We exist in a greater reality which also contains what we call physical reality. And when our bodies die, we don't die. "Death is the next rebirth that is given to us as a gift in the spiritual universe" (Bert Hellinger, *Natural Mystic: The path of knowledge*).

We, as seities, are eternal.

When the designer of a robot claims that the feeling is identical to the symbol-for-the-feeling, if he is not in bad faith he is not *aware* of what he is saying. As such, he has lost contact with his inner life. *A robot has no feelings.* Period. And when we disconnect from our feelings we will act as robots. The *vital* difference is that we have the privilege of being able to behave as sentient beings as well as robots. That choice is ours and ours alone, and it must come *individually* through the free will each of us has.

It is true that feelings may often make us suffer, but choosing not to feel anything to prevent suffering is senseless. As the German writer Eckhart Tolle says: "If you had not suffered as you have suffered, you would not have the depth, the humility, and the compassion of a human being." We can know ourselves only by first acknowledging and then by following our feelings with our reasoning-and-feeling mind. We need both!

We must not confuse words-as-symbols with the ideas and meaning they represent. If we fail to comprehend the insurmountable difference between symbol-without-meaning and symbol-with-meaning, we confuse the imitation of reality with reality. As Alfred Korzybski states: "The map is not the territory" and "the word is not the thing…Maps and words, small geographical maps of our psyche, are used to move in reality, but if they are too vast they become bulky and dangerous." In fact, the symbolic-only representation of reality, however detailed it may be, can never be reality.

In our study of reality we have fallen into a trap because we have mistaken the symbol for the meaning! We have given to symbols the value of reality and denied reality to the meaning. This happened because we have disconnected from our own feelings, especially when suffering is present. In fact, refusing to face our suffering will increase it, not make it disappear. Suffering is what our lack of comprehension feels like. It can only disappear when it is faced and resolved, not by pretending it out of existence.

Suffering occurs when we are not heeding the call to know ourselves with honesty and integrity. By not facing our inner reality of meaning, we end up living in a virtual reality made only of empty symbols. We may pretend to be happy for a while, until the suffering becomes so unbearable that we are forced to "look at our avoidance" and take care of the real purpose of our existence. Ontology exists only in the semantic-symbolic reality that cannot be separated.

This core misunderstanding must be healed as soon as possible, because it is leading us astray. We are conscious and luminous fields, not machines! The machines are only the symbolic part of Life. The real information is what allows us to know and appreciate each other as conscious human beings, as full expressions of One. I hope that the time will soon come when, as Goethe said: "The inner light will come out of us, so that we will no longer need any more light."

A New Interpretation of Quantum Information

We have seen that quantum information is the representation of knowing (meaning), but that information is not what knowing is. Knowing is *a lived experience*, the conscious experience of a seity that can be *mathematically represented* by a pure quantum state described as an organization of entangled qubits. However, this qubit structure cannot replace the lived experience which is ontological because the seity that knows from within *becomes* what it knows. The description of reality is not reality; the map is not the territory.

This type of knowing (meaning) is linked to existence like the two sides of the same coin, because to exist is to know the meaning, and to know the meaning is to exist. The pure quantum state is just an abstract state that is useful to represent the knowing of the seity that becomes what it knows. The interesting aspect of quantum information is that it has the essential characteristics of what it represents since it is definite and cannot be reproduced, i.e., it is private just like the knowing of the seity is. In this sense, quantum information represents the interiority of the universe! What can only be known by being it.

Whereas classical information is public and can be copied, quantum information is private and knowable only by the "quantum system," i.e., by the seity. In the interpretation offered by QIP, what can be known of the private meaning from the outside is only the live symbolic information that the seity decides to make public. And the comprehension of the meaning of those symbols requires that the receiving seities already know a meaning close to what those symbols are intended to convey.

When we comprehend something new, we create new existence and become more than what we were before: we grow and achieve great fulfillment (joy). The urge to grow belongs to life. "Life is growth. If we stop growing, technically and spiritually, we are theoretically dead" (Morihei Ueshiba, founder of Aikido).

Any new meaning must first occur within our consciousness and then it can be communicated by creating new symbols, just as it happens for a book whose content can only be written after the author has comprehended what he will symbolically express. Said differently, the meaning precedes the symbols that describe it, just like the whole-as-idea (the invention) always comes before its symbolic construction.

If we represent a seity as a quantum system, then her quantum state represents her inner experience which is an indivisible whole. What can be manifested of that experience will be that portion of the whole that the seity has chosen to share with live symbols. Sometimes the seity may manifest a "creative state" represented by a live symbol that never existed before, in which case an external observer could not have assigned a probability prior to measuring it. This situation, however, could only be represented by quantum theory if the postulate of unitarity was not part of it, since this postulate implies that all the possible states that can manifest must be known or knowable before their manifestation. Therefore unitarity is equivalent to eliminating creativity and free will from the universe, since a creative state, prior to its creation for the first time, cannot even be known by its creator.

D'Ariano has recently shown that the postulate of unitarity is non-falsifiable [11]; therefore this postulate should not be part of quantum physics, thus allowing the existence of creative states that could either be caused by free-will decisions or by new comprehensions. Therefore, a more general quantum theory, such as D'Ariano's OPT [7] that does not need such a postulate, allows the existence of *irreversible* non-unitary transformations[7] that avoid the need for the collapse of the wave function and permit the existence of free will.

There can be no laws or algorithms that forbid the open evolution of the universe, the *becoming* of One, which is based on One's free exploration of Its self-knowing. Only the probabilities of symbols that follow consolidated syntactical laws can be predicted, but the emergence of new symbols and new laws that did not exist before cannot be predicted.

---

7   Unitary transformations have been widely adopted by physicists following the mathematical theory of quantum physics developed by von Neumann in the mid-1930s. These transformations are *reversible*, maintain the purity of the quantum state, and require the collapse of the wave function to produce measurable phenomena in spacetime. The transformations performed by quantum computers, for example, are strictly unitary. The collapse of the wave function created the measurement problem that has never been solved.

The Universe as Exploration of Knowing

I open my scuttle at night and see the far-sprinkled systems,
And all I see multiplied as high as I can cipher edge but the
rim of the farther systems.
Wider and wider they spread, expanding, always expanding,
Outward and outward and forever outward.
—Walt Whitman, *Song of Myself*

In summary, I believe that from the Creative Principle follows the logical necessity of CUs emerging from One. These are parts-whole whose purpose is to know themselves, and thus increase the self-knowing of One. CUs are "perspectives," "points of view," or "frames of reference" with which One knows Itself. They are similar to the *monads* introduced in 1720 by Gottfried Wilhelm von Leibniz.[8] As CUs communicate and know themselves, they create a first level of symbols and syntactical laws that eventually lead to a second level of seities and a stable second level of symbols made of combinations of first-level symbols. For example, when the CU corresponding to the quantum field of "up" quarks communicates with the CU that corresponds to the field of "down" quarks, a new combination-seity whose identity symbol is the proton is eventually formed. The new symbol is a combination of the original symbols, but it has very different properties from those of the quarks that combined. The measurable state of the proton field is only a small portion of its quantum state, which is not fully knowable

---

8 Leibniz proposed that the universe is created by the interactions of monads in a famous book entitled *Lehrsätze über die Monadologie*, published in 1720. Leibniz understood that consciousness must be the basis of reality and did not approve, on a purely philosophical basis, of the idea that reality should be controlled by mechanical and coercive laws as proposed by his contemporary, Newton.

from the outside since it corresponds to the private experience of the new seity.

This process is repeated and results in the creation of a hierarchy of levels of seities and symbols. For example, when the "proton" seity communicates with the "electron" seity, they end up creating a second level of syntactical laws and a third-level seity whose identity symbol corresponds to the hydrogen atom.

I am describing a process similar to that of the Lambda-CDM cosmological model,[9] but with a fundamental difference because the first entities that emerge from One are CUs, not the inanimate fields of elementary particles that follow pre-established laws. In the proposed model, the unified Field of physics is the physical correlate of One, the elementary quantum fields are the physical correlates of the CUs, and the elementary particles in spacetime are the live symbols used by the CUs to communicate with each other. The basic laws of quantum physics are the analog of the syntactical laws of symbols that spontaneously and gradually emerged as the CUs evolved their basic language.[10]

For example, the symbols manifested by the seity whose physical correlate is the quantum field of electrons are the states,

9   In the Lambda-CDM model, the universe contains three components: (1) a cosmological constant associated with dark energy (lambda), (2) dark matter called CDM (cold dark matter), and (3) ordinary matter. This is the simplest model that accounts for the following phenomena: (1) the cosmic microwave background, (2) the distribution of galaxies, (3) the relative abundances of hydrogen, deuterium, helium, and lithium, and (4) the accelerated expansion of the universe.

10 In physics, the laws are independent from the fields and are imposed "from the outside," constituting the second "miracle" that has never been explained. In the new model, the laws emerge through the spontaneous communications of the CUs. They represent the syntactical rules that the CUs "negotiated and agreed" in order to communicate with each other.

entangled or not, of such a field. These states we called electrons, which were until recently erroneously considered independent objects. The configuration of these states represents that portion of the meaning of the "electron seity" that she communicates symbolically to the other fields. If we could simultaneously perceive the vast number of states of the electron field and were able to interpret their meaning, we could understand what the electron seity is communicating to the other seities.

I like to point out that what we do when we speak is not much different from what the electron field does: the vibrations we emit are symbols that represent the meaning we intend to communicate. The physical laws that describe the behavior of the air vibrations have little to do with the meaning we communicate, which is what matters to us. These vibrations are related to the meaning they represent, but they are not the meaning.

In this model, the syntactical laws of the seities' languages correspond to the probabilistic physical laws describing the behavior of the states of the quantum fields. These states (symbols) are controlled by the free will of the seities and behave with statistical laws similar to those of the letters of the alphabet of our languages. In this interpretation, it is not surprising that the pure quantum states cannot be copied since they are private, knowable only by the seity, and not by any outer observer, just like our inner experiences are.

In my opinion, the main reason nobody understands quantum physics is because it describes the inner world of private experience and free will, when it was expected to describe the behavior of material objects in spacetime. The quantum formalism is telling us that Nature has a private interiority which is the source of the public exteriority we observe. With this elegant interpretation, quantum physics can finally become comprehensible.

10

The Nature of the Seity

Each of us is a god with the conviction of being contingency, shadow of a dream.
—Emanuele Severino, 'A German handed me the machine gun and ran away,' *Corriere della Sera*, 31 December 2018

As Giordano Bruno expressed: "There will come a day when man will wake up from oblivion and will finally understand who he really is." I also believe that we all have a divine nature which is our true essence, and our task is to try "to bring the divine that is in us back to the divine that is in the universe" (Plotinus).

We are potentially infinite beings that cannot be completely captured by any definition, because to define is to limit by placing rigid boundaries around us. Defining requires attributing certain properties and excluding others. "Man has no limits and when he realizes it, he will be free even here, in this world" (Giordano Bruno). Yet many would like a reality in which everything—including us—can be cataloged, classified, defined, and placed in a box. That is, they would like reality to be entirely digital, bounded, in which everything is reducible to being either true or false. This, however, does not even work within arithmetic, as we have already pointed out when we discussed undecidability in axiomatic systems in Chapter 1 in connection with Gödel's theorems.

There are many thinkers who would like us to believe that we are just machines and that it will be possible to create machines that are smarter than us. However, to become aware of our greatness, we must reconnect with our deepest feelings which are the source of our personal power and vastness. And then we will finally comprehend that if we can create digital machines that perform certain mechanical tasks much faster than us, and without making any mistakes, it is only because we are infinitely "more" than our machines.

We are not digital and finite. We are vastness, potentially beyond all limits. I know it with certainty in my innermost being because I have experienced it, as described in the Introduction of this book. But the description of a pure state with words (shareable symbols) is impossible because a pure state is not reproducible, and thus words will never be able to capture the full meaning intimately disclosed by a sentient experience. We all have already experienced this limitation, and physics is also telling us this much.

Although this new model is still incomplete in many details, I believe it is sufficiently fleshed out for the curious reader to begin grasping the whole vision and to reflect on its deep significance. The effort needed to see reality with new eyes will lead us to freedom from the conceptual prison that has broken our wings. "You were born with ideals and dreams. You were born with a gift. You were born with wings. You are not meant to crawl, so don't do it. You have wings, learn to use them and fly" (Jalal al-Din Rumi).

A Seity Is ... Beyond

To define is to limit.
—Oscar Wilde

In my model, a seity is a reality that goes beyond all categories and all definitions. A seity cannot be defined in the same way that a machine can be, since its properties, namely consciousness, identity, free-will agency, and creativity, are inseparable and do not have sharp boundaries.[1] We have already discovered with quantum physics that reality goes far beyond the one described by classical physics, though we are still struggling to understand. "Nobody understands quantum physics." This is a famous quote by Richard Feynman, who included himself in that statement, expressing the strangeness of quantum physics, for it contradicts our intuitive ideas of how the world works.

I suspect we don't understand quantum physics mainly because we don't want to accept, at the "psychological level," what it is telling us, and we want to continue to believe that the real world is the deterministic one described by classical physics. Quantum reality is instead probabilistic, indeterministic, and contains entanglement, a mysterious property that connects the quantum states (particles) "from within" regardless of their distance. This implies a holistic reality made of parts that are not completely separable. Therefore the quantum nature is already telling us that the determinism and reductionism of classical physics do not exist, and that free will is possible, starting from the elementary fields of which everything is made.

It is surprising to me that, instead of embracing the freedom that quantum physics has shown us to be a crucial feature of reality, most scientists seem to prefer a deterministic and controllable world in which all properties can be precisely defined. I believe that we are all an integral part of a cooperative and magnificent adventure of consciousness, the aim of which is to discover that each of us has One within himself and has a special gift that makes him unique and irreplaceable. This gift is the particular point of view with which One has known Itself

---

1 Wanting to precisely define all the properties of reality as if reality were reductionistic and mechanical is deeply misleading because reality is not made of inanimate classical matter but it has instead two irreducible aspects: the semantic and the symbolic ones that continue to freely coevolve without end.

when It gave existence to each one of us. "Each person is a new experiment in God's laboratory" (Isaac Bashevis Singer), and, as Walt Whitman wrote in *Leaves of Grass*:

Each of us inevitable,
Each of us limitless—each of us with his or her right upon the earth,
Each of us allow'd the eternal purports of the earth,
Each of us here as divinely as any is here.

Moreover, those who appreciate and develop their uniqueness do experience deep joy, love, and fulfillment in knowing themselves in each other.

The Creation of Many Worlds

Let your soul stand cool and composed before a million universes.
—Walt Whitman, *Song of Myself*

The seities can create many different worlds which are all interconnected and exist one inside the other. Their fundamental connections are determined by the *universal* language created by the first-level seities, the CUs. This is the world that contains all other worlds, the language from which all other languages have emerged, and through which One can explore every possibility of knowing Itself.

For example, whenever the seities discover undecidable propositions on the basis of the "axioms" valid in their own world, they can create two new worlds in addition to the existing one: the first is formed by the seities who choose to explore the undecidable hypothesis as if it were true, adding it as a new axiom to the preexisting ones; the second world contains the seities that choose to explore the undecidable hypothesis in the negative. Thus, a portion of the seities decides to reject the undecidable axiom, while two other groups choose to explore two new and logically far less secure worlds.

A striking example of an undecidable hypothesis is found in Euclidean geometry when it was discovered that it was impossible to falsify the axiom of parallels on the basis of the other four axioms. This means that two new, non-Euclidean geometries could be created in which the parallel postulate was false. In Riemann's elliptical geometry the parallels converge, while in Lobachevsky's hyperbolic geometry the parallels diverge. Clearly, certain theorems valid in Euclidean geometry are not valid in elliptical or in hyperbolic geometry, even though all the theorems that do not depend on the parallel postulate are valid in all three geometries.

The seities who decided to reject the new axiom could continue to explore their world, ignoring the two new worlds being explored by the more adventurous seities. The repetition of this process, with the addition of many new undecidable axioms, may eventually lead to the lack of communication between seities who have created logically incompatible worlds.

Nonetheless, the seities who have not accepted any undecidable axioms could still benefit from the new knowledge gained by the others. And the latter could always communicate and understand each other by using only the basic language common to all of them, a language that continues to exist and evolve thanks to the less enterprising seities. It is important to note that the seities who explore these insecure worlds may lose their connection with the world of fundamental and indisputable values, because they may not realize how many undecidable axioms they have taken as true or false.

It is also noteworthy that, starting from any level, the entities and the laws of the next level are not fully predictable on the basis of the knowledge acquired from the entities and laws of the previous levels. The creative nature of the universe is manifested by the repetition of the same open process, which subsequently creates a hierarchy of levels and syntactical laws that describe an unpredictable becoming without end. The universe is open and its future is undetermined. This is a consequence of free will and the inherent creativity of One, which also reveal themselves in the probabilistic laws and in the indeterminism of the symbolic reality.

At the same time, it must be recognized that free will coexists with the laws of symbols, and therefore, as new levels of laws are created, freedom becomes ever more constrained, and this can lead to more mechanical worlds, even in the type of knowing being explored. Classical physics describes precisely those worlds that are *apparently* mechanical,[2] because their objects are statistical combinations of numerous uncorrelated quantum states. In these worlds, with their evermore constrained classical symbols, the danger of confusing symbols and meaning is worsened.

How Does the World of Seities Work?

To get an idea of how this world might work, let's try to imagine a large square with hundreds of people and animals that emit perceptible vibrations like sounds. Vibrations are abstract symbols whereas sounds are the qualia that bring meaning to each entity (seity). The vibrations produced by the various participants spread throughout the square and can be perceived by all present. This creates a "vibration sphere," an objective and shared physical reality, in which all the information produced by the various entities is accessible to each of them.

For example, if we observe Bob and Alice conversing, we know that the goal of their communications is to exchange

---

2   With the expression "apparently mechanical" I also refer to the fact that the determinism of classical physics does not imply long-term predictability, given the chaotic behavior of any sufficiently complex classical system.

meanings using symbols. The symbols are the vibrations of the air produced by the larynx of one that are captured by the hearing of the other. Hearing is extremely sophisticated because it allows the listener to select with free will certain frequencies and convert them into the symbols of interest, while ignoring all the others. The free-will selection made is perceived as qualia and translated into meaning by the listener. In the other direction, the choice of the meaning to be converted into symbols is made by the free will of the sender who generates the vibrations corresponding to the meaning to be transmitted. The symbols that Alice, Bob, and the other entities in the square transmit to each other become a portion of the sphere of objective and shared vibrations from which emerge the subjective experiences of Alice, Bob, and all the others.

Simple actions, like Bob conversing with Alice, involve a very complex sequence of events. Bob and Alice are seities that send and receive live symbols through their bodies. When Bob is the sender, he freely chooses the meaning to convey and creates live symbols to communicate to the cells of his body. From that moment on, his body automatically converts those live symbols into the classical symbols that are the vibrations of the air produced by the complex system of lungs, larynx, throat, tongue, mouth, and their relative muscular systems controlled by the brain. These vibrations are the classical symbols that Bob's body adds to the vibration sphere.

Alice acts as the receiver and freely chooses to listen to the vibrations produced by Bob by sending appropriate live symbols to the cells of her body that control her sophisticated hearing system to automatically tune into those frequencies that correspond to the vibrations emitted by Bob's body. These vibrations are then converted into classical symbols by Alice's auditory system and neural networks, and finally into live symbols within Alice's cells, which her consciousness then translates into the qualia corresponding to the meaning of

Bob's words. This is possible as long as she already knows the meaning of those live symbols.

The roles of Alice and Bob are then reversed in the next phase of the communication cycle during which Alice becomes the sender and Bob is the receiver. The whole cycle then repeats many times until the end of their communication, when the two take their leave.

In this example, each entity constantly repeats cycles of communication consisting of *observation, experience, and action.* Here it can be clearly seen that the inner semantic reality influences the outer symbolic reality, and vice versa. It is also evident that the vibrations emitted represent an influence from the whole to the parts, contrary to the classical materialist view in which the behavior of the whole is entirely produced by the behaviors of the parts. In other words, the movement of the air molecules of the square is also determined by the choices made by the free will of the communicating seities, and only secondarily by the elementary particles of their bodies. It should also be noted that the influences from the inner to the outer world are denied by classical physics since the existence of consciousness as a possible cause of physical phenomena is inadmissible.

At each communication cycle, each entity observes only a small portion of the vibration sphere, ignoring the rest which is considered background noise. This means that what is signal and what is noise are determined by the conscious choices of each observer. For example, my experience while I am talking to Francis will be very different from the experiences of my neighbors conversing with each other. The sounds made by them are part of my background noise, while my sounds are part of their background noise. For the neighboring dog which only pays attention to the barking of other dogs, all other sounds are background noise. So the experience of each observer is different and depends on their decisions about what to perceive, even though the objective vibration sphere is the same for everyone! Reality is therefore even more complicated than we have been told.

According to materialists, everything that happens in the physical world should be "objective." The idea that there is only one objective reality is such an extreme prejudice that it should have been abandoned a long time ago. In fact, quantum physics describes a very different world, which is also consistent with the existence of consciousness and free will. We can say that there is no objective reality independent of consciousness and free will. Instead, there are many overlapping subjective-objective realities that interact with each other.

On the other hand, it could also be said that at each instant there is only one objective reality, because each seity chooses which portion of the same reality it wishes to observe. But the free-will decisions made by the seities about what to observe change reality non-algorithmically,[3] and the free-will decisions of which symbols to emit likewise transform reality non-algorithmically, so that, at any moment, reality can change not only as a result of the laws of symbols but also due to the subjective and free-will decisions of the seities, which are not predictable by any laws.

Consequently, the evolution of the "objective" physical universe must be interpreted as the symbolic correlate of the evolution of the self-knowing of all the interacting seities. In other words, the universe that we can objectively observe is only the symbolic portion of a much vaster semantic-symbolic reality, controlled by the free will of a great number of seities

---

3 I stress that in quantum physics an observation is a measurement that changes the state of what is measured unpredictably. Therefore, the free-will decisions of which states to observe change outer reality based on the observers' inner realities.

that communicate with each other. And each seity can observe reality only from her own particular point of view, and based on her overall experience and intention.

No seity can observe the "objective" reality described by the laws of physics because the equations describing this reality are solvable only when the reference frame of the observer and the initial conditions are specified. This means that the equations must be solved based on the choices and point of view of each observer and will therefore describe different realities. There is no privileged point of view outside this reality from which this "objective reality" can be observed, for all observers are inside and part of this reality. Moreover, each observation changes the observable reality in an unpredictable way based on the free-will choices that are in turn based on the semantic reality of each observer.

In summary, we clearly see that the inner semantic reality influences the outer symbolic reality, and vice versa. We also see that the vibrations emitted or observed in response to the semantic experience of a seity represent an influence from the whole (the seity) to the parts (the atoms and molecules of the air), through the free-will choices of the quantum entity (the seity), mediated by the living organism controlled by her. This can only happen because the seities are not classical systems, and therefore they constitute a whole that is beyond the sum of the physical parts of their bodies. This whole is in fact not part of the body.

A classical system such as a robot, on the other hand, is made up of classical parts that are statistical aggregates of uncorrelated live symbols controllable only by classical symbols. Note that classical symbols are also produced and exchanged by living organisms, which are quantum-classical systems controllable by seities with live symbols. Lacking any "inner experience," the robot's parts cannot create a whole that is more than their sum.

In other words, there can be no "robot" independent of its parts that can control the parts "from the inside," even though the robot could be controlled "from the outside" by a conscious being.[4]

The situation I have described is similar to that of a pilot controlling a drone flying thousands of kilometers away. Information about the outer world and the internal state of the drone is sensed and processed by the drone and communicated to the pilot. The pilot experiences in his consciousness the situation in which the drone is operating and freely decides the drone's next moves by sending high-level commands to it. Note that the commands are based on the pilot's intentions and purposes, not the drone's, since the drone is unconscious and could never make any sense of them. In this example, the drone is to the pilot as the pilot is to the seity. The pilot, however, is a quantum-classical living organism that is much more sophisticated than the classical drone. And the seity is a quantum entity that can only exist in the vaster reality of One that contains both the inner world of meaning and the outer symbolic world of live information.

The Vibrational Universe

Even what seems inert like a stone has a certain frequency of vibrations.
—Pythagoras

We can now imagine generalizing the example of the square to the entire universe, which then becomes an ensemble of communicating seities. The vibrations that they emit and

4   In this case the robot would have to be predisposed by its designer with an interrupt facility that an outside agent could use to control its behavior, and/or some "input" instructions in its program that ask an outside agent to intervene.

observe, however, can no longer be described as classical atoms and molecules in the square, but as quantum vibrations that combine and create a vibrational space similar to the one formed by the electromagnetic waves (photons) and quantum waves of the other elementary particles. This is the space of live information.

Let us now imagine that before the appearance of living organisms, there are many seities that communicate with each other in the way I described earlier, but this time using live symbols directly, without the intermediation of living organisms (bodies). Like before, each seity decides which portion of the vibrational space to observe and which live information to add to that space. The repetition of communication cycles therefore leads to the coevolution of the symbolic vibrational space and the semantic and subjective space of self-knowing.

Since we expect correlations and correspondences between semantic and symbolic realities, the hierarchical structure that we observe in the symbolic reality suggests that the seities organize themselves in a corresponding hierarchy, starting from the CUs. The CUs are similar to the fields of elementary particles (quarks, gluons, photons, and electrons) described by physics whose states describe the live symbols they create. The concept of field is the only one we currently have available to describe entities that have no boundaries and exist everywhere in the same spacetime. However, to also represent the interiority of the seities, the fields must be conscious and have free will.

As we already discussed, the seity is a conscious entity that can also "incarnate" in a "body" that she controls. The "process of incarnation" is necessary for the seities to operate effectively within physical reality and achieve the cognitive objectives they set out to attain. It is reasonable to think that the identification of the ego with the body is not a coincidence, but is chosen by the seities to be able to make authentic and deeply felt free-will choices that could not occur if they thought they were part of a simulation. The severity of the identification varies and when the ego only pays attention to the live symbols produced by the body, the ego could completely isolate himself from the seity.

Normally there is a certain communication between the ego and the seity, which manifests in the form of intuitions, ideas, emotions, thoughts, and imaginations. The lower the degree of identification of the ego with the body, the deeper the communication between ego and seity can be. The ego perceives as "objects" what, in the vaster reality of the seities, are complex combinations of live symbols.

When the ego is totally identified with the body, he believes that the only reality is the one perceived by the body's sensory system, a belief that may lead him to censor that portion of the live symbols coming from the seity that do not involve the physical reality perceived by the body. These are the live symbols that the seity intends to communicate directly to the ego through other channels that I expect to be present in the body. It follows that the ego is led to perceive only what he is willing to accept, and this may obscure his ability to understand the nature of his inner reality and further separates him from the seity. Note that the seity and the ego are not directly measurable with instruments in spacetime and can interact with macroscopic physical objects only through a quantum-classical living organism.

Experience Is Quantum

All living beings are different phenomena of a single universal substance; they draw from the same metaphysical root, and their difference is quantitative, not qualitative.
—Giordano Bruno

I realize that these ideas may meet strong resistance from those who have embraced the materialistic and reductionistic view of reality. However, as Lord Byron said: "Opinions are meant to be changed, otherwise how can one get to the truth?"

Quantum physics has created a deep bewilderment among physicists indoctrinated in classical physics, to the point where most of them have not yet accepted its profound messages. Albert Einstein himself observed that: "The more successful quantum theory is, the more it seems nonsense." But if we take seriously what quantum physics is saying, we should take into consideration the unorthodox view I am advocating.

In a letter to Oskar Pollak dated January 27, 1904, Franz Kafka wrote:

If the book we are reading does not wake us up like a fist hammering on our skull, why are we reading it? ...what we need are those books that deeply disturb us...a book must be like an ice ax that breaks the sea of ice that is inside us.

If we consider that reality has two aspects, one inner and one outer, just like we experience, we can overcome the interpretative difficulties and the prejudices that prevent us from understanding quantum physics. And, "This is how things suddenly become clear. And then you realize how obvious they have always been" (Madeleine L'Engle).

This model is consistent both with the experimental results of physics and with the ordinary and extraordinary conscious experiences lived by those who have deeply explored their own inner reality. Only in our innermost being can we discover that the universe and life have meaning and purpose. The study of mathematical symbols alone can never reveal this truth. The experiments of physics and our mathematical theories have already said all that they can say when they revealed that: (1) the "waves" of quantum physics are probability amplitude waves, *not physical waves*; (2) the actual state that will manifest cannot be known, unless its has probability 1 of manifestation; (3) there are *distance-independent correlations* called entanglement; and (4) quantum information cannot be cloned. It is up to us to correctly interpret further these mathematical symbols.

If we accept that quantum physics describes the characteristics of inner reality, the next step should no longer be so surprising, namely, accepting the idea that we are seities that interact with the physical world through our quantum-classical bodies. The body can be compared to a semi-autonomous drone or an avatar operating in a virtual reality. The information revolution allows us to experience, and thus understand for the first time, the ability to interact "inside" virtual realities. Consequently we are now in a position to deepen the comprehension of the nature of reality and the nature of conscious experience. Moreover, the same reasoning capacity that led us to create computers and virtual realities allows us to understand that life must be both quantum and classical in order to allow seities to operate in a physical world of 3+1 dimensions.[5]

In early childhood, our consciousness has been conditioned to perceive the symbols produced by the body as "reality," making us forget little by little the symbols of our native reality. This process led us to identify with the body and partially separate the ego from the seity. Since the ego pays most of his attention to the live symbols produced by the body, he ends up believing that his intentions, emotions, and thoughts originate in the body, forgetting that he is part of a vaster reality. Qualia

5 The statistical organization of many uncorrelated live symbols forms the physical support of classical symbols such as the bits and logic gates of the computer hardware. A living cell is instead a quantum-classical structure made of highly correlated live symbols that can communicate directly with a seity with live symbols, and with the classical world using classical symbols. The presence of live information in a cell can be amplified and transformed into classical information just like our particle detectors can amplify the weak effects produced by elementary particles.

do not exist in the body, even though they have physical correlates within it.

I think it is plausible to hypothesize that we have incarnated into this physical reality to know ourselves more deeply and to facilitate the discovery that we are an integral part of a greater seity.

Consciousness, Identity, and Agency

Seities are fields that share the same dynamism, holism, and Creative Principle with One. Their properties have no definable boundaries; they are unlike any classical object, including many of the mathematical abstractions we have invented. Identity, free-will agency, and consciousness are inseparable and coemergent properties of seities. This means that identity could not exist without consciousness and agency, and the same is true for the other two. In other words, these are *indivisible* and *irreducible* aspects that are an integral part of each seity. I will therefore describe them without attempting to define them since they are inseparable.[6]

Consciousness includes the ability of the seity to have an inner conscious experience made of qualia and to recognize it as her own experience (self-consciousness). The notion of identity is implicit in this description since identity is that perspective that allows the seity to know herself as the owner and director of her own experience. Identity is what gives self-consciousness, unity, purpose, and meaning to the seity, allowing her to also recognize herself as distinct from the other seities. Finally, agency is the ability of the seity to act with free will through symbolic communications with other seities. Clearly, free

---

6 Insisting that we must define the concepts that belong to the inner reality, as we define mathematical objects, changes the nature of what we should comprehend. When we impose our vision of reality upon reality, we no longer study reality but a model of reality that is not reality.

will implies the existence of identity, intention, and purpose. The intention expresses the ultimate goal of the seity, while the purpose is the immediate goal. And the two are generally aligned and coherent with each other.

In the physical world an action generally involves pushing or pulling. However, without a body an elementary action is the free-will choice of which meaning to convert into live information to add to the vibrational space, and which portion of the vibrational space to observe and translate into meaning. Since the meaning refers to the quantum information representing the entire state of the field, live information refers to the outer state of the field, i.e., the symbols, shapes, or vibrations of the field in spacetime. The objective physical universe is therefore created from the set of these "vibrations" in spacetime.

11

The Evolution of the Seities

Birth and death are just a door through which we go in and out. Birth and death are just a game of hide and seek.
— Thich Nhat Hanh

Understanding the nature of life and consciousness, especially in connection with the death of the body, has always occupied human minds. What happens when we die? Is it the end of everything or is there something about us that survives death? The various theories that have been advanced range from one extreme, "When the body dies it is the end of us," to the other, "Our consciousness is eternal." Clearly, the body dissolves when it dies. If something survives, it must be part of the seity; therefore it is inevitable to ask: "What is the relationship between matter and consciousness?" "What is consciousness and where does it come from?"

Among the various theories, panpsychism stands out as the most natural and ancient. According to it, consciousness has always been part of the ontology of the universe. Therefore, everything that exists, such as a grain of sand, a stone, a plant, an animal, a planet, and so on, must be conscious. As scientific discoveries have clarified over time the nature of reality, various forms of panpsychism have succeeded one another. The most recent version is based on the atomism of classical physics, but it has been discredited because of the "combination problem," which has proved to be unsolvable. David Chalmers puts the problem this way: "How can micro-phenomenal properties combine to form macro-phenomenal properties?" This is the same kind of criticism that the American psychologist William James made of panpsychism at the beginning of the twentieth century, when he asked: "How can the minds of a hundred individuals agglomerate into a single compound mind, when no one has ever observed such a phenomenon?"

The Combination Problem

The panpsychism based on classical physics requires each atom to have its own individual consciousness. When two atoms combine and create a molecule, what happens to their consciousness? There are two possibilities: (1) the consciousness of the molecule is the sum of the consciousnesses of the two atoms, (2) the consciousnesses of the two atoms combine and form a third consciousness, that of the molecule.

In the first case, the consciousnesses of the two atoms do not combine at all, therefore it is impossible to explain the existence of any consciousness higher than that of the individual atoms.

In the second case we have two possibilities: the atoms lose their consciousness in the combination, or, the atoms retain their consciousness. If we accept the first possibility, we can explain the existence of a higher consciousness, but how can the two atoms lose their consciousness if this was their constitutive property? In the second possibility, there are three consciousnesses starting from two. Where does the third one come from?

This problem cannot be solved in the context of classical physics and it is precisely this impossibility that allows us to say that consciousness cannot emerge from a computer or a brain as classical structures. We have already seen that a classical system is deterministic and reductionistic, therefore its behavior is the sum of the behaviors of its parts, and there cannot be a whole that is independent of the sum of the parts. This is the reason why a classical system could only be conscious if its atoms were also conscious. But in this case no higher combination of consciousnesses could exist, exactly like in the first case described earlier.[1]

There remains one last idea to solve the combination problem, namely that consciousness may be a quantum phenomenon. This hypothesis was advanced as early as the 1930s by John von Neumann and others, when he stated, some say half-jokingly, that the observer's consciousness could be the cause of the collapse of the wave function. However, this hypothesis has remained infertile, because no one has ever managed to find a meaningful connection between the properties of consciousness and those of quantum physics.

The Solution of the Combination Problem

To my knowledge, QIP theory is the first theory that clearly recognizes the strong similarity between consciousness and a pure quantum state. QIP identifies a pure quantum state as the mathematical representation of a conscious experience by the system that is in that state. As such, it is a panpsychist theory that does not, however, have the combination problem.

To better clarify how QIP solves such a problem, let's take a molecule of sodium chloride (NaCl) as an example. NaCl is the *quantum* combination of a sodium atom (Na) and a chlorine atom (Cl). The molecule of NaCl resulting from this combination is a new entity with completely different properties from those of the two constituent atoms. In fact, the interaction of very many NaCl molecules forms a hard crystal, whereas many sodium atoms combine into a soft solid, and many chlorine atoms form a gas. The transformation of the properties of a single sodium atom and the properties of a single chlorine atom into the

---

1   Within classical physics the combination problem does not exist because atoms are not supposed to be conscious. However, the unsolved problem is the following: "If the matter of which we are made is unconscious, how come we are conscious?"

completely new properties of one molecule of sodium chloride is a quantum phenomenon that classical physics cannot explain. Within classical physics, the state of a system composed of a sodium atom and a chlorine atom that bounce elastically against each other would simply be the sum of the two. Instead, their quantum combination creates a new entity with an entirely new set of properties in which the two atoms have *lost their former identity*.

If each atom were conscious, the quantum combination of the two into a molecule would lead to the elimination of the consciousness of the atoms that combined. If the molecule were later split into its two component atoms, the consciousness of the molecule would be lost and be regained by the two atoms. This makes the idea that atoms and molecules are individually conscious inconsistent. However, we already know that the elementary particles of which the atoms are "made" do not exist as objects separate from their corresponding fields. Therefore it is reasonable to assume that the conscious entities are the fields and not the particles, which are simply the states of the fields that are inseparable from the fields.[2]

The combination problem arises only when we do not recognize *that consciousness is a quantum property of a field and not a property of the states of a field.* When the "sodium" seity (a field) found a way to combine with the "chlorine" seity for the first time, the two gave birth to the "sodium chloride" seity, which is a new field with semantic and symbolic properties completely different from those of their components. The sodium chloride molecule is then a state of the NaCl seity, and therefore it is not conscious, for it is a "form" within the NaCl field. The field is the conscious entity, not the states of the field. When a NaCl

---

2   A state of a field can be imagined as a wave in the sea. The wave is a ripple on the surface of the sea that cannot be separated from the sea. Therefore, the consciousness of the ripple would be a property of the sea.

molecule is divided into its component atoms, it no longer exists as a state of the NaCl field; however, the consciousness of the field does not undergo any change, just like our consciousness would not disappear if our body were destroyed.

The combination of two seities into a higher-order seity can be explained as a quantum phenomenon due to the superposition and entanglement of two fields that would lead to the formation of a new field of higher dimensionality. The identity symbol of the new field is the quantum combination of the identity symbols of the component fields, with new and unexpected properties, like in the example of the NaCl molecule. In other words, two seities are two distinct fields that can give birth to a new field, without ceasing to exist. We must not confuse the quantum combination of the identity symbols with the combination of the fields (seities).

The combination problem can therefore be solved in the context of QIP theory, since consciousness is a quantum phenomenon and the quantum superposition of two pure states creates a new pure state with very different characteristics than their components. This would be impossible if consciousness were a classical phenomenon. *Consciousness is purely quantum, and so is free will,* as we will see later.

The attribution of consciousness and free will to quantum systems that are in a pure state with the conversion from quantum information to live information, and vice versa, has enormous consequences in science, philosophy, and spirituality. In this theory, free will and consciousness coexist and allow the existence of systems capable of transforming meaning (represented by quantum information) into live information, and vice versa. This is based on the capacity of such systems to direct their own conscious experience with free will.

How could a pure quantum state that is not knowable by anybody correspond to any reality? Stipulating that a pure quantum state can be *known* by the "system" that is in that state gives a reason for the existence and purpose of quantum information, leading to a completely new interpretation of the nature of reality that returns meaning and purpose to the universe.

Semantic and Symbolic Spaces

If we start with the assumption that there exists a vaster quantum reality made up of seities that communicate symbolically with each other, then the universe currently described by physics represents only the symbolic aspect of the communications of the seities. With this new assumption, what we call spacetime could be directly linked to the specific representation of reality created by the body used by the seity. In other words, the "objects interacting in spacetime" that we perceive and believe to be reality are primarily determined by the nature of the information sensing and processing performed by the particular body through which the seity observes and acts within the symbolic reality.

It is therefore useful to introduce two concepts that will help us visualize the reality of the seities prior to the existence of spacetime, the nature of which is probably less fundamental than it is now considered in physics. I call these two concepts *C-space* and *I-space*. C-space is the space of the private conscious experiences of the seities that collectively make up the subjective inner world of experience. I-space is the symbolic space of live information constituting the objective vibrational space shared by all seities as previously described. C-space and I-space are indivisible and represent the two subjective-objective, semantic-symbolic, and inner-outer aspects of the basic reality of the communicating seities. These spaces are extra-physical and do not need to be tridimensional.

We have seen that the communication of each seity consists of an *observation* phase, during which the seity chooses which shared symbols of I-space to observe, followed by an *experiential* phase in which the seity translates the observed symbols into subjective meaning in C-space. Then the *action* phase follows, in which the seity chooses which portion of her meaning to translate into objective and shared symbols to be added to I-space. Then the communication cycle of each seity describes the transformations from I-space to C-space, and vice versa, controlled by her free will. In this model, the interactions between inner and outer reality play a fundamental role in the evolution of One. Free-will agency, identity, and consciousness express the intention and ability of each seity to guide her own experience and pursue her self-knowing. At the same time, each seity also contributes to the self-knowing of the other seities in a deeply cooperative enterprise. The self-knowing of One is the superposition of all the self-knowing of the seities that have emerged from It.

As the seities know themselves, the live symbols evolve and transform, creating ever more sophisticated languages suitable for representing their ever-growing self-knowing. This evolution is a process similar to that of our languages that spontaneously coevolved with our knowing. The symbols and the symbolic laws that created what we call the inanimate universe represent the first stage of the coevolution of symbols and meaning of the seities.

The next stage created biological life.[3] By studying live symbols, the seities realized that the formal properties of the symbols could help them deepen their own self-knowing. Through a highly cooperative process, this study gradually led to the creation of increasingly complex symbolic structures which culminated in the creation of the first living cell. Cells are semi-autonomous symbols that reproduce and allow the seities to explore I-space, the objective world of symbols, through them.

---

3   Life in the broad sense of the term is the fundamental property of One
    to create CUs that reflect Its image and likeness, a property that the CUs
    also inherit.

The invention-development-evolution of biological life has allowed the seities to deepen their own self-knowing through the exploration of I-space, a symbolic space that reflects the inner structure of meaning in the outer structure of its live symbols and syntactical laws. Therefore the study of I-space helps the seities know themselves, just like the study of our languages helps us know ourselves.

By following a similar path, we have learned to use matter (classical information) to create the technologies that have made possible the building of computers, drones, and immersive virtual realities accessible with special headsets. In this manner human beings are able to explore objective symbolic worlds by using their own consciousness. These virtual realities, built with classical information, exist as small subsets inside the sea of live information that forms I-space.

Biological life reflects the need of the seities to recreate at the symbolic level, through the exquisite workings of living organisms, the semantic structures they recognize within their own direct self-knowing (meaning). This is an extraordinary cognitive opportunity, deriving from the homomorphism between the symbols and their meaning that spontaneously emerged in the coevolution of the two. This is also what happens when we use poetry or music to find a deeper expressive capacity in our ordinary symbols, allowing us to translate what we feel by going beyond the ordinary limits of classical symbols. "Every poem is mysterious. Nobody fully knows what they have been allowed to write" (Jorge Luis Borges). And the poet Alfred Tennyson observes that:

Words, like Nature, half reveal
And half conceal the Soul within.

I think that the creation of biological life represents the crowning achievement of a collective cognitive process by the seities through which they discovered that their live symbols and symbolic laws allowed them to create self-reproducing live symbols![4] *Reproduction* is the fundamental property with which One created the CUs in Its own image and likeness. It is the origin of Life! This capacity has been inherited by the seities, for they also can create other seities out of themselves. Reproducing reproduction at the symbolic level is an expression of monumental creativity and intelligence that allows open-ended cognitive progress in new directions.

In the proposed model, we can imagine a CU like a single cell, a seity like a multicellular organism, and One like the environment that contains, sustains, and connects all biological entities. In this analogy, living organisms are part of the physical environment (I-space) and yet they are inseparable from it since they are open and dependent on it. These organisms are patterns of interactivity within, and of, the environment, for their borders are wide open and live information is constantly exchanged between each organism and the environment. Yet, every organism is conscious, has a unique identity, and can act with free will to pursue its own experiences.

These latter properties, however, do not exist within I-space but in C-space, the vaster semantic space that "contains" I-space and can be represented with quantum information. C-space contains seities, i.e., fields that can transform qualia into live symbols, and vice versa, to communicate with each other directly, or to communicate with living organisms which behave like immensely sophisticated drones. In other words, each organism is only a dynamic pattern of live information that exchanges information within I-space. Some of the informational exchange is between the organism and the seity, though the organism is

---

4   The creation of the first living cell represents an achievement equivalent to that which humans will make when their scientific progress allows them to integrate information technology with biology.

not conscious and thus it has no way to know where the I-space symbols it observes are coming from, just like in the case of a drone in spacetime.

The evolution of living cells made possible the creation of a huge variety of virtual worlds in which the seities could "incarnate" in different forms (live symbols) and explore symbolic worlds within I-space. Each virtual world has its own live symbols and symbolic laws and serves to deepen specific aspects of self-knowing of the incarnating seities. I call P-space the "physical world" experienced by the seity that believes herself to be the organism in which she is incarnated. P-space will then mirror the specific informational reality of I-space that is observed and processed by the organism. This reality derives from the unique sensory-brain-actuators possessed by the organism and through the free-will decisions of the seity in C-space that controls the organism and experiences the live information created by it.

Therefore, the true causes of the events occurring in P-space cannot be found in either P- or I-space. The real causes are the free-will decisions of the CUs and seities occurring in C-space. It is important to realize that One does not have any exteriority and cannot be found anywhere in either I-space or P-space.

There Is Much More Than Physical Space

I envision the experience of a non-incarnated seity in C-space to be a completely natural process in which the transformations from live symbols to meaning, and vice versa, are automatic, and the seity knows her conscious experience based on qualia. In other words, the seity does not need to know anything about the "mechanisms" by which she naturally interacts with the live symbols of I-space. We could compare this experience to that of a child who knows nothing about the functioning of the world in which he finds himself. He follows his inclinations and impulses, choosing the things he wants to pay attention to and the actions to take.

Without a body, the actions of a seity are communications, i.e., automatic transformations from meaning to live symbols, and vice versa, spontaneously performed by the quantum seity interacting directly with I-space symbols. These live symbols are the "objects" that populate the "universe" in which the seity exists. It is likely that initially the seities didn't know anything about the live information they emitted and observed. Their *rational* capacity to pose questions and find answers was probably a later conquest allowing them to investigate "from the outside" the inner structure of their own meaning reflected in the symbols of their natural language.

This conquest was probably a direct consequence of their comprehension that the live symbols could also be used as long-term memory to store the meaning of their experiences. This crucial achievement would allow the seities to develop a form of metacognition that led to the gradual evolution of rationality, a process that humankind repeated with the invention of writing.

Comprehension combined with rationality then made possible the creation of new symbolic structures capable of representing their increasing self-knowing, leading to the gradual development of living cells as their proficiency in the manipulation of live symbols increased. These marvelous structures allowed the seities to examine the "functioning" of the symbolic world *from the point of view of another symbol*.

This new creative and intellectual development led the seities to eventually evolve human bodies to capture and expand their ever-higher level of comprehension. Operating through human bodies, the seities could then create new types of *classical symbols* that could not happen by chance. I am speaking of our machines, computers, artificial intelligence, and robots that would allow, once more, the dramatic extension of the range of virtual realities that the seities could eventually explore with new types of bodies that combine live and classical symbols. We have now arrived at the threshold of this possible future for humankind.

The creation of the first living cell allowed seities to have a *conscious* experience of the symbolic world, as perceived through the "senses" and the "processing" of live information made by cells and increasingly complex multicellular living organisms. A seity comprehends the live symbols within a cell, and can interpret them from the point of view of the cell through her unique qualia. Moreover, the seity can manipulate these live symbols inside the cell, while respecting the probabilistic syntactical rules of the live symbols. In other words, the seity controls a cell as if it were a drone belonging to I-space.

This situation is similar to that of the early video games in which the screen represents a virtual reality with an avatar, which is the equivalent of a drone, seen from the outside. The player (the seity) controls the avatar by perceiving the avatar, the virtual reality, and the physical reality in which the screen and the computer exist. By manipulating remote controls, the player directs the avatar according to her will and observes the virtual reality, well aware that such reality is part of a larger reality that contains it.

The next step in the evolution of video games is represented by "immersive" virtual realities in which the player wears a headset and a costume that allows him to observe the virtual reality, and act in it, entirely from the point of view of the avatar. By moving naturally, the player controls the body of the avatar automatically and, if she is in a quiet room, she will perceive only the signals coming from the virtual reality. Under these conditions, the player might easily identify with the avatar and end up paying attention only to the signals coming from it, forgetting—if only for a short period of time—that she actually exists in a greater physical reality containing the virtual reality.

She will certainly notice this fact if the signals coming from the virtual reality were to suddenly cease (the "death" of the avatar), a situation that would be like waking up from a vivid dream. A similar condition also applies to a seity embodied in a living organism when she becomes completely identified with the symbolic reality perceived by the organism. Believing herself to be the organism through which she operates in the physical world, she will only pay attention to the symbols produced by the organism. Only when the organism dies can she realize that she had not been paying attention to the other symbols of the vaster reality in which she existed (I-space). She had been so captivated by her adventures that she forgot her true nature.

The Nature of P-space

The physical space and the objects experienced by the seity during her "incarnation" in P-space result from her "coloring" the symbolic representation of I-space made by the organism with her native qualia. In other words, the seity that has identified with the organism ends up interacting only with the live symbols that form the representation of I-space created by the organism, forgetting that such a world is a secondary, reduced reality, contained in the greater fundamental reality of I-space. This interpretation naturally leads to the sensible hypothesis that the physical reality we believe to be foundational may only be a vastly reduced reality produced primarily by the information processing performed by our physical body.

However, the body could in turn be a symbolic structure that is part of another more fundamental symbolic structure also existing in I-space, in Chinese-box style. The world of dreams and the worlds explored by those who "leave the body" through an OBE (Out of Body Experience) could then be explained if our physical body were itself contained within an "astral" body existing in a greater symbolic reality that is not yet the fundamental reality.

In this case the astral reality would be contained in I-space and there would then be three different kinds of live symbols: physical, astral, and mental, producing respectively the physical, emotional, and mental qualia experienced in C-space by the seity. Physical symbols would then be combinations of more fundamental astral symbols, and these would be combinations of even more fundamental mental symbols, the latter being the native symbols of I-space. The evidence of OBE and lucid dreams, in which the dreamer's ego knows he is dreaming and can partially control the progress of the dream, could then be explained by this type of hypothesis.

With the death of the organism, the seity loses her identification with P-space and realizes that she exists in another reality where she enjoys a different and greater freedom. Of this we can have an intuition thanks to the evocative power of Giordano Bruno's verses in *Of the Infinite, Universe, and Worlds*:

Therefore safe wings I offer to the air
nor do I fear intrusion of crystal or glass;
but I fly the skies, and to infinity I rise.

In this view, dying is nothing more than waking up from a "vivid dream" in which the seity was convinced she existed, and opening up to a vaster experience while retaining the same identity.

If this is the case, then truly the day of death becomes a *dies natalis*, as Lucius Annaeus Seneca writes in *Moral Letters to Lucilius*:

This day that you fear as the last is the birthday into eternity... The day will come in which the mysteries of nature will be revealed to you, the haze that surrounds us will dissolve, and a radiance will strike us from all sides, combining and merging within itself the light of the stars. No shadow will disturb that serenity and the sky will shine with the same light: day and night alternate only in this lowest part of the cosmos. We will become aware of the darkness of this mortal life when, with our whole being, we will gaze at all the splendor that now comes to us, and only minimally, through the too-narrow passage of our eyes. What will that light look like to you when you will see it in its source?

Precisely because we all dream, we can all understand how we can become engrossed, identified, with different realities to the point of believing that only those realities exist. Within this context, an incarnation may severely limit the degree of freedom available in our native reality since the body is a symbol subject to the stricter laws of the virtual reality in which it exists and operates.

In summary, P-space exists only as the experience of the ego of the live symbols produced by the organism he controls. The ego is that portion of a seity's consciousness that believes himself to be the organism. The objectivity of P-space is only apparent, for it is shared only by all the egos that interact with I-space through a body of the same species. Different organisms such as a fish, an eagle, a lion, or a tree allow a seity/ego to explore a vast range of different P-spaces. And when the organism dies, the ego "returns" to the vaster reality from which he actually never "moved" away.[5]

P-space is like a virtual reality created by the organism— even though the qualia with which such reality is perceived are those native to the seity. The crucial difference between the native reality and the one experienced by an embodied ego is that the native one comes from the seity's direct interaction with

---

5 In the book *Silicon* [1] I introduced this same conceptual framework called the *CIP framework*, in which C stands for Consciousness space, I stands for Information space, and P stands for Physical space.

"unprocessed" I-space symbols while P-space comes from the I-space symbols produced by the living organism that observes I-space with its specific sensory-brain system.

Finally, it is worth noting that, if we start from the hypothesis that CUs and seities existed before physical reality, the concepts of space, time, matter, and energy, which are considered primitives in physics, must be reconceptualized as deriving directly from the nature of the seities' interactions with I-space. This new vision requires a complete rethinking of what we have hitherto accepted as fundamental axioms. The result will be an immensely significant new science that unifies our inner and outer realities. I believe the union of science and spirituality is the necessary step to solving the outstanding problems we are facing at this critical juncture in human history.

12

Knowing, Life, and Information

Knowing is a light of the soul.
— Meister Eckhart

The dream of contemporary physicists is to be able to find a theory of everything that explains all phenomena, starting from a unified field and a universal law. This is not very different from the materialistic assumptions of classical physicists who tried to explain everything starting from elementary particles which were thought to be the simplest possible *objects*. Now the objects have become states of quantum fields, a more abstract concept, but the essence of the new plan is a *physicalist assumption* not much different than materialism since it assumes that the universe is an information-processing system, i.e., an abstract machine ruled by an algorithm. Therefore, everything contained in the universe is another abstract machine.

In my opinion we are still too influenced by classical physics which tells us that the world is made of separate parts, and comforts us by saying that at the macroscopic scale the world works perfectly well as described by it. Here it is in the words of 1988 Nobel Prize winner, American physicist Leon Max Lederman: "When enormous quantities of atoms unite to form macroscopic objects (airplanes, bridges, and robots), the disturbing and counterintuitive quantum phenomena, with their load of uncertainty, seem to cancel each other out and bring the phenomena back into the precise predictability of Newtonian physics." This is only partially true, however, given the indeterminism and nonlocal nature of quantum physics and the presence of chaotic systems.[1]

However, quantum physics, from which classical physics emerges as a subset, tells us instead that there are neither separate parts, nor particles as objects; nor does probability exist as we imagined it in classical physics. Therefore, there is *becoming* in the universe which cannot be predicted by any equation or algorithm. This means that the universe could have evolved in an infinity of possible ways using exactly the same laws. In fact, these laws contain 25 physical constants that need to be adjusted with extreme precision to create the universe in which we live, based on *a posteriori* knowledge. How did those parameters happen to have those specific fine-tuned values we assigned to them to match what we now measure in our universe?

Finally, I point out that the union of quantum physics with an adequate theory of quantum gravity, as now proposed, would still not be able to explain the origin of life, consciousness, and free will—and therefore it would not be a theory of everything— unless these properties were incorporated into the properties of the unified field, which would then become what I call One. Then the evolution of the universe no longer needs to be dictated by impersonal laws with 25 predetermined fine-tuned physical constants whose origin cannot be explained. In fact,

---

1 In note 9 of Chapter 1 we saw that the equations of classical physics describe nonlinear systems that are chaotic, i.e., systems that are deterministic but unpredictable after some time because their behaviors are very sensitive to their initial conditions. This means that the behaviors of two identical systems differing only by a tiny change in their initial conditions end up being very different after a sufficiently long time. Moreover, any minor disturbance along the way, impossible to predict in an open and interconnected system like our universe, would add other sources of exponential change as the systems evolve.

each of these constants acts like an axiom within the current Standard Model of particle physics.

In the current scientific methodology, we have replaced the comprehension of reality with an intellectual understanding of the mathematical theory of reality, as if the two were the same. Thus, the comprehension of reality is exhausted by saying: "It is this way because the mathematics says so." This attitude would be almost correct if we were sure that the mathematical theory of reality accurately describes *all* reality, but we know instead that the current theories leave out life, consciousness, and free will, the very aspects that give meaning to the universe.

Moreover, mathematics can only describe the symbolic aspect of reality, not the semantic aspect. Mathematics is only descriptive and not prescriptive, as it is widely believed. Mathematics is not ontology and cannot create conscious seities. Mathematics cannot give birth to a brain, whereas brains guided by the creativity of seities can give birth to mathematics.

To create a model of physical reality we need a body capable of interacting with reality and equipped with a brain controlled by a sufficiently evolved seity to be able to create valid concepts starting from observations and interactions with reality. Only seities can evolve the brains that, properly supervised, can then create the mathematics that explains the symbolic reality they collectively created in other ways. It makes no sense to think that the seities designed the universe starting from mathematics. In this model they started by communicating with each other, following their own nature, and evolved a universe that reflected that nature. Mathematics could much later describe the self-consistency of the observable reality for the simple reason that, for a universe to exist, it must be logically self-consistent. But mathematics alone can bring neither the universe nor itself into existence.

In the previous chapters I have portrayed a very different reality from the one described starting from materialistic assumptions. This different reality seems to function more like a living organism than a machine because it is made of *parts-whole* like the seities. We generally think that the elementary particles make up the whole by combining, as in classical physics; however, this is not the case because the ontology belongs to the quantum fields. The fields are the parts-whole and the particles are simply their states that are "connected from within." From the outside the particles appear separable, but in reality they are entangled in an unknowable way.

In the previous chapter we have seen that the conscious comprehension of a seity allows her to gradually perceive the invisible links forming the inner structure of the meaning she feels. The desire to communicate that meaning then renders visible and objective a portion of the meaning through *the complexity* of the symbols necessary to *represent it*. Thus, symbols take on a structure that is homomorphic to the inner structure of the meaning. The most complex live symbol we know to exist is the ecosystem of our planet, which consists of about 10^{41} atoms closely interacting with each other!

The World of Knowing

During the last 20 years we have realized that quantum information cannot be cloned, and therefore it represents a world that is invisible and unknowable from the outside. But what is the sense of "information that is unknowable" if it does not make sense at least to the system that holds that state? In the new axiom of QIP, a pure state represents the "experience" or meaning of a quantum system that is in that state. The ontology is thus the meaning of a *private experience*, and since the representation must reflect the ontology, and not vice versa, the mathematical representation of a private state must be a non-clonable state, a state that cannot be known from the outside.

All that can be known must then follow Holevo's theorem, i.e., it cannot be more than a classical bit for each quantum bit contained in the pure state.

Note that the existence and the properties of pure quantum states have been imposed by the properties of Hilbert space, the only mathematical structure we found to be adequate to display the behavior of quantum systems. To describe these systems, we must use the concept of non-clonable information, which would make no sense if it did not represent something significant for such systems. It is therefore perfectly fitting to attribute consciousness to a quantum system that is in a pure state, even though this attribution brings interiority into physical reality.

On the other hand, how can we explain the existence of consciousness if we do not admit the existence of interiority? As the philosopher Joseph Levine states: "No explanation given entirely in physical terms can ever account for conscious experience." Consciousness is something that cannot be explained in simpler terms than itself, therefore it must be an elementary constitutive property of a private reality, just like the particles (excited states of the quantum fields) are the elementary constitutive properties of a public reality. This simple starting point avoids having to later explain what would otherwise require miracles.

Within QIP theory, the inner and the outer realities are connected by stating that the conscious experience of a seity (a quantum field) can be represented by a pure quantum state. We thus have a suitable mathematical representation of inner knowing, or meaning. This theory can then explain for the first time a baffling mathematical fact about the quantum world: the existence of information that cannot be reproduced. I claim that such information represents the private meaning of a field whose excited states are the symbolic, shareable information with which the field expresses a portion of its meaning.

With this interpretation, the entire philosophical conception of physics changes, because the existence of an inner, private reality implies that there is a purpose and a meaning in the universe, a position that physics has never before accepted as valid.

With this highly plausible axiom, unexpected new possibilities arise to answer the many unresolved questions we have accumulated so far. I believe that we can now finally solve the measurement problem that has puzzled physicists since the beginning of quantum physics. The "collapse of the wave function" which occurs with an irreversible transformation from a quantum state to a classical one can now be interpreted as a free-will decision by a seity that creates a state that cannot be predicted by any algorithm.

The World of Life

As we have already discussed, life is another major unsolved problem of science. If the universe were indeed like it is described by the laws of physics, it would have to be inanimate, just like all the other planets in the solar system appear to be. The existence of life on our planet is a huge "anomaly" that has never been adequately explained. And the more we know about quantum physics, the more it seems impossible that life could have self-organized out of natural phenomena.

Molecular biologists have always considered life as a phenomenon explainable with classical physics. Only in the last 20 years has a small avant-garde of scientists started to study life as a quantum phenomenon. I think that life is both a quantum and a classical phenomenon, with new and unsuspected properties that will lead us to a deeper understanding of the nature of reality. To me, life is the fundamental strategy with which One can know Itself, for self-knowing must be a "lived" experience, and life is therefore the process through which each seity progressively comprehends the meaning of her own experience and knows herself. Each seity gradually makes her self-knowing explicit, first inside and then outside herself, via symbolic constructions made of live and classical information. This information can be copied and therefore communicated, leading to the proliferation of meanings (comprehensions) that were originally private, each known only by a single seity.

This knowing feeds the collective cognitive processes, accelerating the self-knowing of One. The great mystical poet Jalal al-Din Rumi wrote:

Do you know what you are? You are a manuscript of a divine letter.

You are a mirror reflecting a noble face.

This universe is not outside of you.

Look inside yourself; everything you want is already there.

I note that we also use a similar process to comprehend. For example, when we want to clarify an idea, we represent it on a piece of paper, or we may build a physical model, or write a computer program that makes a dynamic simulation of it. The marks we make on a piece of paper, on a computer memory, or on a physical model represent the long-term memory of the "symbolic construction" that represents our comprehension using classical information. When the construction "works," it means that we have understood. This comprehension then applies not only to us but also to many other people who would not have been able to comprehend on their own. They do so by observing the functioning model that is shareable because it is made of classical information. The classical model functions then like a "mental enzyme" that lowers the "barrier" to comprehension.

To me, this is the essence of the creative process with which lived experiences lead to the *coevolution of quantum information (meaning), live information (life), and classical information (matter).*[2] This process also explains why classical physics must exist since it allows the creation of long-term memory, and shareable dynamical models that spread the comprehensions among the seities. Thus, the seities do not forget their experiences and can *cooperatively* continue to deepen their meanings by communicating with live and classical symbols. If the purpose of One is to know Itself, all Its self-knowing must be preserved and deepened.

The lived experience is that obtained through the embodiment of a seity into a living organism. The organism transforms the classical information of the environment into live information which is then experienced and comprehended by the seity as a reality that illuminates and accelerates its self-knowing process. This process requires two distinct classes of transformations: (1) transformations of live information into quantum information, and vice versa, performed by the embodied seity that communicates with the organism, and (2) transformations of live information into classical information, and vice versa, performed by the living organism interacting with the world of live and classical information.

The world of classical information is purely symbolic and represents the material world that has hitherto been considered "everything that exists" by science. The world of live information is represented by atoms and molecules "organized" into living organisms. Living organisms are parts-whole that can maintain their self-coherence for some time and reproduce. Such

---

2 Coherent (i.e., correlated, ordered) combinations of live information create other live information, while classical information is created with incoherent (uncorrelated, disordered) combinations of live symbols to which we attribute meaning through agreements.

organisms require live information and could not exist in the world of classical information that is supported by incoherent (disorganized, uncorrelated) matter.

Live information is something in between quantum and classical information. Something that so far has not been clearly identified. I imagine it as information that could only be represented by a dynamical classical system with infinite precision. As such, it could only be partially *simulated* by a computer but not *emulated* because something would always be left out, given the limited precision of any computer. Here is where the "infinity" of the qubits intrudes into the finiteness of any classical representation.

Live information has not lost its connection with the wholeness of the quantum world that describes the ontology of experience. Our consciousness can sense that infinity and respond. A computer cannot. A living organism passively reflects that infinity into its functioning since it is made of live information. Thus a living organism, even as a physical system only, cannot be fully simulated by a digital computer.

The World of Classical Information

The classical physical world can be described with classical information represented by collections of large numbers of uncorrelated quantum states forming macroscopic "objects." When the probabilistic behaviors of those quantum states are averaged, their collective behavior ends up obeying the deterministic laws of classical physics. Therefore, within a classical system, the concept of information makes no sense at all since the next state is always determined by the application of a deterministic algorithm to the previous state. Thus, the next state has always probability 1 to occur.[3]

---

3 Note that the amount of information carried by a symbol (state) is defined as the cologarithm of the probability of observing that state. Therefore, the

If we analyze the amount of information carried by the state of a classical computer, we will find that the evolution of its state is predictable by those who know the program and how the computer works. Therefore, the amount of information conveyed to them by each of its states is 0. For those who are ignorant, the next state is unpredictable, and therefore it may carry a lot of information. For those who have partial knowledge, the amount of information has an intermediate value. Therefore, the assumption that the quantity of information is objective, as we have been generally told, can only be true if all observers are equally ignorant, or do not exist. But what would be the point of information if there were no observers? To proceed any further it is necessary to reexamine the concept of probability.

What Is Probability?

Probability is expectation founded upon partial knowledge. A perfect acquaintance with all the circumstance affecting the occurrence of an event would change expectation into certainty, and leave neither room nor demand for a theory of probabilities.
—George Boole

The concept of probability, which most physicists consider objective and which underlies not only classical statistical physics but even more subtly quantum physics, has never been satisfactorily resolved. According to the famous statistician and mathematician Bruno de Finetti, *probability does not exist*, and I completely agree with him. I think that probability is a human

---

amount of information carried by a state that has probability 1 of occurring is 0 since the cologarithm of 1 is 0. But the definition of information assumes that the probability is objective. Is that true? The next paragraph in the main text will tell.

concept, inextricably linked to the degree of knowledge of a conscious observer who wants to act based on his predictions of the next state. This concept makes no sense for an unconscious, deterministic (classical) system which has no way to change its future state.

Probability cannot be objective, because it is closely linked to the expectations of a conscious observer endowed with free will, for knowing is a property of consciousness, and knowing the probability without being able to act based on that knowledge would make no sense. In other words, probability is largely subjective.

Considering probability a concept independent of the consciousness and free will of the observer, as if it were an objective *physical* variable, is, in my opinion, another big misunderstanding that has largely contributed to the incomprehensibility of quantum physics in which this concept is central. Probability is about knowledge, and only consciousness can know. Therefore probability has relevance only if consciousness exists! The fact that quantum physics is about probability is saying that the physical universe is about knowing! The white elephant in the room is thus consciousness!

Probability is a fundamental variable in quantum physics because the wave function represents the "probability amplitude" of a quantum state whose square gives us the probability of its manifestation. In other words, quantum physics does not describe the evolution of the actual state of a system like classical physics does, but rather the evolution of the probabilities of all the states that we might measure, i.e., know. Therefore, quantum physics primarily represents what we may be able to know about the system rather than how the system will actually behave.

An unconscious robot may be able to calculate probabilities, but only if the human programmer *so determined* in its program. This fact does not give objectivity to probability since the robot is blindly obeying its program to compute what we call probability and does not know what it is calculating. The robot does not make any prediction based on its judgment because it has none of its own. We are the ones who made the estimate we have called "probability" and are forcing the robot to comply, for a robot is totally unaware. Thus, the robot is not responsible for the consequences of its actions. The responsibility is only ours.

I would also like to point out that Shannon's definition of information, which refers to classical systems, would be inconsistent if it did not secretly refer to *conscious observers* held to be *separate* from the observed system, and thus unable to affect what they observe. This assumption actually works well with classical systems because the observation can occur without appreciably disturbing the system. However, with quantum systems that are described by quantum information, the observation deeply affects what is observed, and thus there is no longer independence between observer and observed. Therefore, when the observer cannot be separated from the universe, his decision of what to observe changes the universe. Moreover, since information is the cologarithm of probability, quantum physics ultimately deals only with quantum information, and thus with knowing (conscious experience).

Note that since probability only makes sense if it implies the existence of consciousness and free will, the problem of consciousness—which has been kicked out the door—comes back through the window in the form of the subjective probability of quantum physics. Only when we recognize that quantum information describes the knowing of conscious observers can quantum physics be understood.

Information Makes Sense Only if There Is Consciousness

We have seen that within a deterministic system the concept of information makes no sense because every action is perfectly predictable. Moreover, if the universe were deterministic, the notions of observer and probability would make no sense whatsoever, for inside such a universe everything is preordained, and outside it no observer could exist. Curiously, there is an ontological interpretation of reality called *Block Universe* that is endorsed by the physicists who consider the theory of general relativity as fundamental. In such interpretation, the universe has always existed as a sequence of three-dimensional "frames" along a four-dimensional direction that represents time. Time therefore does not exist, for which reason this interpretation is also called *eternalism*.

According to the Block Universe, our experience of existing in a three-dimensional space and moving in time with free will is an illusion. Therefore the Block Universe has eliminated from reality the only part of us that knows about existing and Existence! If the Block Universe existed, the one who came up with the idea of the Block Universe should not exist. In other words, the existence of our consciousness falsifies the hypothesis that the Block Universe exists.

At this point it should be clear that the concepts of observer, consciousness, knowledge, meaning, probability, information, and symbols are intimately interconnected and would make no sense if the Whole were deterministic and reductionistic. Treating these concepts as if they were separable is logically inconsistent. For example, the probability that defines classical information makes no sense unless there are conscious observers inside a deterministic universe, but such observers could not be part of that universe! In fact, to contain a conscious observer with free will, the universe must be indeterministic. Therefore, the deterministic portion of that universe, if it exists, should be contained as a special case within the indeterministic universe.

The concept of information makes sense only in connection with the concept of open-ended knowing, never completed, concerning conscious observers with free will. Omniscience would spell the end of consciousness and the end of existence because there would be nothing more to know! Moreover, the existence of a universal consciousness without the existence of other conscious entities, each with their own individual consciousness, would not make sense because in this case there would only be One observing Itself and no other. But this hypothesis cannot be true because we are here and we are conscious. And each one of us is a part-whole of One, and One is also "within" each of us.

Consciousness only makes sense if it belongs to observers who wish to increase their own knowing. And this requires the existence of new, creative states, i.e., of new meaning and new symbols, and therefore of new information. But this type of information is more like a combination of live information and quantum information that for the time being I will call Information with a capital "I." It can therefore be said that the necessary and sufficient condition for the existence of Information is the existence of consciousness! But consciousness would not make sense without entities who want and can know more by directing their own knowing toward increasing Information. This is the reason why free will and the open becoming of the universe must exist as well.

This Information is what I earlier called C-space and I-space, the irreducible interiority and exteriority of the universe, One. I-space is the collection of the states of the Field, the unified field that theoretical physicists are currently trying to define. These states are inseparable from the Field, and the Field currently is not intended to have free will and consciousness. The Field with consciousness and free will is a completely different entity that I have previously called One. The self-knowing (meaning) of One is represented by the pure quantum state of the Field, which is the superposition of the pure states of all the fields that have emanated from One, which I have called seities. The excited states of the Field represent the vibrational sphere, i.e., the ensemble of all the live symbols used by the fields (seities) to communicate and explore their meaning.

Consciousness, observer, knowledge, pure quantum states, and meaning are an integral part of the aspect that I have called *interiority*, while live information, probability, mixed states, and symbols are part of the other aspect that I have called *exteriority*. But these two aspects must be indivisible, because consciousness and information, as well as meaning and symbols, make sense only if both exist together. Without conscious observers, each having their own unique point of view and capable of symbolically communicating with each other, there would be nothing to know, nothing to discover, nothing to rejoice with, and nothing to love.

This is the reason why the universe cannot be classical. If it were, we could not exist, because consciousness and free will cannot exist in a classical universe. And yet a classical universe is intimately connected with live information which is homomorphic with quantum information and indivisible from it. The classical universe emerges from live information (statistical ensembles of uncorrelated states of live information), like live information (entangled quantum states in spacetime) emerges from quantum information (pure quantum states) that represents the ontology of meaning that can only be known privately within the fields (seities). The classical universe has the same type of existence as a virtual reality created by a computer. Moreover, the existence of entanglement tells us that all the parts of the universe are interconnected, that there is becoming, and that free will allows us to explore the world of meaning and transform new meaning into new symbols. *This is the essence of our individual and collective creativity.*

This is also why the knowing of a highly evolved seity can only be adequately expressed with a complex live symbol such as a human being, i.e., an organization of 10^{28} atoms, and the knowing of a much more evolved seity that is much greater than ours could be expressed using the ecosystem of our planet, a live symbol that uses 10^{41} atoms. The complexity of these symbols gives us a measure of how vast is the knowing of the seities that communicate with each other!

Knowing and Live Information

We have seen that knowing can only occur through *lived experiences* that cause the seities *to become* what they know. Organic life exists to enable the seities to make new experiences through living organisms which, in this view, *are creations of the seities that coevolve in step with their self-knowing*. This process creates a virtuous circle in which each new knowing leads to more complex symbols that make possible more new knowing. This process is endless because it tends towards an infinity that can never be reached.

From an informational point of view, a living organism is a live symbol, an informational vehicle that allows a seity to experience the world of classical information. This symbol represents a small fraction of the knowing of the seity, for that is represented by a pure quantum state that evolves in Hilbert space. Live symbols with the complexity of 10^{28} or 10^{41} atoms are astounding, yet they represent small fractions of the number of entangled qubits that would be necessary to represent the pure state of a seity expressing herself through such a symbol! According to D'Ariano's OPT, it takes many thousands of entangled qubits to describe an elementary particle and therefore atoms and molecules are extremely complex informational structures.

If we take seriously what the QIP theory is telling us, we have before us an undiscovered world of such complexity and wonder that, in comparison, the recent achievements of artificial intelligence are little more than toys. Once we accept that consciousness and free will exist as fundamental properties of nature, our worldview changes irreversibly and enriches us immensely. This vision restores the purpose and meaning of the universe denied by classical physics, and is deeply aligned with the thinking of perennial philosophy which has always recognized the inestimable value of consciousness and knowing.

This new interpretation, which involves consciousness from the very beginning and is much broader than what our rational mind has been telling us, gives us a glimpse of a world still to be explored and discovered *both scientifically and experientially*. It was the rational mind that suggested we are machines because that mind could only understand how things "function." Knowing the functioning of things certainly allows us to design complicated mechanisms, but we are infinitely more than mathematical "operations"! *Each one of us is a part-whole of One that wants to know the Whole that we carry within.*

It should be noted that a seity that communicates with other seities does not have to know what quantum information in Hilbert space is, just like we do not have to know Fourier transforms when we converse with each other. In other words, with the same naturalness with which we automatically transform the vibrations of the air into a sound and its meaning, a seity directly perceives the live symbols as an experience, and can directly translate a portion of its experience into live symbols.

Meaning Is the Essence of Knowing

I have a naïve faith in the universe...that at some level everything makes sense, and we can get glimpses of that sense if we try.
—Mihaly Csikszentmihalyi

Meaning is the essence of the seities' self-knowing and it is only partially represented by the live symbols they use to communicate with each other. We have seen that the coevolution of knowing and live symbols occurs through the repetition of communication cycles. This process also produces new seities, new seities' combinations, new symbols, and new symbols' combinations. The laws by which the symbols manifest and combine are probabilistic, and their meaning is generally specified by which symbols are chosen (words), and their order (sentence), as determined by the free-will choices of the seities. This is typical of any language and is also the profound reason that explains why quantum laws are probabilistic and indeterministic.

The probability of appearance of each symbol in a sequence is independent of the meaning expressed. For example, in the sequence of symbols "the gray cat ate the red mouse," the probability of each word is perfectly predicted by the symbolic laws of English. If the sequence had instead been "the red mouse ate the gray cat," the same probabilities would have been observed, but the two meanings would be quite different.

Note that quantum physics laws, just like the syntactical laws of any language, predict the probability of appearance of their symbols but not their order! However, the fact that the probabilities of symbols are independent from the meaning expressed by them does not mean that the language is meaningless. Quantum physics can only describe the probabilistic rules that are necessary, but not sufficient, to express and explore meaning. But the free-will exploration of meaning cannot be predicted by any mathematical theory.

The "objects" described by quantum physics are the symbols of a universal language that manifest in spacetime and represent the "letters," "words," and "phrases" of conscious entities that communicate with each other. In this context, everything written on paper, or in the memory of a computer, is made up of classical symbols representing only the memory of a knowing that is always evolving and is characterized by a deep and irreducible dynamism.

Before symbols there is the meaning that formed them, and meaning has much more depth and breadth than any possible symbolic expression might hope to capture, especially the meaning connected with emotions and creative thoughts. We are holistic beings, and this is also the reason why our words have more than one meaning per symbol. Therefore, when we combine many words in a sentence, the number of possible meanings grows exponentially with the number of words.[4] Therefore, deciding which of the many meanings is the correct one requires comprehension. Without it, verbal communications would be impossible. We also comprehend poorly worded sentences because meaning comes first for us. Comprehension is also responsible for the creativity that has allowed us to invent computers and the algorithms that make them useful.

Computers cannot understand ambiguous sentences nor can they program themselves because they do not comprehend the limitations of algorithms. There is no path from meaningless symbols to meaning for the same reason that electrical signals cannot be translated into qualia without consciousness. Furthermore, each *new* meaning must be expressed with a new combination of symbols that never existed before. Syntactical laws allow such combinations, but they cannot prescribe them because the real cause of a new combination is the conscious comprehension of a seity that exists outside the domain of classical symbols.

The widespread idea that the laws of physics can predict all of physical reality is dead wrong. It would be like saying that

---

4   If we have a sentence of m words, where each word has n meanings, the number of possible meanings is n^m. For example, a 12-word sentence in which each word has 10 possible meanings has a trillion possible meanings (10^{12}), versus only one meaning (1^{12}) if each word has one meaning (n = 1). When n >> 1, understanding a sentence requires a non-algorithmic decision impossible for a computer.

the syntactical laws of English can predict all the new ideas that will be written in the future. The symbolic laws can only predict that the symbolic expression of future new ideas will obey them, but cannot anticipate which ideas will make sense. The driving force behind any new meaningful combination of symbols is not their syntax, but the ontological reality of the meaning that created it. For example, whatever is the meaning of the book I will write in the future, we can be sure that the letters of the alphabet I will use will obey the syntactical laws of the language in which such book will be written. However, symbols alone cannot create new meanings because meaning comes first. Yet we often value symbols (form) and ignore meaning (substance).

The probabilistic laws of quantum physics, which describe how elementary particles combine, work similarly to the syntactical laws of the symbols of our languages that describe probabilistically how the letters of the alphabet combine. Likewise, the quantum laws do not determine the order of the particles and atoms that appear, but only their probability of appearing, just like the choice of words and their order in a book is not determined by the syntactical rules of the language.

Physical reality without new creations would be like having books written by computers: the syntax would be perfect, but there would be no new meaning because the computer does not know how to judge meaning. A computer cannot have new ideas beyond the ones we have inserted into its algorithms. If an idea produced by a computer seems new to us, it is only because we had not completely "unrolled" the algorithm that we put into its program. For example, if we have developed an algorithm to generate various images of snowflakes by assigning random values to a number of open parameters, the computer may generate a snowflake so beautiful that we might believe the computer is an artist! In truth, the artist was the programmer together with the person who recognized that the "snowflake" produced by chance by the computer was a work of art. The computer did not know what it was doing. David Hume said: "The beauty of things exists in the mind that contemplates them," and that's exactly how it is. It is time to stop attributing human qualities to what does not have them! When we think that the ontology of the universe resides only in its symbols, we describe a meaningless universe. Physics can only grasp the objective meaning of symbols, just like Shannon's information does, but it cannot do any more. On the other hand, seities build symbolic realities from the inside out, going from conscious meaning to symbols. And their capacity to go from symbols to meaning depends on their prior comprehension of the meaning that can only *creatively*, and not algorithmically, arise from their consciousness.

Information Needs to Be Redefined

Meaning cannot exist in a physical reality described only by symbols and symbolic laws without meaning. And this is what current physics does. In such apparent reality, consciousness, life, and free will are nothing more than epiphenomena.

In the proposed new worldview, meaning, which is the essence of knowing, comes before symbols, yet symbols serve the purpose of communicating and exploring meaning, which is the reason for their existence. Thus, without meaning there is no reason for symbolic information to exist. Surprisingly, *quantum information describes the knowing, i.e., the meaning that was excluded in the original definition of information!*

Moreover, the symbolic laws of quantum physics admit the existence of an extraordinary dynamic symbol that is a living cell. However, that cell was not "written" by the laws of symbols but by the seities who, little by little, discovered the "meaning of life" and expressed it with the same symbols they used to comprehend it. These symbols "obeyed" the symbolic laws of live information in the construction of the first cell in the same way that Dante obeyed the syntactical laws of Italian

259

in his *Divine Comedy*. However, the symbols were not the blind authors of this sublime work, nor was it Dante's physical body who wrote it. The real author was the embodied seity who chose the most appropriate symbols (words) and their order to express the meaning she felt, while at the same time obeying the syntactical laws.

Therefore, to express a complex thought, the choice of words and their order is determined neither by chance nor by the laws of symbols but by the meaning the ego/seity desires to express. In fact, the symbolic laws can only predict the probabilities of the symbols emerging from seities, but those probabilities have nothing to do with meaning. Likewise, the ideas of life and computer cannot have emerged from chance combinations of symbols but from the deeper reality of meaning. The physical universe which exists in I-space emerged from C-space, the semantic space. We must not confuse the symbols with their meaning! Information exists to communicate meaning, and can only exist if meaning exists.

Symbols are the physical shareable structures with which the meaning is collectively expressed and explored by seities and with which increasingly complex symbols are constructed to express the ever-new meanings emerging anew from C-space. It is the new meaning that "informs" the seities on how to construct the new symbols that express it. Only the intention, comprehension, love, and care of the seities can sense the potential of an idea not yet fully comprehended, which must be gradually expressed symbolically through a creative process that will coevolve symbol-and-meaning.

In this creative process, chance has no important role to play. Therefore, this idea differs enormously from the natural evolution doctrine that entrusted to chance the source of creativity we recognize in the universe. With Oscar Wilde I also think that "chance is simply a synonym of our ignorance." Often the artist can probe deeper than the scientist.

From Observers to Actors

In classical physics, probability is used primarily when dealing with systems made of huge numbers of *classical* particles obeying deterministic laws. It is called statistical physics, and the concept of probability refers to the lack of knowledge of a state that already exists or *has probability 1 to exist later*, but is unknown. In this case the knowledge of the deterministic laws allows us to use a variable to represent what is *certain but unknown*. This is the "objective probability" that can later be averaged and eliminated, allowing the derivation of another deterministic law valid for the ensemble.[5] In other words, within classical physics, the lack of knowledge is not lack of existence of what is unknown.

In the case of quantum physics, however, the theory describes only the information that can be known about reality, not reality. Therefore, the unknown variable is the probability of what will be measured. This probability represents something that is *inherently uncertain and unknown*, a very different concept than objective probability (the future state is *certain* but *unknown*). This is by some called "subjective probability" and refers to information that does not yet exist because the state that will manifest is determined only at the *moment and by effect of the measurement*.

We have seen that this state is completely unknowable before the measurement because it has not been *decided* yet. In fact, it has been proven that no hidden variables exist that could determine that state prior to its decision. Only a free-will decision and/or non-algorithmic randomness could be its source. Therefore, the probability of quantum physics represents a genuine creation! And genuine creations cannot be predicted. Thus quantum

---

5   The first major example of use of probability in physics was the development of the classical theory of gases that derived from first principles the empirical Boyle's Law, and gave birth to statistical physics.

physics is the best possible representation of a creative universe. As such, it cannot predict the future because that future has not yet been created.

In other words, no one can actually know the state that will be found when we make a measurement because that state does not literally exist. Thus quantum probability refers to the lack of existence of what may be later known. This also explains why the quantum laws can only predict the probabilities of the possible states that might manifest, but not the actual state that will occur, because what will show up is determined by either non-algorithmic randomness or the free will of some quantum agent. In both cases, it is not decided by a deterministic law.

Classical physics purported to describe reality directly only to discover that it was mistaken, for it only described what our classical sensory systems or instruments revealed about *outer* reality, without recognizing that outer reality emerges from a deeper and more fundamental reality that cannot be directly known. There are indeed hidden variables, but those are behind classical physics, not quantum physics!

I believe that our inability to comprehend quantum physics originates from a hidden expectation or desire that the universe should be deterministic instead of creative. This *prejudice* has caused a fundamental misunderstanding about the nature of reality, as revealed through the mathematical formalism of quantum theory. Quantum physics may account for the past but cannot predict the future of physical reality because it can only tell us what we can possibly know about the future.

I think the deep message of quantum physics is that: (1) quantum information is the representation of the inner experience of quantum systems, some without and others with free will. That experience can only be privately known by each quantum system and is the creative source of outer reality; (2) live information represents the symbolic, shareable information that can *directly* communicate a portion of the private experience of quantum systems to other quantum systems. Live information can also be organized as living organisms; (3) classical information is the symbolic, shareable information representable by statistically significant ensembles of uncorrelated live symbols that behave deterministically. Classical information cannot be organized as living organisms. It can only be used to create virtual worlds.

The observer of a classical system is an *idealization* of someone who can know the objective state of the system without disturbing it. Therefore, such an observer can only exist outside the observed system, like passively watching a movie, because he cannot exist as a cognitive observer *inside* a virtual reality. The observer of a quantum system, instead, cannot observe without drastically disturbing what he observes, and thus changes it. Therefore, *he is not an observer but an actor*. Moreover, no observer can know the state of a quantum system even in principle since quantum information cannot be reproduced. Quantum physics is therefore telling us that *there are only actors!*

The notion of observer in physics has to be eliminated and replaced with the notion of *quantum actors* because inside a quantum universe there can only be quantum actors. And quantum actors are conscious, according to QIP, and interact with other quantum actors which are also conscious. Therefore the entities that interact within a quantum universe are like the thoughtforms and the seities that I have postulated and described. I recall that thoughtforms are quantum systems that are conscious but do not have free will and thus do not have an identity, whereas seities are self-conscious entities that have an indelible identity and free will. Obviously, there may be many other types of quantum actors, for now unexplored, since the notion of quantum actor has not been fully explored.

13

Lived Knowing

> Beauty is life when life reveals itself. Beauty is eternity that is contemplated in the mirror, and we are eternity and the mirror.
> —Kahlil Gibran

The initial goal of science was to explain natural phenomena, not life or consciousness. When scientists convinced themselves that mathematics alone could give us a detailed description of reality and that our sense-based intuition was fallacious, the ideas that life is mechanical, consciousness is epiphenomenal, and free will does not exist became widespread. This is exactly like saying that the universe is without meaning and purpose. Moreover, some even proposed that the mathematical description of reality is reality, i.e. that mathematics is ontological, even though it is a creation of our human minds.

It is good to remember that Galileo said that mathematics is the language of nature, not that the language of nature is nature. But today there is an increasing tendency to believe that reality is made up of meaningless symbols. But how can empty symbols replace lived experiences? For example, the word "compassion" cannot replace the "experience of compassion." True compassion is the "descent into shared suffering" (Pope Gregory the Great). The meaning is in the lived experience, not in the words or other classical symbols that represent it, and the experience belongs only to those who live it.

Rationality Is Not Enough

> Reason is nothing without imagination.
> —Descartes

The need for ever more complex mathematics to describe our world has increasingly distanced us from our lived experiences—the only true source of knowing—and led us to consider rationality the only mental capacity useful in the study of reality. For example, we have tried to understand quantum physics using only our rational minds without the creative inputs of intuition, emotion, and imagination. If quantum physics primarily describes the interiority of reality, as I propose, mathematics alone can never lead us to the necessary comprehension. Quantum physics is homomorphic to the qualities of our inner experience, not the measured physical quantities of the symbolic classical world.

Interiority is represented by a pure quantum state that cannot be reproduced and can only be known by its owner "from within" in the form of qualia. Such experience, being subjective and private, can never be symbolically transmitted in an objective way. Its description using classical symbols will always be an approximation, for the inner structure of meaning contains a portion that will remain ambiguous and undecidable even within the conscious experience itself, as we all know so well.

I am convinced that our intuitive mind and emotions have access to a fundamental meaning that can lead us to the truth when guided and combined with all our other capacities, which include rationality of course, but a rationality inspired by the heart. If it is true that One wants to know Itself, it would be inconsistent to think that we, as seities, lack the capacity to do so. By not trusting our intuition and our heart, we tend to mainly use our rationality. However, for as long as our *knowing* remains only at the symbolic level, it will only be *knowledge*, and cannot be complete. When we say "It is so because mathematics says so," without going beyond the *operational* understanding of what mathematics is telling us, it means that we have stopped at the surface of things. Facts and rationality are only the first step, absolutely necessary for sure, but not sufficient for full comprehension.

By stating that the universe is open, I mean that any algorithmic description of reality can only be approximate and incomplete, and that it will never be possible to know the whole future. Believing that the future can be described by calculating the limit to infinity of an algorithm is not possible, in my opinion, because, if everything is interconnected, there cannot be separate algorithms that describe separate portions of reality.

This is also the lesson we learn from chaotic systems, where a tiny difference in the initial conditions of two otherwise identical systems leads in the long run to a macroscopic and unpredictable difference between the two. If everything is interconnected, there must be tiny connections among all the algorithms that collectively describe the Whole. These connections will change the behavior of each isolated algorithm and will take it beyond its mathematical definition. Therefore, even though these connections can be initially neglected, they can later produce a completely different behavior from the one expected by the algorithms in isolation, well before reaching infinity.

Infinity is unthinkable, because the portion that remains outside any finite part is infinitely greater than that part, no matter its size. In mathematics, many of our most important results have been achieved by calculating the limit to infinity of a series (an algorithm). Since reality is all interconnected, the various mathematical theories that we should use to describe it should also be all interconnected, i.e., each theory should be able to influence the others, even though to a small degree.

Our total reliance on mathematics as a tool to describe a *holistic* reality, especially with regard to mathematical extrapolations to infinity, must be reconsidered in the light of the holism revealed by quantum physics. Mathematics is a valid mental construction, yet, if it is made of separable parts, it cannot *possibly* describe a holistic reality. The fact that pure quantum states are not knowable "from the outside" is already an extraordinary result, which indicates the secret connections of mathematics with a non-algorithmic, open, and unknowable universe. *The mathematics of physics cannot erase the mystery of a universe that evolves based on free will.* It is likely that our need for power and control may subtly drive us to believe that we can know the future that even One does not know.

Beyond Rationality

As André Weil observed in his *Apprenticeship Memories*: "Mathematics is just one of the many mirrors in which truth is reflected, albeit perhaps with more purity than in other mirrors." However, it was not mathematics that created our world, and therefore there must be deeper reasons for the world to reflect so well in the mathematical models we have invented/discovered. Such reasons can only be found by studying ourselves and investigating who we really are, since we are also the inventors of these models. After all, each of us carries within the "genome" of One.

To comprehend our true nature, the computational and mechanistic models that are rapidly gaining the upper hand in the sciences are not sufficient. Not even logic alone is sufficient, though necessary. We also need the other aspects of our nature, such as our emotions, imagination, creativity, courage, empathy, free will, curiosity, and the incredible capacity to comprehend through our lived experiences. If each of us reflects the whole, our knowing must also include these non-algorithmic properties, which go far beyond the purely rational knowledge we rely upon almost exclusively today. I am convinced that if we disconnect from these fundamental aspects that distinguish us from our machines, we run the great risk of becoming machines ourselves, not by nature, but by choice.

We have also seen that there is no trace of meaning in the probabilistic symbolic laws of our languages, and the same is true in the language of matter, i.e., the language of classical symbols. However, the existence of meaning is evident for each of us in our conscious experience, and is reflected in the subjective nature of quantum probability and in the nature of the pure states that we have discussed. Moreover, the expression of meaning is not governed by any physical laws, and therefore the laws cannot describe the lived experience, which is what matters most to us and to all the innumerable seities created by One. I believe this is also the reason why quantum laws must be expressed with subjective probabilities that do not allow us to know ahead of a measurement which symbol will show up, because that symbol is decided by free will and not by an algorithm.

As Albert Einstein states: "It is possible that everything can be described scientifically, but it would not make sense; it would be as if we were describing a Beethoven symphony as a variation in the pressures of the waves." For sure, a piece of music is not just the musical score and the frequency spectrum of the air vibrations: "The music is not in the notes, the music is between the notes" (Wolfgang Amadeus Mozart). The Music is also the subtle meaning contained in the emotions and the joy it brings, not to mention the pleasure of reproducing it with our own voice or with an instrument, if you are so lucky as to be able to do it. The objective structure and characteristics of a piece of music are not enough to describe the lived experience of it, which is enriched immeasurably when you play it with other musicians you love to be with. That is a cooperative work of art and discipline.

Music as physical vibrations is only its symbolic dimension. The experience of music is its semantic dimension, and the two can be conceived as the indivisible and correlated faces of the same *creation*. Music, together with speech, provides us with a striking example of the close link that exists between the inner and the outer worlds. "Where words fail...music speaks" (Ludwig van Beethoven). And, "Music is perhaps the only example of what could have been—if it had not been for the invention of language, the formation of words, and the analysis of ideas—the communication of souls" (Marcel Proust, *The Prisoner*).

A New Interpretation of Physical Reality

I think that a complete theory of information should start from the general principle that the purpose of information is to communicate meaning, even though we didn't think so 75 years ago when Shannon wrote his famous article [12]. The principle of "correspondence of meaning with quantum information" expressed by the QIP theory fundamentally changes the interpretation of quantum physics, and therefore our ideas about the nature of reality. I think that what we have imagined as a blind evolution based on chance has instead always been guided "from within" by seities.

It was not the physical laws that formed the universe; these are instead the result or effect of the progressive self-knowing of the seities reflected in the syntactical laws of the symbols they used to explore and memorize their ever-growing self-knowing. These laws result from the cooperation of the seities and from the dynamic order inherent in the nature of One as reflected in each of them.

In vain we tried to explain consciousness as an emergent property of unconscious matter. The QIP theory now fully supports the idea that what we have conceived as matter is an emergent property of conscious quantum systems (seities), not the other way around, since pure quantum states have all the characteristics of conscious experiences, and classical physics emerged from live information, which in turn emerged from quantum information. This implies that consciousness cannot be explained with any simpler concepts than itself because it always existed. It is spacetime and matter-energy that can be explained with consciousness, because consciousness has always been guiding the evolution of the universe.

In this new worldview, *matter reflects the symbolic aspect of conscious entities that communicate meaning with each other.* Symbols and meaning are the two irreducible aspects of a holistic reality.

At some point the place of honor that belonged to meaning has been given to symbols, together with the idea that the laws of symbols must predict all of reality. This is profoundly misguided because symbols alone will never be able to predict the evolution of meaning that is open and creative. The current laws of physics can only predict that the symbolic expression of any new meaning will not be contradictory with the symbolic expression of any previous meaning. However, *new* meaning may create new laws since meaning is not algorithmic, and the complex symbols needed to represent it are just as creative and unknowable prior to the emergence of the new meaning.

For example, the laws of physics did not predict the invention of the computer. The computer is simply a human creation, *allowed* by the laws of physics, but originating from the imagination, creativity, love of knowledge, and commitment that has always inspired and guided us from within.

Meaning, Live Information, and Classical Information

The discoveries that have required the development of quantum physics have subverted the classical worldview and, so far, have been impossible to interpret correctly. However, it is essential to fully comprehend the message of quantum physics to make further progress. Shannon information is the cologarithm of the probability of classical symbols that can be used to represent the meaning that conscious agents have agreed, though there is no connection between symbol and meaning in its definition. The existence of meaning only makes sense if there are conscious observers interacting with free will. And, as we have discussed, these observers cannot exist in the classical world.

The homomorphism that exists between live information and pure quantum states (meaning) does not exist in classical information, for it has been averaged away in the uncorrelated live symbols that constitute the deterministic classical matter. Since classical symbols emerge from live symbols and live symbols emerge from quantum information, we can clearly say that the origin of classical, objective, and public information is the subjective meaning represented by the private quantum information.

When physicists tell us that the probabilities of quantum events are objective and therefore reality has no subjective meaning, this is just like saying that a human language has no meaning because the probabilities of its symbols are objective. Well, we know that our languages exist to communicate meaning and therefore the syntactical laws must leave the expression of meaning unregulated. Thus, the fact that quantum physics is structured like the syntactical laws of a language strongly validates the hypotheses that physical laws evolved over time, and that quantum information represents the "meaning of information" that is missing from Shannon information.

At the end of the previous chapter I concluded that the observers in quantum physics should be banned and replaced by actors that are integral parts of the universe and whose observations, experiences, and actions affect both the universe and them. A fundamental class of actors are the seities that communicate with each other using live symbols. As their knowing increases, live symbols get ever more complex until they reach the level of a living cell. With the invention of living cells the seities could then create virtual worlds made of classical symbols in which they could have novel experiences that gradually became ever more engrossing, and led to the creation of multicellular life.

Multicellular organisms become able to experience fully immersive virtual worlds like the one we are currently experiencing. These organisms transform live symbols within their cells into the classical symbols necessary for their body to act in the world of macroscopic objects. The transformations from classical to live symbols are also performed by living organisms to communicate the "reality" of the classical world to the seities.

Classical symbols are like the ink droplets with which books are printed, or like the bits of our computers. But the reason why books and computers exist is to allow embodied conscious entities to experience the near-infinite possible worlds that can be cocreated and explored to better know themselves through knowing each other.

Ideas Come before Symbols

The vase can break, but its pattern will continue to exist in the mind.
—Tibetan proverb

To create an invention, we need to start from an idea. However, the idea is not enough by itself. Only if it is sufficiently articulated can the inventor begin to build the object of his invention. Through the construction of the object, the inventor refines his idea, which in turn allows him to refine the construction (another example of a "snake biting its tail").

It took millennia to invent the computers with which we now can interact with virtual realities of our own creation. The computer was not born by chance, but through a conscious process of exploration, comprehension, and realization that started from a conscious idea that already existed in its embryonic form long before its realization. Likewise, any creation must always start from a general idea before arriving at any specific realization, and not vice versa.

Note that the idea is often born from a *desire*. For example, the desire to fly must have emerged within human consciousness at the time of the hominids, presumably by observing birds and imagining the joy of being able to fly like them. It took hundreds of thousands of years to gradually develop the technologies and the knowledge needed to build an aircraft. The first flight on a fragile contraption took place in 1903. In 1947, the sound barrier was broken, and in 1969 humans landed on the moon!

However, the aircrafts that exist today are not the result of random combinations of matter that self-organized naturally "from the outside" without any idea of the intended whole. They are instead due to the desire, intention, imagination, courage, and tenacity—inner skills—of generations of human beings who gradually achieved the goals they had envisioned and set for themselves.

In the physical world there is a tendency toward disorder that is encoded in the Second Law of Thermodynamics. In current science, the principle of *random* variation and selection is the only creative principle allowed to explain the natural evolution of complex systems. This is certainly a valid principle, but only if among the random variations there is at least one that is "fitter" than the ones that previously existed in the pool of variations. Otherwise, there is nothing better to select.

Suppose, for example, we randomly change the state of a bit in a computer program. What is the probability of improving the program? Almost zero. It would already be great if the computer continued to properly function. Suppose that to significantly improve a program, it is necessary to change 100 bits in the right place. If we randomly change 100 bits and the probability that each bit contributes to an improvement is 1% (an extremely optimistic value if the program has more than 10,000 bits), the final probability would be $(0.01)^{100}$, a value so small that producing an improvement by chance would be practically impossible.

We certainly make improvements through a process of variation and selection, for which reason the principle is valid, but in our case each variation, even if only in our thoughts, is the best idea we have, already knowing the function we want to achieve, and what we need to improve. Random or accidental thoughts are immediately discarded by our conscious comprehension. Despite all this, the selection made by the "market of ideas," which plays the same role as the ecosystem, discards many of our ideas, including those we believed were good. This is why we have been able to create and improve airplanes and computers over time.

To make these ideas more understandable, let's consider a concrete example: in England in the 1690s there were many flooded coal mines containing a large potential supply of coal. Freeing them from the water using animal force alone was a long and tiring job. There was a need to solve that problem and there were also technologies sufficiently developed to get the job done. It was known, for example, that steam could be used as a propulsive power, and this led Thomas Savery to invent, build, and sell the first commercial steam-powered pump in 1698. This was the spark that ignited the industrial revolution.

The invention of the steam pump, which may seem trivial today, had to be first conceived in its entirety to guide from top to bottom the visualization of the parts needed, their interactions, and finally their physical realization and assembly. The overall meaning of the invention was already contained in Savery's imagination in the moment he first conceived of the idea. Later, he had to translate an overall image into appropriate mental symbols by visualizing the entire functioning and assembly of the machine. This process of analysis and synthesis may have been repeated many times, starting and guided from that initial intuitive spark.

This mental simulation is generally aided by some symbolic processing performed on paper, and typically ends with a plan that is then translated into a physical structure that works. Such a plan, even if it did not physically exist, should exist in some form in the inventor's consciousness.

From the outside, the whole seems to emerge from the bottom up, as the parts are formed and assembled. But the whole had to exist as an idea before the parts were shaped and then assembled.

The same process also applies to life. It is absurd to think that simple organic molecules, which represent an infinitesimal fraction of the complexity of the simplest known bacterium, could naturally self-assemble to form an organism capable of reproduction without any guidance and any idea of the intended result. If simple organic molecules were like the transistors in our computers, the simplest bacterium would be like a microscopic robot made of ten billion transistors, including the "software" needed to make it function autonomously and reproduce.

How can we expect the first living and self-reproducing cell to have emerged by chance, without the prior existence of a conscious and intentional idea? How can a hierarchy of precise subsystems self-assemble and form a living organism of incredible complexity through natural and random events that have a natural tendency to disorder? We know that despite knowing the intended result, already possessing all the necessary atoms and molecules, and having the most advanced tools, no bioengineer would be able today to assemble a functioning bacterium. The origin of life is a miraculous event! If a computer were to miraculously self-assemble through natural events, that miracle would be puny compared to the first one, since the complexity of a computer is insignificant compared to that of a bacterium. Yet, many insist that "nature" has done this miracle with her eyes closed and without knowing what she wanted? That nature would be more powerful than God!

Just like One created us, we collectively "invented" and developed biological life and the human brain in step with our comprehension and to help improve it. Yet our scientists expect nature to use a mindless method to create mind. I think that every creation begins from an overall idea motivated by a desire. Combining the idea with the will and the means to pursue its realization, we can gradually arrive at its working implementation through a process of variation and selection. No creative structure like a machine or a cell is realizable without a conscious intuition of what is wanted. How can a living cell self-assemble as a result of natural processes without any idea of what is intended?

In my way of thinking, and consistently with the QIP principles, the first living cell did not self-assemble by chance but was instead the result of the enormous collective creativity and knowing of the seities. Moved by the need to comprehend the existence of the self-reproduction with which they were created and were themselves creating, the seities may have been able to cooperatively manipulate the live symbols of their language to the point of gradually developing a new symbol capable of self-reproduction! The first living cell! We have used the same method employed by the seities to create airplanes and microchips. And we have now reached a level of comprehension that will soon allow us to make machines that can automatically assemble other machines, though using classical information rather than live information. *We have worked like them for the simple reason that we are them!*

What Is the Purpose of Life?

We are all visitors of this time and place. We're just passing through. Our job here is to observe, learn, grow and love... Then we go back home.
—Aboriginal Australian proverb

We have seen that our consciousness allows us to tune into the "vibration sphere" of the reality we want to live and know, and that direct knowing implies "becoming" what we experience. During our first year of life, when the rational mind was not yet developed, we learned to tune into the signals produced by the body. Through this process, the ego emerged as that small portion of our greater consciousness that believes itself to be the body, oversees it, and comprehends the situations in which the body operates. The ego also supervises the automatic learning of our brain, so that we can properly learn to recognize new situations, often with just one example.

The ability to learn, and therefore recognize a new complex situation with one or a few examples, is one of the striking differences between human and artificial intelligence (AI). Consciousness comprehends first and then forms new quantum correlations to symbolically represent the new meaning, whereas a machine can only find classical correlations by mechanically processing many examples of the same situation. In ordinary reality nearly all circumstances are unique, and we are the ones with the *comprehension* to decide which situation to call "the same as before" or "a new one." An AI program cannot learn a new pattern with just one example because it does not have the non-algorithmic comprehension that alone can tell it that such a situation is new and what is new about it. Hence, AI's versatility is much less than that of humans. On the other hand, AI can do much better than us in most repetitive problems. AI is actually complementary to human capabilities. If used well, it will be a great advantage for humanity; if used poorly, it could even create existential problems.

In other words, the immeasurable and unbridgeable difference between human and artificial intelligence lies in the ability to comprehend of the ego/seity; a quantum property that is not accessible to digital computers. But there is more to human intelligence, because it not only makes use of the superb non-algorithmic comprehension and the information processing performed by the "head," but also uses the creativity, motivation, and courageous action that come metaphorically from the "heart" and the "gut." These metaphorical centers are not separable from each other, and collaborate because true human intelligence is the combination of head, heart, and gut. The head is the mental, the heart is the emotional, and the gut is the physical or action aspect of a seity. This metaphor will be further discussed later.

We are incarnated seities, a still-mysterious combination of seity and physical body. This arrangement greatly complicates our comprehension of both our algorithmic and non-algorithmic aspects. Much of what we ordinarily do can be explained by the "mechanisms" of the body, even though the body is quantum and classical, and therefore far more sophisticated than a computer. Occasionally we behave like a seity, at other times like a machine, and almost always like a combination of the two. It is therefore quite difficult to distinguish between the two aspects at the current state of our comprehension of reality, especially given the materialistic prejudices still dominating our worldview.

In a previous chapter, I mentioned that our body is like a quantum-classical "drone" controlled by the ego. The ego can also direct a classical drone through the intermediation of his body. He can do the same with an avatar that is part of a virtual reality created by a computer. The avatar is an example of a symbolic reality entirely constructed out of classical symbols though existing within a greater symbolic reality made of live symbols. This situation suggests the possibility that there may be additional levels of nested realities. Our psychological masks, of which there are several, one inside the other, are another example of nested realities through which we conceal our deepest intentions, often even from ourselves.

I think the purpose of life is to get to know ourselves through the knowing of each other, and this also involves knowing our shadow areas. Here I speak of hatred, racism, violence, and above all, the need to be superior to others.

For logical consistency with the proposed model, I believe that shadow areas must also exist within One, albeit in a far more abstract form, representing inevitable gaps and distortions in the process of self-knowing that occurs through the seities. I imagine that these distortions occur because the self-knowing must rely on live and classical symbols that cannot reveal the full meaning of the experience. Moreover, to comprehend, the ego needs to already understand a meaning similar to the one intended by the sender. This requirement can lead to *misunderstandings*, the result of which is what we call "evil." Just like it happens with human communications, the encoding and decoding of the symbols cannot be perfect. The impossibility of creating a one-to-one correspondence between meaning and symbols among seities is the fundamental cause of distortions.

One of the main purposes of physical life, then, could be to understand the origin and the "shape" of the distortions that exist within each of us, a prerequisite for eliminating them. In other words, evil does not exist as a fundamental reality, but only as a distortion of reality—a misunderstanding that is not reality. Thus, its elimination reveals the native reality that is free of any "evil." Part of this "purification process" needs to take place through experiences lived in virtual realities, allowing us to discover and experience the unknown origin and the nature of the misunderstandings we accidentally carry within us.

According to this interpretation, our earthly life corresponds to a "session in a simulator" designed to reveal and dissolve our distortions through a deep comprehension of our desires and intentions. In the simulator, the ego controls a "character," the physical body, with characteristics that allow the seity, the greater entity we are, to see clearly the nature of the problem manifested through the free-will actions of the ego. Once the problem has been identified, the seity may become aware of deeper intentions and desires that have determined the ego's choices, since the ego shares the essence of the seity. This strategy allows the seity to trace back and remove the underlying causes of her own misunderstandings.

This process of "amplification of distortions" is fundamental, because it makes them visible through the consequences they cause within human society. In fact, we all know that to solve a problem we must first recognize it and accept it as ours, and this is often the hardest part. And then, "The moment we accept our problems, the doors of solutions open wide" (Jalal al-Din Rumi). Thus, little by little, the ego realizes that the reality in which he exists is not the deepest reality; and comprehends— by experiencing it—that he is more than the body. This type of experience is necessary to free the ego from the self-induced trance of believing itself to be the body. This is also the reason why our intellectual-only understanding of reality is not enough to free us.

The opportunity to experience that there is a vaster reality than what appears to our physical senses can also be obtained through a particularly vivid lucid dream,[1] or through some extraordinary experiences of consciousness, as long as one has developed an open-enough mind to take those experiences seriously and critically.

---

1 A lucid dream is a dream in which the ego "wakes up" within the dream and realizes that he is dreaming. In some cases, the ego can even direct the dream as he would direct his body in ordinary life, with the difference that in the dream there are generally fewer physical constraints. For example, one could fly by simply wishing it.

The Evolution of Scientific Thought

Each new theory is first attacked as absurd; it is later recognized as true, but obvious and insignificant; finally, it is considered so important that its adversaries claim to have discovered it themselves.

—William James

After having analyzed for a long time the fundamental parts of which physical reality is made, a small portion of humanity is ready to move away from the materialism of classical physics to the new holistic vision offered by quantum information. Quantum information is compatible with the existence of a profound spiritual dimension of reality that in the past has fueled myths and religions. In fact, we are beginning to realize that the behavior of the whole cannot be explained only by the behavior of its parts, because reality, unlike what we imagined, is not made of separate parts and is not as objective as we thought. The *Tao Te Ching* starts with this verse:

The Tao that can be told
is not the eternal Tao.

This is the poetic description of:

The symbol (classical information) that can be told
is not the eternal Meaning (quantum information that cannot
be reproduced).

Quantum physics has revealed that the smaller the parts, the more inseparable from the whole they become, and therefore the whole must be invisibly present in all of its macroscopic parts. Nothing is closed and separated from the Whole, and even the most abstract symbol of quantum reality—the simplest of which we have called a *qubit*—is information of a special kind, because it remains intimately connected (entangled) with the other qubits it interacts with.

This is also the crucial property of our semantic, inner, and private reality that cannot be explained abstractly because the meaning can only be *intimately* known by those who experience it subjectively within themselves. This ultimate reality is not algorithmic and reproducible and has been so far neglected by science in the belief that everything that exists must be objective. This *prejudice* has eliminated from existence the very essence of the universe. To comprehend and appreciate who we are, we must embrace and integrate our physical, emotional, intuitive, and spiritual aspects into a lived whole.

Three Fundamental Centers

Everyone says that the brain is the most complex organ in the human body; as a doctor I might even agree. But as a woman I assure you that there is nothing more complex than the heart; even today all its mechanisms are not known. If there is logic in the reasoning of the brain, there are emotions in the reasoning of the heart.
—Rita Levi-Montalcini

The metaphor, "We are a whole made of heart, head, and gut," serves to describe the type of union that I experienced in the awakening described in the Introduction. I believe it is necessary to integrate and harmonize the "head" with the "heart" and the "gut," i.e., the intuitive and rational thinking with our deepest unitive feelings and with our capacity for courageous and right action. These three centers are metaphorical, of course, and are neither separate nor separable, because each of them also contains a portion of the other two. Therefore, even an intellectual person who appears to only live inside his head cannot be completely disconnected from his heart and gut.

If we examine the head center, we can recognize that the intuitive and creative powers are our highest mental abilities. We also possess a rational mind, i.e., the ability to reason logically on the basis of the presumed validity of assumptions (both explicit and implicit). The choice of assumptions, however, is mainly based on the level of our conscious comprehension of the whole. Finally, we also have a mechanical aspect, i.e., the ability to recognize patterns and to learn and follow procedures, just like computers that use artificial neural networks (we have copied those networks from the brains of mammals). For example, after the brain has learned to drive a car under the ego's supervision, we can then drive using mainly these quasi-autonomous and automatic learned processes.

As for the heart, it is the center of our feelings, desires, intentions, empathy, love, joy, passion, curiosity, honesty, ethics, and self-fulfillment. Its highest expression is unitive, because no fundamental distinction exists in reality between the observer and the observed when all the "parts" are parts-whole. At the level of our ordinary experience, our feelings are generally neither too strong nor particularly vivid, though they are aware and present. Finally, there is the "mechanical" aspect of the heart, represented by the quasi-automatic, habitual emotions and feelings that have limited awareness and depth, and include the usual sensations of shape, color, sounds, smells, and tastes associated with the physical world. Therefore, the experience of the heart ranges from the habitual semi-automatic level of ordinary feelings to the occasionally vivid and extraordinary feelings enlightened by the sense of unity, love, and fulfillment.

The gut is the focus of our physical actions, and it is the least understood of our centers. Its mechanical aspect is expressed by those physical acts that we perform almost unconsciously, for example, when we walk or ride a bike. The next level contains ordinary, intentional, and free-will actions. Finally, the highest level includes behaviors guided by deep comprehension, ethics, love, and courage; thus they contain the comprehension of what is right, the love that comes from the heart, and the courage and determination of the gut to act with integrity. The union of the heart with the head and gut is manifested in just, loving, and courageous actions. Sometimes these must go against the interests of the individual, to the point of putting property, reputation, or even life at risk, in order to honor the universal values that are deeply felt and cannot be shortchanged.

Head, heart, and gut may also refer to three different types of knowing, because we can learn mentally, emotionally, and interactively. The interactive knowing is based on physical action, knowing "from without" by interacting with objects and observing the actions of others, just like an apprentice learns by observing and imitating his master, or the scientist learns by doing experiments.

Emotional knowing is mainly knowing "from within," based on the sensations and feelings (qualia) we experience by observing the world and ourselves. At the ordinary level, this experiential and empathic knowing can lead us to superficial judgments, while at a highest level, when the knowing is direct, it makes us become what we know. Direct knowing also involves mental knowing and inspires right and courageous actions.

Mental knowing is knowing "both from without and from within." We get the first kind by reading and studying books, for example, or by listening to parents, teachers, and the media. We get the other one through the comprehension and creativity that is based on intuition and imagination. Symbolic knowledge from without and semantic knowing from within represent the ordinary aspects of mental knowing, while knowing "from within" based on creativity and comprehension is instead the superior aspect of mental knowing.

We actually know through the *integration* of all three ways of knowing, because it is impossible to separate them.[2]

A robot possesses only the mechanical aspects of both mental and interactive knowledge, and it completely lacks the knowing that comes from the heart and represents the essence of the non-algorithmic and unified aspects of knowing that markedly distinguish us from robots. If we only had the mechanical aspects, we would also be machines. Instead, our ordinary mind integrates the mechanical aspect of understanding with the ideation, creativity, and comprehension that only comes from the higher mind. Our full mind is then united with the love, joy, passion, and compassion that come from the heart and with the courage, leadership, and right action that come from the gut.

Those who have lived a unified experience open up much more to the knowing and creativity of the seity to which they belong, and this leads to a noticeable improvement of their creative abilities, and to a deeper union of the head and gut with the heart. *The heart is the deepest source of our human, non-algorithmic capacities.* And "Whoever goes to the end of his heart knows the nature of man. Knowing one's human nature means knowing the sky" (Mencius).

---

2   Incidentally, our educational system mainly uses the ordinary mental knowledge of facts, instead of promoting the deeper comprehension that requires the full integration of the three modes of knowing.

Conclusion

If the stars are unreachable
this is no reason not to want them...
How sad the paths
if it were not for
the magical presence of the stars.
—Mário Quintana, *Dreamers of a New Humanity*

How sad and how dark are the paths of life if they are not illuminated by the magical presence of consciousness! Using metaphorical language, we can clearly say that consciousness is the North Star that guides us through the paths of life.

Unfortunately, the consciousness of a large part of humanity is nowadays immersed in a self-induced trance that obscures Love, which is the fundamental Law that governs and connects all the parts-whole of the universe: "the love that moves the sun and the other stars" (Dante Alighieri). That is likely the same universal love that I felt in the awakening experience, the love that opened my heart and revealed for the first time the existence of direct knowing.

The heart is the symbolic center of intentions, emotions, and intuitions that informs and unites the head (rationality and creativity) and the gut (courageous and right action), allowing us to achieve "virtue and knowing," in Dante's words again. Only the heart makes it possible to unite the inner and the outer worlds so that *being* and *knowing* become one; a world in which science and spirituality will finally be able to integrate, allowing humankind to comprehend what love is by becoming love and joy and peace: "The ultimate meaning of everything that surrounds us...is the joy that is the source of all creation" (Rabindranath Tagore). And that is what ultimately matters.

Knowing Must Be Lived

Discursive knowledge does not serve to go beyond the illusions of the world, just as darkness does not cease to exist just by mentioning a lamp.

—Kularnava Tantra

Scientific knowledge, whose object of study is the outer world that can be known through the measurement of physical quantities and their mathematical relationships, is absolutely necessary, but it is not enough to lead us to lived knowing. In my thinking, the ultimate goal of knowing—to which science has made a fundamental contribution—is realized only when the observer lives the experience of himself and of the world in an integrated way, because true knowing goes way beyond *knowledge*, the symbolic aspect of reality.

At the peak of lived knowing, the seity becomes one with her own experience, just like we, as children, identified ourselves with the games we were playing to such an extent that we became the game. It is important to underscore that the nature of the "scientific" observer who limits himself to making accurate measurements, remaining detached and dispassionate from what he observes, is quite different from the nature of the actor-observer who "knows what he lives and lives what he knows." The first does not feel part of the observed phenomenon since he assumes that the world is a machine that obeys mathematical laws, whereas the second participates—gut, heart, and head—in the cocreation of the reality that he observes, acts on, is acted on by, and fully lives. As such, he deeply knows that he is responsible for his own experience.

Blaming others for what ails us is how we keep ourselves from recognizing our responsibility as cocreators of our own experience and that of others. When our mind, obscured by the desire to be special, includes everybody else but us in the list of cocreators of our experience, we prevent ourselves from recognizing the special way in which we feel *superior* to them and to the rest of Nature. We must wake up from this selective consciousness and comprehend that we are Nature and that Nature is within us. I believe that feeling superior to Nature is the primary source of our distortions, and the root cause of our suffering. In my experience, becoming aware of our primary responsibility about what happens in our experience is the first fundamental and indispensable step on the road of healing, because our awakening depends on this crucial self-awareness.[1]

Scientific knowledge can only tell us what is factual and possible. However, to make the right decisions, we cannot rely only on science; we must also add the comprehension and the values that only the heart can give us—values like those that filled Immanuel Kant with emotion and wonder: "Two things fill the soul with ever new and growing admiration and veneration...the starry sky above me, and the moral law within me." *Without these values, man counts for nothing.*

Rita Levi-Montalcini said that:

The absolute evil of our time is not to believe in values. It does not matter whether they are religious or secular. Young people must believe in something positive and life deserves to be lived only if we believe in values, because these remain even after our death.

---

1 There is a story in the Jewish tradition that says that the world rests on the shoulders of 36 righteous people, and it is only thanks to them that humanity is not destroyed. The point is that nobody knows who they are, including them. Thus, the fate of humanity depends on each of us, for we might be one of them!

The Biggest Obstacle to Union
Is the Need for Superiority

> There is nothing noble in being superior to another man.
> True nobility lies in being superior to the person we were
> until yesterday.
> —Hindu proverb

The World can only be known when it is observed, acted, and
lived, for we are an integral part of the World and the World is
also within us. The reason we limit ourselves to looking at the
World only from the outside, as if we were not part of it, may
be because we feel superior to it. And this need is also implicit
in the principle of the survival of the fittest that allows us to
blame Nature and others for our lack of love and respect for
others. I think we do so mainly because we feel—and want to
be—superior and special.

I consider this "wanting to be the first" the hardest obstacle
to achieving union, especially since in our society strong
competition is considered a desirable thing. In fact, the entire
economy, public education, our sports, and most institutions
rely primarily on strong competition. The evolution of the
species is also exclusively attributed to win-lose competition
through the "survival of the fittest" principle that provides a
natural justification for our selfishness and aggression.

I should point out here that there is a type of friendly
competition that is indeed desirable and promotes personal
excellence when it stimulates in us the desire to be *superior to
the person we were until yesterday,*" rather than the desire to win
to show that we are *better* than the others. Friendly competition,
however, can easily become win-lose competition, especially
when the attention of the press or the people we care about goes
only to the winner.

At the basis of competition is the need to feel "special," which almost every human being feels. Each of us is indeed special because each of us is unique and unrepeatable, that special point of view or perspective with which One knows Itself. The problem arises when one wants to be more special or more unique than all the other points of view of One. This need for superiority is a great distortion of the legitimate desire and pride to be unique, which is who we are. "We are divine, and we must live not by the survival of the fittest, but in a way that supports everyone and everything on this planet" (Bruce H. Lipton, *The Biology of Beliefs*).

The hard competitive mindset is the ever-present threat that prevents us from being spontaneous, creative, and at ease with ourselves, with others, and with the world. While competition divides, cooperation unites. By cooperation I do not mean "doing good" to feel better than those we help, but the "virtue" that recognizes the value of committing to being an active part of society that cares and intelligently provides for those who cannot keep up, especially by teaching and by example. Competition is the natural progeny of superiority. It is also what hinders the movement towards union, which alone can bring integration to our physical, emotional, and mental health.

The time has come to use our powerful technologies for the good of all, rather than for the delusional good of the self-proclaimed fittest. The idea of separation, which finds its expression in the reductionism of classical physics, must be replaced by the experience of union and inclusion already evident in the holism of life. "There is not a single isolated fragment in all of nature, each fragment is part of a harmonious and complete unity" (John Muir). Only by recognizing this crucial interdependence can humanity go beyond the repetition of the same dysfunctional patterns that have caused so much unnecessary suffering to our species and to the ecosystem.

Many sages throughout history have suggested that we are beings of light that will not die with the death of the body, because we are here to learn and grow. I think we are here to learn to collectively create new worlds in which to operate at a much higher level of cooperation, creativity, and fulfillment than we now can at this early stage of our spiritual evolution. The possibility of experiencing our true nature is already supported by the enlightened personal experiences of millions of people around the globe, and by countless "anecdotal" facts and events that science hesitates to investigate. If we open ourselves to this potential that is dormant in us and ask our greater self to show the way, we may soon be able to experience an unsuspected unity in our lives, the early signs of humanity's awakening to its true power and purpose.

Union Is in the Heart

Follow the advice of your heart, because no one will be more faithful to you than him.
—Book of Sirach, 37.13

I think that the positive forces that will create our future will not be the forces and the laws of matter, but those of conscious cooperation, comprehension, and love for others that all beings in existence must sooner or later manifest because these values are the essence of our deepest nature.

I also think that the most effective way to achieve union is through a process of collective and cooperative creation of a just, empathic, and loving society through right and courageous actions informed by the heart and by the intuitive and rational mind. Then our experience and knowing will grow in our hearts and they will guide our individual actions through an ever-higher level of consciousness. Unfortunately, today there is the real danger of letting ourselves be seduced by the spreading culture of digital ontology and digital consumerism that replaces true and profound relationships with virtual and superficial ones, thus halting, if not reversing, our spiritual development.

Social networks designed to bombard people with suggestive messages, often personalized to reinforce personal biases or based on false information or on presumed conspiratorial theories, generate groups that can become alienated from reality in self-isolating worlds. Nikola Tesla said that "progress must serve to improve the human race; if not, it is only a perversion."

Technology must be used to help us discover our true nature, not to further imprison us in meaningless virtual worlds designed to enrich the richest. We have come to the point where we can truly unite as *humans* no matter where we were born, or stay divided in warring factions with ever-increasing destructive technology on our side.

Only when we truly comprehend that we are responsible for our experiences and that the choice is ours alone, can we begin to truly know ourselves and the world.

To know ourselves more and more, we need a new *empathic science* that can convert scientific knowledge into deep lived knowing and from it generate new scientific knowledge. Similarly, we need a new *rational spirituality* that can convert lived knowing into new scientific knowledge and from it generate new lived knowing. These two disciplines can then intertwine in endless and mutual crescendo.

This is the essence of the Creative Principle of One. Within this vision, empathic science and rational spirituality, integrating and interweaving, will evermore increase our loving, joyful, and fulfilling union with the Whole.

Glossary

Agentivity. The capacity of each seity to interact with other entities with free will, for the purpose of deepening her own self-knowing and the knowing of each other as herself.

Axioms vs. dogmas. In mathematics, axioms are self-evident statements presumed to be true. In physics and science, axioms are typically derived from observations and experiments. Axioms must be falsifiable at least through their experimental predictions. Religious, political, or philosophical dogmas are indemonstrable beliefs that are accepted on faith without being questioned. Dogmas are rarely falsifiable, and thus create a belief system that imprisons the healthy evolution of self-knowing and comprehension.

Bit. The bit is an abstract mathematical entity that can be used to represent a binary variable, i.e., a variable that can only have two states, "1" or "0," "true" or "false," "up" or "down," etc. The meaning of the two states is not inherent in the bit, but is convened and may depend on the context in which the bit is found. For example, a bit may represent the state of truth of a hypothesis (true or false); the simplest possible distinction, such as right or left, exists or doesn't exist; the digit 0 or 1 of the binary number system; and so on. (See also Chapter 4, What Is a Bit?)

The information processed by computers generally consists of a sequence or string of bits the length of which typically consists of multiples of four bits (4, 8, 12, 16, 24, 32, 64). A 4-bit string is called a nibble and can discriminate 16 (2^4) possible states. An 8-bit word is called a byte and can represent 256 (2^8) different states.

The bit can be represented by a physical device that has two stable states, for example an electronic flip-flop, or two bands of electrical voltages at the input or output of an electronic circuit, as explained in Chapter 4.

CIP framework. The acronym CIP is formed by the initials of the words Consciousness, Information, and Physical to specify a framework in which C-space is the space of conscious experiences, I-space is the space of live information, and P-space stands for the physical space perceived by an embodied seity. The CIP framework [13] postulates that the fundamental nature of reality is constituted by a field that has an irreducible semantic and symbolic aspect called C-space and I-space respectively. In this conceptual framework:

1. C-space is the *subjective and private semantic space of consciousness*. It is an extra-physical experiential space and time—not the spacetime of physics—made by the qualia experiences of all conscious entities. C-space is inseparable from the symbolic space of live information (I-space). Together they form the ontology of One. Every entity that emerges from One possesses both aspects. Within D'Ariano-Faggin QIP theory, a quantum system in a pure state is a conscious entity experiencing its own state within C-space.

2. I-space is the *objective and public symbolic space* that contains the live information in which the seities have translated a portion of their meaning to be symbolically communicated to other seities. I-space contains both uncorrelated and correlated live symbols. The uncorrelated constitute the classical symbols that behave deterministically, whereas the correlated form the atoms, molecules, and macromolecules that hierarchically combined quantum

particles and interact in accordance with the laws of quantum physics. In I-space there are also very complex symbols, both live and classical, which can process live and classical symbols to create other symbols. Two examples of complex symbols are: the electronic brain of a self-driving car, and a living organism that creates within itself a symbolic representation of the outer world.

3. P-space is the physical world experienced by the ego, i.e., by the portion of the seity's consciousness that believes himself to be the body in which he is "incarnated." The nature of P-space depends crucially on the type of information processing performed by the species, and on the specific qualia of each ego. The organism controlled by the ego selects a portion of the I-space information to be perceived. This information is sensed and processed by the body and transformed into live information, which the ego perceives and "colors" with his distinctive qualia, experiences, and comprehensions. In turn, the ego transforms a portion of his meaning into live information within the cells of the body to produce the intended actions (symbols) in the physical world. The ego therefore controls a body (an I-space symbolic structure) that acts as an intermediary between the C-space of experience and the I-space of other live symbols. The space of classical symbols is a subset of I-space whose symbols are uncorrelated mixtures of live symbols that behave deterministically, like a computer system for example.

Classical information. Information is an abstract concept that refers to the capacity of a physical event to inform a conscious observer. This concept connects the world of shareable physical events to the subjective meaning that the same event carries for each observer, since we know that the same event informs various observers differently. Only by assuming that all observers are identical, and that they do not disturb what is observed, can information be quantified in the form of Shannon's information. This kind of information can only describe the deterministic world of classical physics exemplified by digital computers. Conscious observers and free will cannot exist in such a reality.

Classical physics vs. quantum physics. According to the OPT theory (Operational Probabilistic Theory) developed by Giacomo Mauro D'Ariano and his collaborators, quantum physics and classical physics can be derived from six postulates that are entirely informational. Five of these postulates are in common. The sixth postulate prescribes entanglement for quantum physics and its absence for classical physics.

Collapse of the wave function. In quantum physics, the evolution of the state of an isolated system is represented by the evolution of a unit vector in a complex N-dimensional Hilbert space whose direction changes over time. When a quantum system interacts with a measurement system, it produces a classical observable in spacetime; for example, it activates a sensor designed to detect a specific particle or atom at a certain time and place. The mathematical theory of quantum physics only predicts the probability of the possible states that will be measured, but it does not predict the state that will manifest. The lack of a theory that specifies the actual state that will manifest when the "collapse of the state vector (or wave function)" occurs constitutes the so-called measurement problem that has never been satisfactorily solved.

Conscious entity. This refers to any "system" or entity that has an inner experience made of qualia. In the text, the terms *thoughtform, consciousness unit (CU),* and *seity* are used to indicate specific types of conscious entities.

Consciousness unit. According to the CIP framework, each new self-knowing of One creates a consciousness unit (CU). Similar to Leibniz's monads, CUs are elementary seities that represent the unique point of view, or perspective, with which One has known Itself and continues to deepen its own self-knowing. CUs can know themselves and other seities, can create other CUs like themselves, and can combine with other CUs to create a hierarchy of seities. Each seity, elementary or combined, is a part-whole of One possessing all the fundamental properties of One.

Dualism. Term that refers to the Cartesian mind-matter dualism in which everything that exists is considered to be composed of two different "substances": mind and matter. Philosophical dualism is in opposition to *monism,* which asserts that everything comes from a single "substance," for example matter (materialism) or mind (idealism).

Entropy. The concept of entropy refers to a measurable property of a physical system that is associated with a state of disorder, randomness, or uncertainty. The term "entropy" was first used in classical thermodynamics. The concept was then extended to statistical physics and information theory. A closed system out of thermal equilibrium naturally and *irreversibly* evolves toward thermal equilibrium, i.e., toward a stable state of maximum entropy, or maximum disorder, in which the transformations are *reversible.* Any closed physical system that has not reached thermal equilibrium is in a state in which entropy is less than the maximum possible and will spontaneously and naturally evolve until it reaches its maximum value (maximum disorder).

Epistemic. Refers to what can be known about reality. In the context of the QIP theory, a quantum system that is in a pure state is in an "ontic state," i.e., is in a well-defined state, only knowable as a conscious experience (qualia) by the system that is in that state. On the other hand, an outer observer of such a system is in an "epistemic state." In this state, the observers can only know the probabilities of manifestation of all the possible observables of that system. The actual state that will manifest is generally not knowable and the ontic state is strictly private.

Fluctuations of the quantum vacuum. Random variations of the state of the quantum vacuum which can occur at any point in space. These fluctuations are a consequence of the uncertainty principle but are *not directly observable*, although their collective presence is the cause of many observable phenomena. They always appear as *virtual particles*, created spontaneously as particle-antiparticle pairs that are annihilated within a time shorter than that established by Heisenberg's uncertainty principle.

Free will. The ability of a seity (quantum system) to decide which state to manifest next. A classical system is deterministic, and therefore cannot have free will. The indeterminism of quantum physics makes the existence of free will possible, although most current interpretations of quantum physics do not allow it. Quantum entanglement is incompatible with the notion that the state that will manifest exists prior to the measurement. As proposed in the QIP theory, it is possible for a quantum system to decide which state to manifest. In this case, the future state is only known by the system immediately after its decision but prior to the manifestation. For the external observer the future state is only a probability until it manifests. Free will requires that the state that will manifest cannot be *algorithmically* derived; it is a creative state.

General relativity (GR). The geometric theory of gravitation published by Albert Einstein in 1915. This theory generalizes special relativity and replaces with a local theory Newton's universal law of gravitation, which requires action at a distance. It is a mathematical theory that links spacetime in four dimensions with the distribution and flow of mass, energy, and momentum using a system of partial differential equations. Within GR the gravitational force becomes an *apparent* force observed in non-inertial reference frames. General relativity is the basis of all contemporary macroscopic cosmological models, and predicts the generation and propagation of gravitational waves that have recently been experimentally detected.

Hilbert space. A vector space that generalizes the notion of Euclidean space to N-dimensions, either real or complex. A complex number is the sum of a real number and an imaginary number $(a + ib)$, where a and b are real numbers and $i = \sqrt{-1}$. Introduced by the famous mathematician David Hilbert at the beginning of the twentieth century, this space has provided an enormous contribution to the development of functional and harmonic analysis. Thanks to the definition of complex Hilbert space, it was possible to formalize the theory of Fourier series and generalize it using arbitrary bases. The properties of Hilbert spaces are often counterintuitive and extraordinary. They allow us to describe all salient properties of quantum fields and their interactions.

Identity. The property of a CU or seity who knows that the experience she is having is hers and hers alone. It is a form of "double reflection," or self-consciousness, in the sense that the entity, by knowing she is experiencing her own state, can direct her own experience "from within." Having identity is a necessary condition for having free will and true *autonomy*, i.e., the capacity for self-determination.

Knowing vs. knowledge. In this book there is a crucial distinction between conscious and unconscious knowledge that is generally neglected in the scientific literature. I have pointed this out in the Preface of the book, and I concisely repeat the explanation here for convenience. The confusion is facilitated by the lack of appropriate words in the English language to discriminate the two kinds of knowing. In the Italian language there are two verbs, *conoscere* and *sapere*, instead of only "to know," that allow us to distinguish the two types of knowledge, even though in common usage the two verbs are not always used consistently. In my English translation I have consistently used "knowing" to translate *conoscere*, with the meaning "conscious knowledge," and "knowledge" to translate *sapere*, to mean "unconscious knowledge." This distinction is essential to discriminate between the symbolic-only knowledge of computers or brains and the semantic knowing of a conscious entity.

Knowing. This refers to conscious knowledge (comprehension) and conscious knowing (meaning), of which there are three types:

1. *Conventional knowing.* The conscious knowledge that has been implicitly or explicitly convened among human beings. For example, the meaning of words and other symbols that require comprehension. This also refers to being conscious of the *mechanical knowledge* obtained through the automatic learning processes of the brain. It is important to realize that what we often call meaning

is another symbol used to "explain" the meaning of a word we do not understand. This can only work to the extent that the actual meaning of the other symbol is already known. If the basic concept or experience is not yet comprehended, words alone will be powerless to explain it.

Note that the meaning of scientific terms is a fully operational "relational knowledge," which does not explain the true meaning of the terms per se and produces circularity. For example, energy is what produces motion, and motion is what is produced by energy, but no one can explain what energy or motion really are. Furthermore, most of our reasoning and thinking involves the manipulation of symbols and not of meanings. This process produces mechanical understanding instead of deep comprehension, exemplified by a statement like, "It is so because the math says so." In other words, we too often behave like machines.

2. *Indirect knowing.* The type of knowing obtained by a conscious entity based on the observation of the live symbols created by another entity to express her own knowing. The comprehension of these symbols is related to the meaning already existing in the receiving seity, since the meaning comes before the symbol used to represent it.

3. *Direct knowing.* Refers to a seity's endogenous comprehension of the meaning that spontaneously emerges out of her own qualia experience. The seity may later generate a live symbol to communicate a portion of that new meaning. This type of knowing is an entirely quantum phenomenon that does not exist in a classical system such as a computer. It is possible only through a

lived experience, which allows the seity to "become" what she knows. Chapters 12 and 13 discuss this crucial subject.

Knowledge. Refers to the *unconscious knowledge* possessed by computers or living organisms in the form of data loaded into their memory, acquired/learned patterns, and action-reaction patterns created by artificial or biological neural networks, or by inference engines. This is also the type of knowledge of a human brain when it operates mechanically without the free will and comprehension that can only come from self-consciousness. This knowledge is *mechanical knowledge* or symbolic-only knowledge in which conscious meaning is irrelevant. Human beings or animals may be conscious of their mechanical knowledge. However, unless their conscious free will changes the behavior informed by their mechanical knowledge, they behave no differently than unconscious robots.

Live information. The type of information used by seities to communicate with living organisms. It consists of elementary particles, atoms, and molecules that interact quantumly and self-organize based on quantum rather than classical laws of physics. Live information makes no sharp distinction between energy, matter, and information. Systems made of live information are correlated organizations of live symbols such as atoms, molecules, and biomolecules interacting individually inside living cells. These types of interactions are for the moment poorly understood since living organisms have been studied as if they were classical biochemical systems rather than quantum-classical information-processing systems.

Locality. Refers to systems that obey the *locality principle*, which states that an object can only be influenced by its immediate surrounding environment. This principle requires that any action at a distance be mediated by waves or particles, the maximum speed of which is the speed of light. The principle of locality, when applied to objects that behave probabilistically, leads to statistical limits established by *Bell's theorem*. Nonlocality implies the existence of correlations that violate Bell's theorem. This happens routinely with quantum systems because, when they interact, they become *entangled*. Entanglement is a *nonlocal* property that does not exist in classical systems (see the *Quantum entanglement* entry in this glossary).

Materialism. A philosophical concept stating that matter is the substance of which everything is made, *including mental states*. According to materialism, consciousness is an epiphenomenon of matter. Materialism is now more often called *physicalism* to indicate that everything that exists is physical, in recognition that in quantum physics matter has become increasingly abstract, and ontology has shifted from elementary particles to the quantum fields of which particles are states rather than separate objects. Materialism or physicalism is a monism in opposition to idealism. Idealism is also a monism because it affirms that physical reality is a mental construction, i.e., matter is a phenomenon produced by the mind.

Meaning. The essence of the knowing that is carried by qualia within a conscious experience. Meaning can also be carried by classical symbols in conventional knowing, as explained under *Knowing* in this glossary. Meaning is what symbolic information is supposed to convey. The information handled by computers has no meaning to them, though it has meaning for their creators. Machines are indeed proxies of their creators. The fact that we attribute meaning or intention to a robot is a grave human misunderstanding that must be rectified.

Much of the meaning of the objects that surround us was intuitively learned as children and then refined through education and experience, both at home and at school. For example, a stone may represent itself, or it may have an implicit meaning linked to its usefulness (a defensive weapon, or building material), or derive from an explicit agreement, for example, "If you see a stone in front of my front door, it means that I'm in my office." The meaning of physical objects is very different from the endogenous meaning of thoughts and feelings. For example, the meaning of a new idea or the meaning of the love I feel for my child come entirely "from within"; they are not agreements, implicit or explicit.

Monism. A philosophical concept claiming that at the foundation of reality there is a single fundamental principle or "substance." Monism is opposed to dualism or pluralism.

Morphism. Indicates the existence of a map between one structure and another of the same or of a different type. For example, in set theory, functions are morphisms. In category theory, objects don't necessarily have to be sets and their relationships don't have to be just maps. In mathematics there are various forms of morphism with different properties, for example homomorphism, isomorphism, automorphism, epimorphism, etc.

Observable. In physics, an observable is a quantity that can be measured. If the system is governed by classical physics, the state of the system can be known directly because it is described by a real-valued function. If the system is quantum, however, the state of the system is not directly knowable (no-cloning theorem). What is observable can be obtained by transforming the quantum state of the system with a mathematical operator associated with the observable. However, this transformation produces a probability distribution of measuring each of the possible values of the observable, not the state that will be observed.

One. The totality of what exists, both in potentiality and in actuality. One is irreducibly holistic, dynamic, and creative. One is the interiority that connects all Its creations "from within." One wants to know Itself and self-actualize. Consciousness units (CUs) emerge from One each time One knows Itself with a new perspective about Itself. CUs communicate with each other and combine, thus creating all realities, both inner and outer. What we call matter is the outer aspect of reality made up of the symbolic forms created by CUs and seities to represent the meaning they exchange with each other to know themselves ever more.

Ontic. Refers to what is real, what really exists. In the context of QIP theory, a quantum system that is in a pure state is in an "ontic state," i.e., in a well-defined state that can be known as a conscious experience (qualia) by the system that is in that state. The impossibility of cloning (copying, reproducing) a quantum state ensures that this state is *private*, only knowable "from within" by its owner. Note that the ontology is in the private experience, not in the *representation* of the experience that is what we call a pure quantum state. A seity is represented by a quantum system that is in an ontic state that evolves by maintaining the purity of its state. A seity can transform live information (shareable symbols) into quantum information (experience, meaning), and vice versa, with free will.

OPT (Operational Probabilistic Theory). This is a theory of theories based on information, considered to be the ultimate abstract entity out of which physical theories emerge. It is due to G.M. D'Ariano and his collaborators [7]. OPT derives all the fundamental equations of classical and quantum physics, from Maxwell's to Dirac's, based on six purely informational postulates. Within OPT, quantum physics supervenes on quantum information, and classical physics supervenes on quantum physics.

Panpsychism. The idea that the mind or some other mental aspect—consciousness, for example—has always been an integral part of reality. Panpsychism is one of the most ancient philosophical theories, already proposed by the Vedas, by Thales, Plato, Plotinus, Spinoza, Leibniz, Russell, and many others. The QIP theory claims that a quantum system in a pure state consciously experiences its state. With QIP, panpsychism becomes for the first time a falsifiable physical theory. According to QIP, consciousness and free will cannot exist in any classical system because they cannot derive from any deterministic system, no matter how complex those systems are.

Part-whole. A part that also contains the essence of the whole. Two examples are (1) a seity that contains the essence of One, and (2) each cell of a multicellular organism that contains the genome of the fertilized egg that created the entire organism.

QIP (Quantum Information-based Panpsychism) theory. A quantum panpsychist theory developed by G.M. D'Ariano and F. Faggin [10], defining consciousness, for the first time, as the ability of a quantum system that is in a pure quantum state to experience its own state in the form of qualia. The theory also establishes that a conscious system can transform quantum information into live information, and vice versa, using free will, thus allowing communication with the classical world to be mediated by living organisms that translate live information into classical information, and vice versa.

Within QIP theory, the phenomenology of a conscious experience is highly similar to the phenomenology of quantum information since an experience is definite, private, and cannot be reproduced, just like a pure quantum state. Therefore, quantum information can properly *represent* a private state only known by the system that is in that state (ontic state). The state of knowledge of an external observer of a system in an ontic state is called an *epistemic state* because the observer can only know the probabilities of manifestation of the observables.

Qualia. This term refers to the sensations and feelings that emerge in the consciousness of an entity following the perception of information. The first theory that specifically identifies a plausible physical correlate to qualia is the QIP theory. According to QIP, qualia can only originate in a quantum system that is in a pure quantum state that evolves by maintaining the purity of its state. Special quantum systems called seities can also direct the evolution of their pure state using free will, and communicate with other seities using live information. This involves free-will transformations from quantum to live information, and vice versa, performed by the seities without the need to have a physical body. Within QIP, the long-term memory of a conscious experience requires live or classical information [10].

Quantum computer. A physical system that exploits quantum entanglement as a computational resource. This allows operations to be performed exponentially faster than what is possible with a classic computer, at least for some algorithms.

Quantum entanglement. A phenomenon that creates nonlocal correlations between the states of the fields that have interacted. This phenomenon does not exist in classical physics. When two quantum systems interact, they become entangled by creating a new system whose state is "more" than the sum of the states of the parts. This means that the interacting systems are no longer independent from each other even after they have separated. Therefore, the measurement of the observable of one of the systems *simultaneously* determines the value of the entangled observable of the other system, *regardless of their physical distance.* The correlations of entangled quantum systems may exceed the so-called Bell bound, which the correlations of classical systems never violate. The Bell theorem establishes the maximum percentage of correlations (the Bell bound) that are possible in a classical probabilistic system when we repeat the same measurement process on many systems prepared the same way. Entangled quantum systems may inexplicably exceed such a bound.

The only way to explain this phenomenon is that the state that will be measured cannot exist prior to the measurement, but must be *created simultaneously for both systems* during the measurement process. How these nonlocal correlations can happen is still a mystery, because they would require superluminal communication between the two distant systems, thus violating the locality principle upon which special relativity is based.

In spite of the presence of instantaneous correlations, the probabilistic nature of the measurement outcomes does not allow superluminal communication because whoever communicates must know the state he needs to encode his message before the measurement, but that is impossible.

Quantum information. The amount of information contained in the quantum state of a quantum system. Quantum information can be manipulated in quantum computers using special techniques that make the state of a quantum system evolve deterministically. Note that there is a fundamental difference between quantum and classical states: the former are private, i.e., non-reproducible, while the latter are public, i.e., shareable.

Quantum mechanics. By quantum mechanics we mean the physics of systems described by the Schrödinger equation or by Heisenberg's matrix mechanics; two formalisms that turned out to be equivalent. Quantum mechanics is non-relativistic and has been superseded by quantum physics represented by Dirac's relativistic equation, which is the foundation of quantum field theory. In G.M. D'Ariano's OPT theory [7], quantum physics supervenes on quantum information and classical physics supervenes on quantum physics.

Quantum nonlocality. Refers to the violation of the *locality principle* in quantum physics. This phenomenon is entirely due to quantum entanglement (see *Quantum entanglement*).

Quantum vacuum. The state of lowest energy of empty space (vacuum). However, this energy cannot be zero due to Heisenberg's uncertainty principle. This causes fluctuations in the vacuum energy with measurable collective consequences, even though the individual fluctuations are not measurable. For instance, the *Casimir effect* is an attractive force between two plates very close to each other due to such fluctuations.

Qubit. The qubit or quantum bit is the elementary unit of quantum information, i.e., it is the quantum version of the classical bit. While a classical bit only represents two possible states, the qubit represents the quantum *superposition* of two complementary state vectors in a two-dimensional Hilbert space, conventionally represented as $|1\rangle$ and $|0\rangle$, $|up\rangle$ and $|down\rangle$, or $|right\rangle$ and $|left\rangle$. This superposition creates an infinity of possible states that can be imagined as all the points on the surface of a sphere of radius 1 (called the Bloch sphere). Examples of qubits are the spin of an electron, whose two states are $|up\rangle$ and $|down\rangle$, and the polarization of a photon, whose two states are vertical and horizontal polarization, $|^\wedge\rangle$ and $|>\rangle$. Qubits can be entangled—a property not found in classical systems—allowing certain computations to be made much faster than is possible with classical computers. Over the past decade, the international race to develop a viable quantum computer has dramatically accelerated.

Randomness. Refers to a total lack of predictability of an event. A sequence of events that is not predictable by any algorithm is called *random*. The collapse of the wave function is a random event. When the same quantum experiment is repeated, even though each individual event is random, the *frequency* of certain patterns can be predictable. For example, when two "quantum dice" are thrown simultaneously, the probability of getting 7 as the sum of the two outcomes is three times that of getting 2. In this sense, randomness does not imply complete lack of any pattern. This is particularly relevant in quantum physics since individual events are random, but the repetition of random events may create highly reproducible patterns. In fact, the deterministic classical physics of macroscopic objects—which are made of huge numbers of quantum events—emerges from the randomness of quantum physics.

Seity. Seity is a quantum entity with three irreducible and indivisible fundamental properties: consciousness, agency, and identity. The elementary seities, which I have called consciousness units (CUs), emanate directly from One.

The combination of communicating CUs, each with its own consciousness, identity, and free will, gives rise to hierarchies of seities. By communicating with each other, the seities create layers of symbolic and semantic organizations that increase their self-knowing.

Semantics. Deriving from the Greek *sema*, meaning "sign," semantics is that part of linguistics that studies the *meaning* of individual and combinations of words (signs).

State of a system. The state of a classical system is formed by the position and the momentum (velocity multiplied by the mass) of each classical particle that forms the system. This state requires six degrees of freedom for each particle and can be precisely known in principle. The state of system composed by N particles can then be represented by a vector in a real space of 6N dimensions. By analogy, the state of a quantum system can be described by a vector in a complex M-dimensional Hilbert space. The differences between a real and a complex M-dimensional space are, however, enormous, especially when the variables are probability amplitudes rather than ontological variables like actual positions and momenta. A quantum system can be described by a well-defined state, called a *pure state*, or by a mixture of states, called a *mixed state*.

Symbol. The term "symbol" indicates anything (sign, gesture, object, animal, person) that can represent a meaning other than that offered by its immediate sensible aspect. The meaning associated with a symbol can be either explicitly convened or intuitively understood (implicit meaning). To communicate, it is essential that the symbols be reliably recognizable. An object can represent more than one meaning if it can support two or more states that can be reliably discriminated. For example, a coin can represent two states (one bit of information), a die can represent six states (2.59 bits of information), two indistinguishable dice can represent 21 different states (4.39 bits), a computer memory of N bits can support 2^N different states.

Thoughtform. Within QIP a thoughtform is a quantum system that exists in a pure state. Thus, it has a qualia experience for as long as it exists in a pure state. However, a thoughtform is not aware of being conscious, i.e., it is not self-conscious and therefore it has neither free-will agency nor identity. In other words, a thoughtform has no sense of self (identity), and cannot direct its actions with free will (agency). A thoughtform is like a cloud that "goes where the wind takes it," thickening, dispersing, and combining with other clouds, following the laws of the clouds without being able to direct its own behavior.

A quantum computer is an example of a thoughtform, because it performs a series of deterministic unitary transformations that maintain the purity of its state during the execution of the program, but has neither agency (free will) nor self-consciousness (identity). A seity is a quantum field with identity, agency, and consciousness that can direct her own experience with free will. Once created, the seity exists and evolves as a part-whole of One for as long as One exists.

Truth. I think that everything that One knows about Itself defines truth, since One cannot have internal contradictions. Given the holistic and dynamic nature of One already reflected in the fundamental nature of the physical universe we know, truth cannot be made of separable and static parts. Truth must be composed of parts-whole connected from within and evolving by ever deepening their own self-knowing without end. In my opinion this is why the mathematical theories we create to represent the physical world show unsuspected "connections" between them.

Unitarity postulate. In the mathematical theory of quantum physics developed by John von Neumann in the mid-1930s, all state transformations in a quantum system are assumed to be unitary, i.e., they are represented by a unitary operator. Such transformations are reversible, maintain the purity of the quantum state, and are deterministic with respect to the probability amplitudes, which are the state variables in quantum theory. This means that the unitary evolution of a quantum system occurs entirely within Hilbert space. To produce a measurable event in spacetime it is necessary to have the "collapse of the wave function," a phenomenon that is not predictable by quantum theory. G.M. D'Ariano has recently proven that the unitarity postulate cannot be falsified, therefore it should be discarded, for it unnecessarily limits the types of quantum transformations possible and creates the "measurement problem" that no one has ever been able to solve.

Vedas. Religious and philosophical texts that originated in India more than 3500 years ago. Written in Vedic Sanskrit, they are the basis of Hinduism. There are four Vedas: *Rigveda*, *Yajurveda*, *Samaveda*, and *Atharvaveda*. The word *veda* means knowing, knowledge, or wisdom.

Bibliography

1. Faggin, F., *Silicon: From the invention of the microprocessor to the new science of consciousness*, Waterside Productions 2021.
2. D'Ariano, G.M., 'Quantum Holism,' arXiv: 2102.01438, 2021, forthcoming in *The Quantum-Like Revolution: A Festschrift for Andrei Khrennikov*.
3. Faggin, F., Klein, T., Vadasz, L., 'Insulated Gate Field Effect Transistor Integrated Circuits with Silicon Gates,' in *International Electron Devices Meeting*, Washington, October 1968, p. 22.
4. Engel, G.S., Calhoun, T.R., Read, E.L. et al., 'Evidence for Wave-like Energy Transfer through Quantum Coherence in Photosynthetic Systems,' in *Nature*, 446 (7137), April 2007, pp. 782–6.
5. Del Giudice, E., *Memorie nell'acqua?*, see the following video: https://www.youtube.com/watch?v=0MAPKRB8qno&t=26s.
6. Arndt, M., Nairz, O., Voss-Andreae, J. et al., 'Wave-Particle Duality of C_{60} Molecules,' in *Nature*, 401, 14 October 1999, pp. 680–2.
7. D'Ariano, G.M., 'Physics Without Physics: The Power of Information-theoretical Principles,' in *International Journal of Theoretical Physics*, 56, 2016, pp. 97–128.
8. D'Ariano, G.M., Perinotti, P., 'Derivation of the Dirac Equation from Principles of Information Processing,' in *Physical Review A*, 062106, 2 December 2014, p. 90.
9. Chalmers, D., 'Facing Up to the Problem of Consciousness,' in *Journal of Consciousness Studies*, 2 (3), 1995, pp. 200–19.
10. D'Ariano, G.M., Faggin, F., 'Hard Problem and Free Will: An information-theoretical approach,' in *Artificial Intelligence Versus Natural Intelligence*, Springer, New York 2022, pp. 145–92.

11. D'Ariano, G.M., 'No Purification Ontology, No Quantum Paradoxes,' in *Foundations of Physics*, 50, 2020, pp. 1921–33.
12. Shannon, C., 'A Mathematical Theory of Communication,' in *Bell System Technical Journal*, 27, 1948, pp. 379–423 and 623–56.
13. Faggin, F., 'Consciousness Comes First,' in *Consciousness Unbound*, ed. E.F. Kelly, P. Marshall, Rowman & Littlefield, Lanham, MD 2021, pp. 283–319.

Acknowledgments

The Italian version of this book with the title, *Irriducibile: La coscienza, la vita, i computer e la nostra natura*, was published by Mondadori in September 2022. I wrote Part I of that book in English and Part II in Italian for the reasons explained in the Preface. Following are the acknowledgments that appeared in the original Italian version.

I thank my wife Elvia for translating the first English draft of *Irriducibile* in Italian, my son Eric, and Andrea Di Blas for reading the same draft and providing useful comments. Special thanks go to Viviana and Irene Sardei, my sisters-in-law, who served as editors of the Italian draft. Their patient work is highly appreciated because it definitely helped improve the clarity of my thinking and the fluency of the text. Viviana then contributed most of the rich quotes that show how my ideas, primarily born from my direct experience rather than from a comparative study of other people's thoughts, are also reflected in the ideas and experiences of many other thinkers and explorers of the inner world from ancient times to our days. There is no doubt in my mind that fundamental values unite all of humanity.

I thank Giacomo Mauro D'Ariano, holder of the chair of Theoretical Physics at the University of Pavia, Italy for the many discussions that have allowed me to better understand the physics of quantum information of which he is a world expert. His scientific rigor and the interest in the study of consciousness that now unites us have allowed me to remain with my feet on the ground, so to speak, in the exploration of such a challenging subject.

Finally, I thank Enrica Bortolazzi, my book agent, and Guido Meardi, CEO of V-Nova, for their appreciated comments. Many thanks go also to Matteo Stroppa, editor of Mondadori, for his final touch.

I translated the printed version of *Irriducibile* into English during the second half of 2022, and I decided to integrate in the main text most of the material of the Notes that were previously collected at the end of the book. I also improved the text with further personal reflections and some of the feedback received from the readers of *Irriducibile*. The English version was reviewed by Elvia Faggin, Edward F. Kelly, Tristan Ze, Andrea Di Blas, Michele Crudele, Franco Ferrant, and Carollyn Sloan Oglesby who are hereby warmly acknowledged. Many thanks go to Mollie Barker for her expert final copyediting.

ESSENTIA

Essentia Books, a collaboration between John Hunt Publishing and Essentia Foundation, publishes rigorous scholarly work relevant to metaphysical idealism, the notion that reality is essentially mental in nature. For more information on modern idealism, please visit www.essentiafoundation.org.